Steve Braunias is the author of 10 books, including *Civilisation* (winner of the 2013 NZ Post award for best book of non-fiction) and *The Scene of the Crime*, published by HarperCollins in 2015. He writes for the *New Zealand Herald*, is the literary editor at *Newsroom*, and serves as life president of the Hamilton Press Club.

Also by Steve Braunias

Fool's Paradise (2001)

How to Watch a Bird (2007)

Fish of the Week (2008)

Roosters I Have Known (2009)

Smoking in Antarctica (2010)

Civilisation: 20 places on the edge of the world (2012)

Madmen: Inside the weirdest election campaign ever (2014)

The Scene of the Crime (2015)

The Man Who Ate Lincoln Road (2016)

The Shops (with photographer Peter Black, 2017)

The Friday Poem (as editor, 2018)

MISSING PERSONS

STEVE BRAUNIAS

HarperCollins*Publishers*

HarperCollins*Publishers*

HarperCollins*Publishers*
Australia • Brazil • Canada • France • Germany • Holland • Hungary
India • Italy • Japan • Mexico • New Zealand • Poland • Spain • Sweden
Switzerland • United Kingdom • United States of America

First published in 2021
by HarperCollins*Publishers* (New Zealand) Limited
Unit D1, 63 Apollo Drive, Rosedale, Auckland 0632, New Zealand
harpercollins.co.nz

A catalogue record for this book is available from the National Library of New Zealand.

ISBN 978 1 7755 4084 7 (pbk)
ISBN 978 1 7754 9121 7 (ebook)

Cover design by Darren Holt, HarperCollins Design Studio
Front cover image Jezz Burdett / EyeEm / Getty Images
Typeset in Bembo Std by Kirby Jones

Printed and bound in Australia by McPherson's Printing Group
The papers used by HarperCollins in the manufacture of this book are a natural, recyclable
product made from wood grown in sustainable plantation forests. The fibre source and
manufacturing processes meet recognised international environmental standards, and carry
certification.

To Minka

The wind whistled in the street and the music ghosted from the piano as leaves over a headstone ...

– Bruce Chatwin, *In Patagonia*

Contents

Introduction

Of course the thing that made me want to write about the missing is that I thought of myself as missing, too, and was actually attracted to the idea of coming to a bad end. I had an image in mind that my life was narrowing to a point. I didn't know what that meant for a long time. 'Things are narrowing to a point!' I'd exclaim, and wonder what I was talking to myself about. It was when I started writing and thinking about the case of Murray Mason that I realised the obvious: the point that things were narrowing to was death. Ideally, a lonely death.

The last thing a journalist ought to do is identify with the struggles or agonies of others to the point where they feel an exquisite pain of their own, and think of the story as really being all about themselves. I wasn't quite that arrogant or insane. The struggles and agonies of Socksay Chansy, the nice guy born in a refugee camp who lay down and died next to an Auckland graveyard by the sea, and Nigel Peterson, whose sad story I wrote about after I saw a 'missing' sign with his face on it on the road between Rotorua and Taupō, and Murray Mason, a good Kiwi joker at the end of the bar

1

who walked into the bush sometime after midnight and died in a shallow creek, were their own tragedies, and the tragedies of those who knew and loved them. But certainly their stories resonated. I almost felt envious. They had managed to disappear.

Things were getting on top of me. I was making other people unhappy. My personal life was a mess, I had an employment upset, there were health issues. The usual failings; plus old age, which for so long had felt like a rumour, was busy furnishing my life with intimations of mortality. Anyway, I took a special interest in reporting these stories of disappearance. I was a lost soul. Self-harm never crossed my mind – I took no interest whatsoever in stories of suicide – but the concept of wandering towards oblivion was very attractive. 'I thought of you as being very jolly,' Emma Bovary says to the calculating Rodolphe in Flaubert's great novel. He replies, 'Of course – that's the impression I give: I've learned to wear a mask of mockery ... But many's the time I've passed a cemetery in the moonlight and asked myself if I wouldn't be better off lying with the rest.' Rodolphe didn't mean it. Probably I didn't mean it either. I lived for my little girl and would never do anything to let her down. The best I could do was gravitate towards the stories of people who had found the horror I was looking for.

A journalist is routinely afforded the privilege and honour of busting in on people's lives at times of great distress. I sat in the living room of Sam Chansy, and he cried while talking about the death of his son. We were in Dannemora, in east Auckland. The houses were new, quite flash, a testament to hard work and the immigrant's ambition. According to the 2013 census, 57.7 per cent of people in Dannemora were born overseas, and the most common birthplace was Asia; after English, the next most common language spoken in Dannemora was Yue.

I sat in the living room of Chris Peterson, and he cried with his ex-wife Eileen, Nigel's mother, while they talked about the probable death of their son. We were in Whakatāne, in the Bay of Plenty. Chris worked as a vet, Eileen wore the company shirt of her employer, the iconic agricultural supply firm PGG Wrightson. They were hard-working Kiwis, familiar with life on the farm. I suppose I identified with them more than I did with Sam, but in neither visit did I dare to identify with their grief. There were times during my two-hour interview with Chris and Eileen when the intensity of their loss and their bewilderment – where was their boy, what had actually happened to him? – was so strong that I had to fight very, very hard not to intrude on their grief and burst into tears. They didn't need that. They lived with their loss and bewilderment. I was in town for the morning.

Later that afternoon, in Rotorua, I followed in Nigel's footsteps, from the top of the driveway of his home to the main street, Fenton Street, where the last absolutely positive sighting was made. It was a sad and wretched walk. It went beside a patch of scrub and a burning inferno of a mudpool; it steamed out of the bush, it was kind of grey, kind of brown, and the only barrier was a small wire fence that even a child could have stepped over. To walk into it would have been to die and to disappear for all time. Ahead was the turn-off towards Taupō, and where possible sightings of Nigel were made. There were great dark forests of pine on either side of the highway. I walked along there, too, for a little while. Much further along was the sign of Nigel – MISSING – that I had seen the previous year, on a family holiday. Every two years we stayed in a strange little motel in Rotorua. We were travelling to Taupō for the day. There and back, I noticed Nigel's sign, gazed at his troubled face, and wondered what it meant, and who it was

3

talking about; it led me to Chris's door. That holiday was our last as a family.

* * *

The fate of Nigel, Socksay and Murray were accidents and mysteries. Something intervened, and took them from life to death: bad luck.

When things start narrowing to a point, you start thinking that you've run out of road, run out of track; some bad end is inevitable. Murray Mason came to a bad end, and when his daughter and his ex-wife heard the news, neither of them was surprised. They had always just thought it would come down to something like that. It wasn't the fate I'd assigned myself – he was out of doors after midnight, stumbling through the Auckland Domain on a cold winter's evening, in the rain; I'm tucked up in bed most nights by 10 – but certainly I imagined my own demise when I followed his story, and pieced together a smudgy, incomplete portrait of someone who was quite assiduous in not wanting to be followed, or pinned down.

We had certain things in common. Like Mason, I worked as a journalist at the *Herald*. Like Mason, I went everywhere on foot, and was a familiar perambulating sight around my neighbourhood. Like Mason, I took an active interest in English football results, read widely, and have been known to like a drink. I followed his footsteps on the night he died. I had a drank at the Albion hotel on Albert Street, and then walked through the city, emerging at the edge of the Domain. That was Mason's journey. His last steps were taken when he stepped into the bush and down a row of steps onto a dirt path signposted as Lover's Walk. I found the little bridge he crawled beneath, saw the saplings he had flattered when he fell – he

4

ran out of track. It was so pretty: the sunlight, the gentle trickle of water, the smell of earth. But I was there in daylight. Mason had died at around midnight.

Our predicament, too, was as different as day and night. Mason had cut himself off from his family, created a new life, almost a new identity. He had taken things to extremes: he had cut his life in two, like a conjuror sawing his assistant in half. This must have taken some considerable courage and caused some considerable anguish. All I did with my life was drift in and out of unhappiness, and I stayed in one piece.

In my previous collection of crime writing, *The Scene of The Crime*, I reported on the murder of Tony Williams. He was a very good-looking Māori musician who went to the Gold Coast and enjoyed the good life. He enjoyed it too much: he crossed the wrong guy, and it cost him his life. But things had already taken a wrong turn. I wrote about him, 'The bachelor pad with the guitars and the surfing pictures, and the kids' bedroom empty most of the week … This wasn't a cautionary tale of what happens when you chase a dream and the dream dies. The yellow brick road had nothing to do with it. This was just the road a man's life can take when none of his relationships work out.'

No doubt I had written that line out of a fear that was the road my own life was going to take, and so it came to pass. 'The kids' bedroom empty most of the week …' I'd walk along the hallway, look in at the teddy bears and various assorted soft hilarious creatures propped up against the pillows, and think of Socksay Chansy giving up the ghost, of Murray Mason stumbling in the dark.

'He just never really caught a break,' Mason's daughter said to me. We were sitting on a bench on the wild shore of Napier. Much of New Zealand's east coast is fastened by shingle; the waves drop

5

heavily, claw and shush at the rocks, suck back out to the Pacific. It got dark. It was cold. I asked her what his good qualities were, and at first she said there weren't any – her relationship with Mason was complex, difficult – but later she softened and pitied him that all his good intentions were undone by bad luck.

The constant moral lesson as delivered by all manner of bores in everyday modern life is that we make choices, and those choices have consequences. Oh, and we have to take responsibility for our choices. It's probably a good and sound way to look at things. It talks to being in control of your own destiny, and having – God I hate this word – agency. We don't seem to allow for chance, for accident, for luck. And yet so much about the sad deaths of Murray Mason, Socksay Chansy and Nigel Peterson came down to luck. If only they turned this way, if only they turned that way … We're taught to think that we make our own luck. Again, that whole idea of agency and choice. But no one makes their own bad luck. In the introduction to *Killings*, the classic 1984 collection of crime writing by *New Yorker* journalist Calvin Trillin, he writes, 'These stories are meant to be more about how Americans live than about how some of them die.' These stories are more about how some New Zealanders go missing – the wrong person in the wrong place at the wrong time.

* * *

'Reporters love murders,' Trillin's introduction famously begins. He concludes that this is so because it gives us something interesting to write about. It's a somewhat flat assessment. Trillin is determined not to give himself or his calling any airs. But I've always been partial to airs, and tried to posit the idea that there was a governing

6

thesis to my 2015 book *The Scene of the Crime* – that its catalogue of violent and sudden death in these islands provided an insight into the towns and cities where the killings took place. Viz, the book's title; viz, these remarks from the introduction: 'A court is a chamber of questions. Who, when, why, what happened and exactly how – these are issues of psychology and the soul; they're general to the human condition, with its infinite capacity to cause pain. The question that very often most interests me in court is: where. It's impossible and pointless to try to put yourself in the mind of a killer, but the setting takes you to the scene of the crime, shows you something about New Zealand. It's not the dark underbelly; it's the dark surface, in plain sight, the road most travelled. There goes Mark Lundy, possibly, driving along the Petone foreshore in the middle of the night. There goes Clint Rickards, definitely, pulling up to a house in Rotorua's gruesomely named Rutland Street ...'

The enduring story – I call it a mystery – of Mark Lundy continues in this collection. And there's a kind of sequel to the story about the murderer, and more spectacularly the attempted murderer, Tony Dixon, he of the methamphetamine death opera and the swinging Samurai sword: it's told by one of his survivors. But the theme of *Missing Persons* is far less concerned with place than with test of character. Everyone in this book had their character tested; and almost everyone failed that test, miserably.

The worst is Jesse Kempson, immediately and enduringly regarded as public enemy number one who killed Grace Millane. Incredibly, it isn't so much the murder he was accused of (which he continues to deny, and is intent on making a second appeal) as the things he doesn't deny that he did afterwards that will forever horrify and appal – fussing around on his pathetic little errands to buy a suitcase from The Warehouse and hire a Rug Doctor ('Bring

7

your carpets to life') carpet cleaner from Countdown. His defence was that he panicked. He was trashed; no one thinks straight when they're trashed. Basically, he tried to get away with it. Nothing novel about that. But he failed every test of common decency; failed, with his shovel in the Waitākere ranges and his stroll around the rubbish bins of Albert Park, any basic measure of character.

Failure, too, in the character of Anna Browne, who committed the ferocious 'Pamper Party Murder' – there was something Victorian about that title, something old-fashioned and gothic – and who then tried to get away with it by passing herself off as a dreamer, a sleepwalker, a fabulous spirit who floated above the menial acts of mere humans, such as picking up a knife and sticking it in someone's head. She, too, was trashed. Strange to think of her, blind drunk, blood on her jeans, stumbling out of the house where she had just plunged the knife into Carly Stewart, and walking down the street in the direction of Henderson Creek. It was a sunny afternoon. Women were screaming. Emergency services were already on their way. At high tide, the creek is a thing of beauty; at low tide, the water sits in low puddles, and the mud reeks. Browne was at low tide, failing.

Malcolm Rewa remains a creature from a black low tidal lagoon. Failure is usually brief, a temporary state of affairs, but Rewa was in it for the long haul – jailed in 1999 for multiple charges of rape, but still pleading innocence in his 2019 trial for the murder of Susan Burdett, who he killed in 1992. I attended his 1999 trial. I attended his 2019 trial. The same old Rewa; 20 years of sticking to his fantasia about a romance with 'Sue', 20 years of total bullshit.

That's the thing about people found guilty of murder: you can say what you like about them, really take them apart, claim perfect knowledge that everything about them is evil and deny them mercy just as they denied it to their victim. But even the wretched Kempson can be viewed merely as a kind of blunderer. He was out of it when he killed Grace Millane, just as Anna Browne was when she killed Carly Stewart. As for Rewa, I got a jolt when I was listening to his lies in his murder trial and he mentioned the name of a woman who I dedicated *The Scene of the Crime* to: May Mackey, a devout Christian who visited Rewa in prison, among many other men convicted of murder. I had last seen her in 2015. She had just turned 95. I wrote, 'May was always out and about at the Parnell shops; earlier that week, she said, she was walking up Parnell Road when Teina Pora jumped out of a café to embrace her. Pora had only recently been released from prison for a wrongful conviction of murder. She remembered him on his first day in prison. "A little person holding his grey blanket, being led to his cell." They became friends in the last 10 years of his imprisonment.' Pora was the man who the police wrongfully framed for the murder of Susan Burdett. Incredible to think of May – small, serene, kindly May, made a widow many years earlier when a madman shot and killed her husband Wally – visiting both Pora and Rewa, and befriending both of them, even though Rewa committed the crime that Pora was jailed for, for 22 years. She spoke fondly of Rewa whenever she mentioned his name in my visits to her little apartment in Parnell. Rewa, too, talked of her fondly at his High Court trial.

No one is all bad. No one is unworthy of redemption. Even Kempson (whose actions after the death of Grace Millane were described by the Court of Appeal with a tone of Victorian rage as 'indicative of a degree of wholly self-regarding wickedness'), even Rewa, even Anna Browne, even – and this is if you go along with the verdict of guilty, delivered at two High Court murder trials, and backed up at length by the Court of Appeal and with scornful brevity by the Supreme Court, and therefore feel justified in saying what you like about him, that everything about him is sickening, monstrous, evil – Mark Lundy.

If Lundy really did butcher his wife and seven-year-old daughter, and then spent the rest of his life playing innocent, this is a little bit more than failing a test of character. It's failing as a human being. It's a betrayal, too, on a cruel and epic scale, of the people who have stuck by him and devoted much of their lives to proving his innocence. But they might be right: the Lundy case might be a gross miscarriage of justice. There is more to come on his campaign for innocence. I would like to read a book about it. I would not like to write that book; better that the author is Mike White, who wrote a lengthy, fulminating piece of advocacy journalism ('Mark Lundy: 20 years of lies, cover-ups and incompetence') in *North & South* magazine in 2020. It was the kind of story that would have ignited a popular demand for a new, independent inquiry into the murder case – except that it appeared just as Covid-19 somewhat distracted the attention of the nation, and the magazine itself was axed almost immediately as part of Bauer's decision to close down its New Zealand operations. You could call that bad luck.

Two stories in this collection are included partly as relief from the other 10 portraits of death. But for Colin Craig and Kim Dotcom there was no entertainment value or anything particularly light-hearted about their court appearances. There was too much at stake. Dotcom continues to fight extradition to the United States, where he will surely be imprisoned; Craig continues to fight to clear his name in seemingly eternal libel trials which all in one way or another come back to his refusal to accept the accusation that he sexually harassed a co-worker, and to his insistence that it was a brief, unrequited romance. But for all his case victories, Colin

Craig only really makes himself look worse with every new claim and counter-claim and counter-counter-counter claim – no one can keep count of the claims.

I've titled the chapter on Colin Craig 'Half the man I used to be'. It's based on a poem he wrote for the co-worker who he was clearly besotted with; the poem worked on the idea that he wished he could be two people, one for the world, and one just for her. It didn't work out very well. Yesterday came suddenly, and his secret self, the one who loved and longed, was ripped out and made to disappear – half of him became the title of this book, a missing person. His fate was to wander quietly carpeted courtrooms seemingly forever and ever.

There was no coming back for the three missing persons – Nigel, Socksay, Murray – who wandered away. But none of them had failed a test of character. Each of them had triumphed. Nigel Peterson and Socksay Chansy were two innocents, two boys who lived alone on their own planet. They never did anyone any harm. They had shown incredible resilience and had gone as far as they could. Murray Mason had long ago caused great harm. He deserted that life and shook off the damaging, noxious character that he had become, and took on a new identity as a noble, dignified man of mystery and learning who wandered the streets of Auckland with a map of fixed destinations in his head, always on the move, always welcome. He had so many options. So did Socksay and Nigel. But things narrowed to a point; the only thing they failed at was luck.

Chapter 1

The murder of Grace Millane: X on trial

The most despised man in New Zealand – a status Jesse Kempson earned not merely by choking Grace Millane to death on the floor next to his bed on the eve of her twenty-second birthday, but more so because of what he did to her afterwards, despicably and, worse, efficiently – only ever appeared in media images as a pixilated blur during his trial, and to tell you the truth he didn't look that much different in person. I gazed at his face quite a lot during his three-week trial in Courtroom 11 at the High Court of Auckland in the early summer of 2019, and for the longest time he failed to make much of an impression at all. His features were vague, smudgy. He had a flat face with a weak chin, small nose and thin mouth. His worst side was either side; he presented a bad profile, his thick neck and squashed features giving his head the appearance of a solid block of wood – i.e. a blockhead. Frankly, he looked like a charmless moron.

But by the third week Kempson's face started coming into view. He was quite a good-looking guy. He scrubbed up nicely in the blue suit he wore every day, and the alternating white open-necked shirt or black open-necked shirt. He carried himself well. He smiled, once, and held it for few minutes, on the final day of his trial, when Justice Simon Moore lightened the mood with a self-deprecating joke. The jury and public gallery had been cleared; that one glimpse of his good humour was in private. The smile animated his face, softened it, gave it shape and focus – the most despised and most despicable man in New Zealand actually had a sweet, even rather tender face.

It would have been the face that Grace Millane saw and liked very much when she met Kempson on their Tinder date in downtown Auckland on a Saturday night. Physically, he was to her specifications; she liked men dark and solidly built, 'the rugby type' as one of her friends put it. She was 21 and he was 26. She wore a black T-shirt dress and a pair of white Converse trainers. He wore a pale jacket and dark trousers. She was from Essex, backpacking her way around the world for a year. He was of no fixed abode and no fixed identity: during the trial and for a long time afterwards, he had name suppression. He appeared in the daily court list stapled on boards at the High Court under the initial of K. But even to print his initial at that time was to sail too close to the wind. He could only be known as the accused, or as X. Not Mr X, just plain X. And not X to flatter him as someone mysterious, but X in the sense of a wrong answer. X, crossed out by the jury when they took just five hours, including a break to eat white-bread sandwiches wheeled in for lunch, to find him guilty; X, aka Jesse Kempson, a deeply and profoundly wrong human being.

Grace arrived in Auckland on 20 November 2018, on the edge of summer. The trial began a year later on Monday, 4 November, in a week of blazing sunshine; on the way to court each morning, I saw backpackers tumbling out of the $17 airport bus and squinting in bright sunlight as they got their bearings, and headed for the hostels offering dorm rooms and cheap drinks. Grace booked into Base Backpackers. It was right in the middle of the city, just off Queen Street. 'The party backpackers,' as Kempson described it; the bar on the top floor has Wet Wednesday T-shirt contests, Thursday is themed as Glow Party. A travel agent two doors down advertises car and campervan deals, $15 per day. After Grace's family reported her missing, police distributed a still image of her leaving Base, taken from a CCTV camera to the left of the front entrance. It was 5.37pm on 1 December 2018. She was on her way to meet Mr Wrong.

The police photographed Kempson with and without his shirt on the night of his arrest. They are pictures of a fat boy with sagging breasts, no waist, and a dim, wide face. He'd evidently lost weight during his year on remand and cut a pretty trim figure that first morning in Courtroom 11. He appeared between two security guards to the right of the court, and behind the witness box. He faced the jury on the opposite side of the room. In between were three rows of media; I sat on the far left, and yes, you could say I was conscious of the fact that I was directly in front of Grace Millane's parents. Each and every session, David and Gillian Millane were always the first allowed into the courtroom to sit in the public gallery. The next person allowed in was a grey-haired gentleman who kept himself to himself at all times: Kempson's father sat in the middle of the row.

There were other regulars in court. Detective Inspector Scott Beard, who headed the Millane investigation, took up the most space – partly because of his height, partly because he had such an immensely grave and serious bearing. Crown prosecutor Brian

14

Dickey, 52, looked younger than his colleague Robin McCoubrey, 44 – partly because of the darkness and vigour of Dickey's black hair, partly because McCoubrey had the prematurely aged look of someone who you imagine wears his suit, tie, waistcoat and possibly even judicial gown to the beach. Dickey had a casual, languid manner. Also, he looked like All Blacks coach Steve Hansen, and had the same demeanour, too, which is to say he came across as a good bastard.

For the defence, Ian Brookie, 43, looked considerably younger than his colleague Ron Mansfield, 52. Brookie had a kind of appealing blandness. It was in contrast to the shrewd, self-contained Mansfield, witty and likeable outside of court, quite intense and certainly very intent inside it. It wasn't so much Mansfield's presence that was felt as his absence: whenever he was away, it felt as though a dark force had vacated Courtroom 11. In recess, he chomped on apples, his little teeth tearing at the flesh.

The finest legal mind belonged to the judge. I remember watching Simon Moore in his past life as a Crown prosecutor. He was very, very good, a persuasive and often physical advocate for the police – ah, how I cherish the memory of when he mimed holding murderer Antonie Dixon's Samurai sword above his head, and his shirt rode up to expose a patch of pink tum. He threw himself into the prosecutor's role, but really it was too narrow for him. As Justice Moore, he called on his experience and relied on his wits to preside over every aspect of a difficult case, and the only time he ever lost his footing was the day he called the Crown prosecutor Mr Tickey. Every trial is a work in progress. The trial of Kempson was very nearly a work of art, Justice Moore's masterpiece.

'Right,' he said, when the jury were selected. 'Good morning.' The public gallery was full, standing-room only. The eyes of the nation were on Courtroom 11. Two nations, in fact; there were hacks from the BBC, *The Guardian*, and the *Daily Mail*. Many murder trials start off as tense chambers of suspense, but relax during recess, when media, court staff and lawyers chew the fat, horse around, gossip. Black humour creeps in, too, because the tension has to escape somehow, somewhere. But there was never anything like that in the trial of Kempson. It remained solemn, hushed, a tense chamber of suspense for the entire three weeks. What Kempson had carried out was so dreadful. It inspired a kind of reverence for the most important person in the courtroom: Grace Millane, the missing person.

* * *

The murder capital of New Zealand is the suburbs. Most violent crime takes place in a house on a quiet street, with junkmail in the letterbox and a tricycle left out in the driveway. The only people who know what goes on in a suburb are the people who live there. But the killing of Grace, and the stations along the way to her murder, took place in the shared space of downtown Auckland, among its bars and romantic pattern of side-streets, plazas and lobbies – everyone in Auckland knows the city, its geographies and night lights. Everyone in New Zealand knows the exact spot where Kempson first met Grace: the Sky Tower.

Much of the trial involved a room full of people doing that thing which has replaced living – watching a screen. Hours of CCTV film and police video were shown in Courtroom 11. It was like a kind of cinema of the damned. Kempson, drinking by himself at a table outside the Bluestone Room pub on Durham Lane on Saturday afternoon, waiting to meet Grace; Grace, walking along Federal Street towards the Sky Tower to meet Kempson.

It's the first day of summer in Auckland, which means it's raining. The roads are slick with water, someone speeds by beneath an umbrella. Grace arrives outside the SkyCity casino entrance. She sends her last message to her parents, a photo of a Christmas tree set up by a nativity scene – it's a historical fact there were pine trees outside the baby Jesus' manger. Someone with a limp walks past, slowly. Kempson arrives at 5.45pm. He holds his arms out wide and gives Grace a quick hug. Her last hours, her appointment with a fat boy who at 26 was already going to seed … The investigation into Grace's disappearance was code-named Operation Gourami. 'There is no magic to that name, is there?' McCoubrey asked a detective in court. 'They are randomly generated, aren't they?' Operation Gourami playing out as a silent movie, the streetlights shimmering on black wet concrete.

Who was she meeting? One of the few times that anything remotely positive was said about Kempson during his trial – very well, the only time – came from a witness for the prosecution when she described their Tinder date.

They flirted with each other by text after they matched. He texted, 'What are you doing?'

'Playing Pokémon.'

'Well I can think of something more fun.'

'Oh really do tell.'

'I'm sure you can think of a few things. What do you like?'

'Do you mean sex?'

'Yes.'

She told him, 'I like being choked.'

The woman put it another way in court, wringing her hands in the witness box, in a clear voice: 'I mentioned I liked rough sex.'

She took a bottle of rum to his apartment. She drank four or five glasses of rum and Coke, he drank maybe the same number of bottles of Heineken. 'We started talking to each other. Like a conversation. A normal conversation.' It was neither dazzling nor boring, it was only there as a preamble to the point of her visit.

McCoubrey: 'Was there intimacy?'

'Yes.'

'Can you describe what happened?'

'He did choke me a bit because that's a preference of mine. He used one of his hands. It was fine. My breath was a bit restricted, but it was something that gave me pleasure. It wasn't too hard that I was gasping for air. It was just the right pressure. He let go when I reached ...' Her voice fell away.

McCoubrey filled the silence. 'So it went okay, did it?'

'Yes,' she said.

Mansfield, in cross-examination, hastened to confirm that it went okay.

'Did you indicate to him that you felt comfortable with the pressure?'

'Yes.'

'You let him know you liked that and enjoyed that contact?'

'Yes.'

'Is it fair to say both of you thought the sex was good?'

'Yes,' she said.

All good. For a brief moment, Kempson was seen as just another single guy hooking up on a dating app; he performed as per requirements, his techniques won a glowing review ('It was fine'), he ordered in pizza after they had sex. But there was a glimpse, too, of something frail, something broken. Kempson fell asleep. The woman was going to stay the night, but decided to dress and catch

18

the bus home. She left her glasses behind and texted him multiple times over the next week to arrange getting them back, but he had another matter he kept wanting to discuss: 'He wanted to know why I left so suddenly after having sex.' His feelings were hurt. He couldn't understand why she would just leave like that. Kempson, anxious; Kempson, alone.

A week later he was able to have the greatest thing in the world – company – when he walked from the Bluestone Room to the Sky Tower. In the film of his first police interview played to the court, Kempson sat down at a small, round table in a small, grey room with Detective Ewen Sewell. Kempson spent the next hour and 38 minutes lying like a flatfish. Like the best liars, he based his fiction on a true story. Sewell began the interview by sifting through a thin stack of papers on his side of the table, and bringing out a photograph of Grace Millane. He said, 'Do you recognise her?'

Kempson said, truthfully, 'Yes.'

* * *

Everything's great when you're downtown. Kempson and Grace enter the casino lobby, walk past a WIN THIS CAR promotion, and travel up the escalator beside a giant silver tinsel Christmas tree. At the top they can see the suckers on the casino floor, feeding coins into the bottomless pits of Megabucks Gold and Oriental Fortune. They take a sharp right, and head for Andy's. It's a fun, busy joint, with pretty lightbulbs set in rows in the ceiling, and a basketball hoop hung over a pair of antlers above the bar. They drink mango passion mint cocktails, then they leave at 7.16pm and walk across Victoria Street West to the Mexican Café. It's fun there, too, an upstairs bar and restaurant, where they sit outside on the balcony with an intimate view of the thrusting Sky Tower. They drink blue margaritas and shots of tequila, then they leave at 8.24pm and walk further along Victoria Street West, turn into Albert Street, cross the road and head down a strange, steep dip beneath two sky bridges. It takes them onto Durham Street West, and then Durham Lane, the dead-end, obscure location of the Bluestone Room. It's a dark sports bar with a low ceiling of exposed wooden beams and two flaming torches on the outside wall. Kempson and Grace take a round table at the entrance. After a few minutes she picks up her stool and moves it to sit beside him.

There's another couple sitting opposite, a man in a white T-shirt who talks very, very animatedly to a woman with long, fair hair. She doesn't move, just sits there, rigid as a post, possibly bored to tears. But Kempson and Grace are into each other. He reaches out and gently touches her hair, and they have their first kiss.

The CCTV film of their night out was played in Courtroom 11 as edited footage. 'A highlights package,' as Ian Brookie put it. He had an idea. He asked that the jury see the entire hour of their date at the Bluestone Room, the whole thing, in real time. I could appreciate his point. It was to show a young couple organically, as it were, having an awesome time, kissing, intimate, happy – above all, consensual. Consent was the magic word that Brookie chanted throughout the trial, from beginning to end, wanting it to work like a spell, carrying with it really the only hope that Kempson had of salvation and a verdict of not guilty. But the reality of having to watch his idea play out on a screen for an hour felt like a total drag and I fled for the political comedy taking place next door at Courtroom 13 in the matter of New Zealand First leader Winston Raymond Peters versus National Party deputy leader Paula Lee Bennett.

My timing was lucky. Bennett herself appeared in the witness

20

box just as I was arrived. Sit-down comedy can be just as good as stand-up, and Bennett was in great form as she rebutted Peters's accusation that she breached his privacy in the leaking to the media in 2017 of his national superannuation payment by an unknown source. Bennett was aghast at the merest suggestion that she associated with anyone who dabbled in dirty politics; she was whiter than white, a public policy purist. There was a break in proceedings after she gave her evidence and we all filed out to strike up lively conversation. There was gossip, laughter, chat. Bennett came over to me and said, 'I'm coming to live in your hood!' She'd just bought a home in Te Atatu. I lied, 'That's great!'

The whole scene felt unnatural, even shocking. I was used to the silence and decorum of Courtroom 11. Even during recess, when the public gallery filed out, no one spoke loudly, no one joked, no one displayed the slightest sign of having a good time. There was a retired pathologist from Sri Lanka; he kept his views to himself. There was a man who made his way through Roddy Doyle's novel *Paddy Clarke Ha Ha Ha*; he never laughed once. There was a well-known and quite vivacious actress; she dropped her voice when we chatted, and it wouldn't be accurate to describe it as a theatrical whisper. Like everyone, she was conscious of the occasion. The trial of Kempson was history in the making, an important reckoning. Grace Millane came to New Zealand as a guest, and had suffered and died. It was a national grief.

Back in Courtroom 11, CCTV showed Grace and Kempson walk arm-in-arm from the Bluestone Room to the CityLife hotel on the corner. It's a distance of 46 steps. Kempson lived on the third floor. He said to Detective Ewen Settle in his police interview that his room cost $380 per week.

'Is it quite comfortable?'

'It's cosy.'

'Just a little shoebox?'

'I would say,' said Kempson, indignantly, 'that it's a decent-sized shoebox.'

* * *

Who was Grace going to bed with? One witness described a foul sexual encounter with Kempson. It was at his room in CityLife in early November. She said she gave him oral sex, but when she lay on the bed, he sat down on her face and she couldn't breathe, fought, feigned unconsciousness, was afraid she was going to die.

She gave her evidence via video from a room somewhere in the High Court. More cinema, more looking at screens. It was deeply unpleasant to watch. She sat on the edge of her chair, and in front of her were three white stones made of paper: wet, rolled-up tissues. She told the jury what had happened to her in revolting detail. And then Mansfield got to work.

His cross-examination was brutal, old-school – destroy the credibility of a woman alleging she had been sexually attacked, accuse her of lying. It made for more deeply unpleasant viewing. Mansfield's line was that she exaggerated Kempson's actions out of disgust when the police told her he was responsible for the death of Grace Millane: 'You didn't want people to think you were into a guy who is now charged with murder.' He set about wearing her down under the slow, steady, exasperating drip of 708 text messages that Kempson and the woman had exchanged throughout November.

It was at once an intimate record and a reminder that texts form the world's most banal literature. A few days after the alleged incident, she wrote, 'I don't want to lose you yet.'

Kempson: 'Didn't think you wanted me. This won't work if you don't like me.'

'I'm willing to give this a fair shot if you are.'

'I want a shot to be your man if you'll let me.'

'Yes. We've got nothing to lose.'

Later, she wrote, 'I hardly know you yet. But I would like to.'

Kempson: 'I would like to know you too.'

'Great.'

Later, he wrote, imagining a night together, 'I could cuddle you.'

'I'd fall asleep in your arms.'

'That would be cute.'

'I'd like that.'

And so on, and on and on, Mansfield reading them out one by one, careful to recite the emojis ('Smiley face … Eyes with hearts'). The woman countered she was afraid of Kempson, didn't want him in her life in any shape or form, and the texts were a litany of falsehoods to avoid making him angry. And then Mansfield would read another of her texts ('How was your day?'), and another ('I've just been to the supermarket'), and another ('I don't want to lose you yet') …

It's not a question of whether a good cross-examination is brutal or confrontational. It's a question of whether it's effective. The Crown introduced the woman as a witness to establish that Kempson was sexually violent towards women, had form; Mansfield's long afternoon of reading out her friendly and encouraging texts was an attempt to raise serious doubts that her story was true. She sat in the room staring blank-faced and hostile at the camera, turning often to look at the clock on the wall. 'It doesn't have to make sense,' she said. Her cross-examination felt like one of the few times the defence had gained any ground.

But its effectiveness was abolished the next day. The woman had broken down in tears when she was told by Justice Moore at 5pm that she had to come back to court in the morning. 'No,' she wailed, and her head collapsed on the desk. Court adjourned. Everyone stood as the judge left; the woman remained on screen, wailing. There she was again in the morning, looking wiped-out, and there was Mansfield, now intent on discussing the exact choreographies of her sexual encounter with Kempson. Where were his knees, where was her head, where was his penis … 'Did you lick and suck his testicles?' Mansfield asked. 'No,' she said in a flat voice. The cross-examination had gone on too long. Everyone wanted it to end.

It ended. Was her story true or false? Was some of it true, some of it false? But if the actions of Kempson seemed in doubt or had been embellished, his character and pleading, desperate nature were once again exposed. She described how he gave a sudden performance of a man in agony, clutching his stomach, and declaring he had cancer. He was going to die. He asked the woman to tell his sister he loved her. 'He started telling me, "You don't want me. Nobody wants me." He was saying it over and over again. "You don't like me, you don't want to be with me, so I just should just kill myself." … He texted later, he was in disbelief that I left and hadn't stayed the night.'

Kempson, lost and alone; Kempson, a total fucking mess.

Kempson and Grace Millane walked into CityLife at 9.40pm. After four hours of drinking, they were likely slaughtered, happy too. The glass doors opened, dividing the frosted image of a Christmas tree. The doors closed as they made their way to the elevator and walked past three luggage trolleys.

* * *

She died in his apartment. He killed her with his bare hands. He was found guilty of murder.

I was never very clear about the likely verdict. The Crown presented a solid case for murder; they had the pathology (the bruising to her neck, the estimate that it would take a prolonged agony of 10–15 minutes to extinguish her life), they had pretty good indications that his state of mind was violent and diseased, they had what happened afterwards. The defence argued that it was an accidental death. They had the pathology, too (the absence of defensive injuries), and the chant that Kempson and Grace were consensual – this isn't a sensitive word to use, and I'm aware it wasn't used at any time in the trial – lovers. There wasn't much they could do with what happened afterwards. 'You may not like his actions,' said Brookie. 'That's understandable ...'

Brookie had called only a few witnesses. They included Professor Clarissa Smith from the University of Sunderland. She appeared on a video link; she wore a dark brown dress, and placed a black coat on a rack. She confirmed that she was co-editor of *Porn Studies* and was an expert in the study of BDSM. 'It's like any hobby people might engage in,' she said. She was very twitchy when she gave evidence. She said that many women liked to be choked during sex. She began to tremble. She said it was known as 'breath play'. She began to shiver and shake. She said that safety 'may not be the focus' if the couple were drunk, and got 'carried away in the moment'. And then she said, 'Would you mind if I put my coat on? It's incredibly cold in here.'

The consent defence got about as far as Brookie could take it. As for motive, he asked, 'Why would this otherwise happy couple end up in a situation where there was anger or violence?' Both were trashed, out of it; was Kempson so trashed, so out of it, that he simply went too far and had no idea what he was doing?

Manslaughter was an option. It was always going to be an incredible option, and might have caused a riot or at least some deep, enduring national malaise, but there were times when it felt like a logical outcome. A very fine legal mind certainly seemed to think so.

Most lunchtimes I strolled across the road from court to the University of Auckland staff common room in Old Government House. It's very nice, very English, quite shabby and genteel, with big armchairs and a high ambient IQ. It's for staff only, but I can easily pass as an academic – old, white, unsuccessful – and it was pleasant to sit there with my thermos of instant coffee and take issues of the *Times Literary Supplement* from a glass cabinet. On the final day of the trial, following Justice Moore's summing up, I ran into a law professor.

'You've come from the Millane trial, haven't you?' he said.

'Correct.'

'Manslaughter,' he said. 'Has to be.' And then he launched into a brief history of acquittals and successful appeals based on the consent defence.

Only minutes earlier I had heard Justice Moore tell the jury very near the end of his summing up: 'If [Kempson] honestly believed she consented to pressure on her neck, he must be acquitted.' For that brief moment it was as though a window was opened which permitted a view of a verdict of manslaughter. Grace liked pressure on her neck during sex, had encouraged an ex-boyfriend, belonged to bondage sites, all that. The night before she had her Tinder date with Kempson, she slept with a guy who appeared as a monosyllabic defence witness and said that he thought he probably applied pressure on her neck.

The Crown objected to that witness. 'It has no probative value,' argued Dickey. Mansfield told the judge: 'It goes to her willingness.' The judge said, 'I think the relevance is sufficient for it to be admitted.' Even so, Mansfield had to work hard to get the witness to say the things he wanted him to say.

He had to walk directly past Kempson to get to the witness box. Kempson had a good, long look at him. They didn't look wildly different – similar build, both tall with dark hair. The difference is that one was confident and assured, professional and successful; also, Kempson blathered endlessly during both of his police interviews, but the witness was a man of as few words as possible.

Twice, Justice Moore had to gently chide Mansfield for putting words into the man's mouth. 'Ask the right question, Mr Mansfield. It needs to be open-ended.' Mansfield thanked His Honour, but soon asked the wrong question again, and was interrupted. 'I'm trying to be careful, Your Honour,' he said. 'I know you are,' said Justice Moore.

'Where,' he asked the man, 'do you put your hands?'

'In what sense?'

He eventually confirmed to Mansfield that he put his hands on the necks of his sexual partners.

'How often?'

'I usually do it.'

'Why?'

'Because girls usually enjoy it.'

'How frequently do you undertake this practice?'

'A lot of the time. It's common.'

'How common?'

'Common.'

'When you usually do that, where do you put your hand?'

'On her neck.'

'Whereabouts?'

'On her neck.'

'Where?'

'Someone's only got one neck.'

Helpfully, Justice Moore suggested that the man demonstrate exactly where he would place his hand. The witness sat in the witness box and put his hand around his neck. The jury looked at the man with his hand around his neck; Kempson, too, looked at the man with his hand around his neck. At various times during the trial, Brian Dickey had stood in court and placed his hand around his neck, too, as had Ian Brookie, Ron Mansfield, and I think Robin McCoubrey, too, although he might just have been adjusting his tie.

It's likely Grace consented to Kempson placing his hand on her neck. But as Justice Moore reminded the jury, consent cannot be given by a person who is already unconscious; the court had heard evidence she may have lost consciousness, but that Kempson continued to choke her. And so as soon as Justice Moore opened the window for a manslaughter verdict, he slammed it shut again.

Many or even most summings up are dreadfully boring. They're a kind of useless appendage, a long and dutiful essay repeating what's already been said. But Justice Moore's summing up was like a delicately engineered calculus. It set things out clearly and exactly. It told the jury that the whole question of consent – that rope the defence clung to, its central argument that it was death by misadventure – didn't even come into it if the jury already established that it was murder by intent: 'Was this an intentional or deliberate killing? If your answer is yes, you will find him guilty of murder and you do not have to consider other questions.'

If the answer was no, there was a second part to the question: 'Are you sure when he applied pressure to her neck, he consciously ran the risk Grace would die as a result of his actions … That he recklessly carried on, and was willing to run that risk?'

Intent is always extremely difficult to prove. Recklessness, less so. 'You do not have to plan murder,' as Dickey told the jury in his closing address. 'But to kill Grace Millane, the gentleman behind me,' meaning Kempson, whom Dickey never once looked at and only ever treated with complete disdain for three weeks, 'would have had to suffocate her. It takes five to ten minutes to cause death by mechanical asphyxiation, or what we call manual strangulation. At some point the victim would have to lose consciousness and you have to carry on to cause death.'

Dickey spoke very quietly throughout the trial, sometimes not much more than a mutter. I chided him a couple of times and asked him to consider those of us who are hard of hearing. 'You have to carry on,' he yelled. 'This is holding a person's throat for an extended period of time and feeling her struggle for her life, and her going limp and unconscious, and,' he yelled again, even louder, '*you just carry on.*'

The death of Grace Millane was violent and awful. What happened afterwards was beyond even that. It was Kempson descending into Hell.

* * *

It was the long night of the damned. He occupied himself with various pastimes and diversions after he caused her death. He watched porn for about half an hour, took 10 minutes to choreograph and take seven intimate photographs of her naked body, and he also used his phone to begin his long and insane little fussy preparations to remove and conceal her. Incredibly, he probably also managed to get some sleep.

It's always shocking when a judge swears. In his summing up, Justice Moore read out the title of the first porn clip that Kempson watched, the rectangle of his phone bright with light at 1.41am: *'Young Teen Arse Fucked in Her Room.'* Kempson also watched *Sporty Youthful Stunner* and *Little Teenager Latina*.

Between 1.46am and 2.09am, he photographed Grace. 'Let's be perfectly clear,' Dickey had said in his opening address. 'She's dead at this point.' Dickey returned to the subject in his closing address. There was more yelling, and he stood in front of the jury and thrust a police booklet at their faces. The booklet published the seven photographs. He was showing the jury pornography. 'He took that photo,' he said. 'And that as well.' He flipped the page. 'He took that one of her.' He flipped another page. 'And he took those.' The yelling ceased. But he continued holding the booklet, and said, 'And do you know what? He told police her legs were straight out in front of her.' He glanced down at one of the photos, and tapped it with his finger. 'They ain't straight out here, are they?'

The defence left it very late in the piece to mention that Grace may have been alive when he first went online at 1.19am. Maybe, Ian Brookie said in his closing address, they were talking about going somewhere the next day, and that's why he searched for the Waitākere Ranges. He didn't hazard another desperate guess as to why Kempson's very next Google search was for 'hotest (sic) fire'. He didn't say anything at all about the porn.

Kempson, dozing in bed with Grace dead on the floor; Kempson, waking up to go back on his phone at 6.01am – did he charge it while he slept? – and further research what he needed to do. He had completely lost his mind. But the intellect remained, and he made pragmatic decisions, set out a methodology. For the next hour, he searched for rental cars, nearby luggage, rigor mortis, and carpet cleaner.

For the next few days, he went about on various errands. He was so efficient, a Nazi bureaucrat fussing around with paperwork as the trains rolled in. Kempson, at the Countdown supermarket on Quay Street opposite the wharf, renting a carpet cleaner for $39.99; Kempson, spending $17 on a taxi to Apex Car Rentals, the driver having to make a detour because city streets were closed for the Santa Parade; Kempson, buying a $59.90 shovel out west in Kumeu from a shop assistant ('He was a nice person to talk to … Tall, chubby build'), on his way to the Waitākere Ranges.

It was lonely work. He needed company. He went on a Tinder date. Text, 8am, Grace dead at his feet: 'Morning! How are you today?'

They met at Revelry, a corner bar on Ponsonby Road. They sat outside. She asked, 'What have you been up to?'

He said, 'Trying to find a large duffel bag.'

Afterwards, driving back to his shoebox with a dead body in it, he texted her, 'Love to do it again if you're keen?'

She replied, 'I'm not sure if we had the connection I'm looking for.'

He wrote, 'All good.'

Back in his apartment, he got to work. 'She was half-in, half-out of the suitcase,' he told police. He stopped to vomit. He zipped up the bag and then he got a luggage trolley. Grace left his room on a Sunday night, Kempson pulling the trolley backwards into the lift. There were times during the trial when some silences were filled with horror; the CCTV film of Kempson in the lift – everyone in courtroom looking at the screen, transfixed – was likely the worst of these silences.

There are two parking spaces outside CityLife. Kempson timed it well, parking there on a Sunday night. He wheeled the trolley towards it and opened the boot. He left the car in a nearby Wilson's parking building overnight. In the morning, he drove to buy the shovel ('Nice person … Chubby'), and then to the Waitākere hills, at a distance looking like 'the rim of a blue painted bowl' as described by novelist Maurice Gee, up close a dense, dark-green forest, quiet and lush.

Who killed Grace Millane? When the suppression order was finally lifted, Jesse Kempson's name joined Clayton Weatherston, Antonie Dixon, Malcolm Rewa, that person you think murdered the Bain family, and a few select others on the list of New Zealand's worst or most reviled killers. His name will be said for years to come and always with disgust. His name will always be associated with the drive out west on a Monday morning with the suitcase in the boot, pulling into a layby, and getting out a long-handled spade; his name will always be dirt: 'I went and got the suitcase and put it in the hole and covered the hole.'

His confession spilled out in his second police interview. Both interviews were filmed, and both were given to Detective Ewen Settle in that narrow grey office. Both were stunningly conducted interviews. Settle employed a particularly brilliant technique: silence. Kempson's confession was made as two long, uninterrupted monologues, one lasting 22 minutes. Settle just sat there, and didn't so much as nod. In the first interview, Kempson had told a series of detailed, long-winded and actually quite boring lies to disguise his whereabouts. He slept in late on Sunday morning after his brief date with Grace, he said, and then he had a pub lunch in town: 'I ordered a Scotch fillet, cooked medium rare, with mushroom and cheese, oh yeah and salad.' Settle took out a photo from his thin stack of papers and displayed it in front of Kempson like a card: he played an ace. It was a CCTV image, he explained, of Kempson leaving CityLife at 8am on Sunday. 'Explain that,' he said. Kempson sat there and looked at the photo. Settle sat there and looked at Kempson. Together they sat there in silence for a full minute. Kempson, cracking; Kempson, busted.

I ran into the detective one morning outside Courtroom 11. Settle is a tall man with very watchful eyes. 'I want to congratulate you on that interview,' I said.

We shook hands. 'Thank you,' he said.

I said, 'That silence you left – that was deliberate, wasn't it?'

He smiled, and said, 'Yes.'

He stood there and looked at me. I stood there and looked at him. Really I was daring him to say something, anything, but Settle could not be beaten at silence and I began gabbling.

Kempson, too, gabbled. He told Settle exactly where to find Grace. That night he sat in the back of an unmarked police car and directed the driver to a layby on Scenic Drive. It was nearly dark. An officer from Search and Rescue was told to enter the bush. He found an area that had been disturbed. It was closed off, and a team went in the next morning. Soil was excavated in strata of 10cm and examined through a sieve. They found a chicken bone. Then they found a suitcase buried in a small puddle of water.

It was removed from the ground at 4.35 that afternoon and lifted onto a plastic sheet covering a table. Police tried to X-ray it to see what was inside but there was too much liquid. Forensic pathologist Dr Simon Stables arrived. He told the jury, 'The suitcase was unzipped just to establish someone was in there.' It was tagged with the notice HUMAN REMAINS.

A photo was taken of the partially unzipped suitcase. It's a brown bag. The zips have red tags. The jury were shown this photograph. I looked at this photograph. There is a body inside the suitcase.

'You're under arrest,' Settle told Kempson back at the police station.

'Yeah,' he said.

'For the murder of Grace Millane.'

'Okay.'

'Do you understand?'

'Yeah.'

Yeah. Okay. Yeah. Kempson, finished; Kempson, on his way to prison for the longest possible stretch; Kempson, already in Hell, stuck in it forever, buried alive, unable to stop the howling inside his head, haunted, hated, and worst and most intolerably of all, alone.

Chapter 2

The search for a mystery: Mark Lundy

One of the most striking things about the case of Mark Edward Lundy – the Palmerston North sink salesman accused and convicted, twice, of the murder of his wife and child, his appeal thoroughly rejected by the Court of Appeal, his appeal of that ruling inevitably rejected by the Supreme Court, and so found guilty four times for that violent and repugnant slaughter – has been that it's hardly ever regarded as any kind of mystery. It's exempt from the catalogue of New Zealand murder mysteries; it's not up to the accepted standards of New Zealand murder mysteries.

The case of David Bain is widely regarded as a mystery, a riddle beautifully expressed by the very first trial judge: 'Who did it? David Bain? Robin Bain?' The case of David Tamihere is commonly regarded a mystery. He was convicted for the killing of two Swedish tourists, but we now know that paid informants – in itself, always a dodgy tactic; Lundy, too, knows about jailhouse snitches – provided false evidence. The case of Scott Watson is regarded as a mystery. Gerald Hope, the father of Ben Smart, who Watson was convicted of killing on the waters of Marlborough Sounds, along with Olivia Smart, met Watson in prison and said to him: 'We never got the truth. We haven't got the truth yet.'

Lundy, though – Lundy doesn't get that same benefit of the doubt. It's as though we've judged him unfit to join the thrilling and perplexing whodunit file of modern, heavily reported New Zealand homicides. 'Guilty,' said the jury at his first, ridiculous trial in 2002; 'Guilty', said the jury at his streamlined, wildly adapted 2015 retrial. New Zealand – the population, generally; the appeal courts, specifically and resolutely – has gone along with the verdicts, consigned him to Hell. Lundy is in Rangipo prison. Long may he rot, that sort of thing.

Why? What's the problem? How come the Lundy killings don't appear to qualify as something unknown, strange, mysterious? Very few people make it public that they actively take his side. There's an intense, driven guy in Kumeu, and an old friend of Lundy's in Matamata, who have both worked to prove his innocence, and he's always been able to count on the support of his sister and her husband in Taupō; but Lundy has a brother who detests him so much that he's changed his surname.

The murders were atrocious. They were committed in the family home in Palmerston North on 30 August 2000. Lundy was away on business. He checked into the Foreshore Motel in Petone and hired an escort for an hour's entertainment. Police said he drove home some time after midnight and picked up a sharp weapon from the garage. Christine, his wife, was hit so many times and with such force that her face was no longer a face (*police report:* 'There appeared to be a piece of skull on her left cheek'); Amber, his daughter, killed in her nightie and little white socks in her parents' doorway (*police report:* 'The forceful blows appears to have occurred with her head no higher than 700mm from the floor'), was seven years old.

I met Lundy in the summer of 2015 when the Privy Council ordered his release and he was awaiting his retrial. He was a big, cumbersome fellow, suspicious, wary, kind of arrogant. He had a cynical laugh and his skin was very pale. It was difficult to warm to him. One day he asked about my daughter, who was the same age as Amber when she died, and said: 'Give her a hug from me when you get home.' I gave her a hug regardless, and marvelled at how little and vulnerable she was, how trusting.

The only correct position to take with Lundy as a journalist was to take no position. I formed no set ideas about his guilt or his innocence, but certainly I thought it was good practice to think very closely about the Crown case against him, and to question whether it was safe. I attended the retrial and thought he was going to be found not guilty. I attended the Court of Appeal hearing and thought his appeal had a reasonable chance. I attended the Supreme Court hearing and thought his appeal didn't have a chance in Hell. It was the only time I got it right.

Lundy didn't appear at the appeals, and there was another absence: the subject of the deaths of his wife and daughter. The killings were only fleetingly mentioned at the three-day Court of Appeal hearing in Wellington. Strange to put so much thought into a double murder and barely refer to the deaths. It was all to do with small details of evidence, of science and psychology, of legal minds forced to think fast. 'Here we are,' said Lundy's latest lawyer, Jonathan Eaton QC, when the hearing began. Eaton, a tall, slim, foppish character, made it sound like an exciting challenge. It was his first time mounting a defence for one of the most hated men in recent New Zealand history. 'Here we go again,' sighed and grimaced Philip Morgan QC, when he opened for the Crown. Morgan had prosecuted Lundy three years previously. His opening sigh and grimace would not be the last time he tried to act the role of a man who plainly viewed the whole thing as a giant waste of time and that the defence was preposterous. It was a bitter little charade, the kind which plays well in front of a jury – people want certainties, an unequivocal position – but I thought it was gratuitous in an appellate court in front of three law lords.

Eaton argued the 2015 verdict was unfair. He counted the ways. There weren't all that many ways. He zeroed in on the very thing – in terms of physical evidence, the only thing – that put Lundy at the scene of the crime, and disputed the 'novel and extraordinary' scientific testing that claimed two small stains found on Lundy's shirt were from Christine's brain. He talked about new evidence which might have convinced the jury that Lundy didn't have enough petrol to drive from his motel in Petone to Palmerston North on the night of the murders. And he also argued that the judge at the retrial ought to have directed the jury to ignore Lundy's body language in a police video, because Lundy's body language and his demeanour were the very things that convinced the general public that Lundy was a lying, murdering sonofabitch.

'Everyone remembers his behaviour at the funeral,' Eaton said. 'The public perception that he feigned distress has entered New Zealand folklore … He has engendered no public sympathy.'

And there it was, seemingly, the answer to why the Lundy case has never been taken especially seriously as a murder mystery. 'People have thought of him,' said Eaton, 'as a big fat so-and-so.' Leaving aside the fact that no one in New Zealand public life has said 'so-and-so' for approximately 50 years, Eaton's remarks struck at something important. Lundy has never inspired public sympathy. But nor do most people accused of vicious killings or violent crimes. David Tamihere and Scott Watson both manifestly failed to arouse any kind of sympathetic response on account of their manifestly unlovely characters. The same went for Teina Pora, wrongfully convicted for the rape of Susan Burdett; he was bad news, a Mongrel Mob gang prospect.

It's not the lack of sympathy and widespread perception of Lundy as a so-and-so that has denied his case the status of mystery. It's the perceived lack of evidence pointing away from him and to someone else. If not David Bain, then Robin Bain; if not Pora, then Malcolm Rewa. If not Lundy, then who?

The police investigation into the killings drew up a list of 82 people of interest. None of them emerged as credible suspects. But small and possibly crucial pieces of hard forensic evidence were introduced at both trials which pointed away from Lundy. The weird thing was how much they've always been overlooked, even disregarded. They were presented at the Court of Appeal hearing, too, but almost in passing. Some of it was astonishing and raised serious questions. And yet it was as though the element of mystery was introduced in stealth.

* * *

The appeal hearing took place in October 2017, during those sunny, halcyon days when New Zealand was without a government, and Winston Peters amused himself with coalition talks. The Court of Appeal is on Molesworth Street, opposite Parliament; I hoofed across the road one day and had a cup of tea with Jacinda Ardern. She didn't know whether she was prime minister in waiting or waiting to resume her role as leader of the opposition, but she did know that either way it involved a lot of waiting, and she was very receptive to a visit to help pass the time. She made the tea, and poured; she raided the pantry for chocolate biscuits; incredibly, she didn't let me in on the secret of her pregnancy.

On another occasion I hoofed up the road to the High Court. These are things a crime writer does for nostalgia. It's where Lundy was found guilty in 2015. It was poignant being back, and I remembered the last time I was there, on the day the jury found Lundy guilty, and wondering whether a great wrong had just been committed. His appeal was an opportunity to put things right. I doubted it would.

They do a better class of seating in the appeal court. It's the business class of the criminal justice system. There is gorgeous wood panelling, and plenty of room at the long bench at the front of the court for the three judges – Justices Helen Winkelmann, Mark Cooper and Raynor Asher – to sit and to stare down upon the masses with all due pomp and authority.

To witness an appeal hearing in action is to experience a strange and surprising spectacle. The judges are given written submissions, containing robust, careful arguments; the paragraphing is numbered, and no doubt the spelling is immaculate. But the appeal court also operates as a kind of oral exam. Counsel for both sides are required to stand and talk, freely, and at length, and to improvise answers for questions they can't possibly expect. The scene is set for a shambles. A fair bit of the Lundy hearing was duly shambolic.

Eaton ummed and ahhhed and stuttered and shook. 'And-and-and-and,' he raved, bouncing up and down on his feet, looking wildly from left to right; sometimes I had the impression that the first he'd ever heard about the case of Mark Edward Lundy was when he got handed a folder at the door of the appeal court.

As for Morgan, he relied on the old trial tactic of expressing scorn for the opponent's allegations. Eaton argued that the stains on Lundy's shirt were from something he ate; Morgan sneered, 'The only explanation the defence ever gave was a photo of some pork chops.'

He repeated his withering reference to 'some pork chops' two more times until Justice Winkelmann said, 'I'm just anxious why you're going on about a plate of some pork chops.'

'I can show you the exhibit photo of some pork chops,' Morgan replied.

'No,' said Winkelmann, 'I don't want to see the photo of some pork chops.'

Morgan banged on yet again about the ridiculousness of some pork chops.

This time Justice Cooper stopped him in his tracks: 'We're not really wanting to concentrate on the business of some pork chops.'

An unsmiling character, patient and intent, with a dark, saturnine face, Morgan made for a powerful jury lawyer. His performance at the retrial was direct and very effective. But appeal court requires a fast and nimble imagination; Morgan swayed from side to side, and merely said, 'Well, sir – there it is.'

He blundered into the same vexed territory of food with central nervous system tissue in it the following day when he made familiar sarcastic noises to dispute the defence theory that Lundy's shirt stains came specifically from a chilli beef and cheese pie. A wrapper was found in his car.

Justice Asher: 'The pie contained ground beef. Ground beef includes central nervous system tissue presumably. He picks up a fork and two drops spill on his shirt.'

Morgan: 'How unlucky can you be to be eating a chilli beef and cheese pie and get a piece of beef on your shirt, and Christine Lundy's DNA has got on the same spot in a large quantity?'

Asher: 'I seem to successfully smear food on occasion into my shirt.'

Was it bad science that did for Lundy? The stains were critical in establishing his guilt. Much of the hearing centred on Eaton's argument that the various testing – conducted in Texas and Holland – ought to have been regarded as laughable fumblings in the dark, and ruled inadmissible. By the by, he also pointed out that surely no other murder prosecution in New Zealand criminal history has relied on the police moving the goalposts so drastically from one trial to the next. In 2002, it was alleged Lundy made his 'killing journey' at incredible speeds in the very early evening; in 2015, police put the time of death at around 2.30am, and now had Lundy driving with caution.

Even more by the by and by, with something almost resembling discretion, Eaton referred to pieces of forensic evidence gathered at the crime scene. Unidentified handprints in the conservatory, where it's argued an intruder broke into the house on Karamea Crescent. Unidentified footprints. Unidentified DNA found beneath the nails of both Christine and Amber, as well as unidentified fibre – which did not match Lundy's famously stained polo shirt. (Even Eaton referred to the possibility of Lundy wearing overalls, but there is no evidence he owned a pair.)

From the 2015 trial, there was this exchange between defence and a forensic expert witness.

'Is this right, there were similarities between the results from the fingernail samples from Christine Lundy and those found on the fingernail scrapings of Amber Lundy?'

'Yes.'

'So does that mean at least one male was common to both sets of fingernails, Amber Lundy on the one side and her mother on the other?'

'Yes. I would suggest that's likely.'

'And the source of course could be skin?'

'Yes.'

The appeal hearing attracted a light sprinkling of media. They included the peerless Mike White from *North & South*, whose very detailed investigations into the case led directly to the Privy Council ordering a retrial, and *Manawatū Standard* reporter Jono Galuszka, who covered the 2015 trial more thoroughly than anyone. But neither had heard of an almost incidental piece of evidence that Eaton mentioned at the Court of Appeal: unidentified hairs, found in both clenched hands of Christine Lundy.

They were evident in a police drawing taken at the autopsy. Christine's hands were wrapped with plastic bags at the crime scene; they were unwrapped at the morgue, and hairs were evident between her fingers. The drawing also indicated defensive wounds to her forearms. There she was, in the last dreadful seconds of her life, holding up her hands to protect her face from the blows; had she also reached up, her fingernails scraping at the skin on her attacker's face, and grabbing at his hair? He had missed with some of his blows, and splintered the headboard. Christine had moved across the bed to get away. Was it in these seconds that she was able to collect fragments from the body of the killer who was someone else other than her husband?

* * *

43

The Court of Appeal threw out Lundy's appeal with some considerable force. I received the information and read its decision in unlikely circumstances: on a family holiday, in Rarotonga, at a resort which just so happened to be hosting the 37th Annual Pacific Islands Law Officers' Conference. Senior officials from the Crown Law Office in Wellington were swanning around in neatly ironed board shorts, and one of them showed me the appeal court decision on his phone. It made for bracing reading. There wasn't an if, but, or maybe about it; every single ground for appeal was summarily, almost sourly dismissed, and the judges concluded: 'In the end we have been left sure of Mr Lundy's guilt.'

As for the hair and the fingernails – again, just like the way they made a cameo appearance at the Court of Appeal, they were dealt with almost in passing. Yes, judges confirmed, DNA from at least two unidentified males was found beneath Amber Lundy's fingernails; yes, DNA from one or more unidentified males was found beneath Christine Lundy's fingernails. And yet: 'We do not consider the evidence about fingernail scrapings to be of significance.' What about the hair? 'This evidence does not assist in resolving the issues we have to decide.' Skin from male or males unknown, found beneath the fingernails of both victims; hair, which did not match Mark Lundy, found in Christine's hands: of no apparent significance, just one of those things, just … a mystery, but not worth worrying about.

The decision of the appeal court was emphatic. But it allowed one victory for Lundy's defence – and an opening to appeal to the Supreme Court. It ruled that a key piece of evidence produced by the prosecution ought to have been inadmissible. It went to the very essence of the Crown case against Lundy: the two small stains discovered on the shirt he wore on the night his wife and daughter were killed.

There are strong parallels with the Lindy Chamberlain case. The forensic evidence which put Chamberlain in jail for the murder of Azaria were two small 'sticky droplets' discovered in her yellow Torana hatchback. 'The Crown said at the trial', Chamberlain writes in her autobiography, *Through My Eyes*, 'that I had sat in the front passenger seat, held Azaria out in front of me and cut her throat … An artery spurted blood producing the spray pattern.' Forensic biologist Joy Kuhl said it tested positive for foetal blood that 'could only have come from a child under six months'. Later tests established the spray pattern in the car was a chemical sealant used to deaden sound.

Lindy, Lundy, and tiny traces of … something. According to the prosecution, the two small stains on Lundy's XXXL polo shirt came from his wife's brain. According to the defence, it might have been food, perhaps a nice hot pie. Two scientific tests supported the brain theory; one of them, Eaton told the Court Appeal, was more or less junk science, and ought never have been admissible. It turned out he was right.

He meant evidence from Dr Laetitia Sijen of the Netherlands Forensic Institute. Her mRNA testing claimed to show that the tissue on Lundy's shirt was human brain and not brain of any kind of animal. I remember her very well in the retrial. She was reduced to a shaking, sobbing wreck in cross-examination. Sijen gave evidence that seven out of twelve tests showed the stain tested positive for human. A lousy 58 per cent isn't exactly a scholarship result; it's barely a pass mark. Besides that, as trial lawyer David Hislop said in court, not a single forensic expert was prepared to come forward to support her mRNA methods or her claims that the central nervous tissue was human. 'Sijen,' trial judge Simon France memorably told the jury in his summing up, 'stands alone.'

And so Eaton hammered her evidence at the appeal court, gave it everything he had. He knew it was a weak spot. But so did Crown prosecutor Philip Morgan. He affected a disdain, almost a boredom for Sijen's findings. They weren't that big a deal, he said. The Crown could have easily done without it.

The appeal court judges agreed with both Eaton and Morgan. They ruled that the evidence ought to have been inadmissible, but that it made no difference. They asked, rhetorically: 'Would Mr Lundy have been convicted notwithstanding the evidence?' They put it another way: 'We are required to conclude whether the appeal should be dismissed on the basis that no substantial miscarriage of justice has actually occurred.' They concluded exactly that. Justice had been served; Lundy killed Christine and Amber; and of course maybe they were right.

* * *

I agree with the Court of Appeal that Sijens's mRNA evidence probably didn't make a lick of difference. Certainly it bored the jury rigid. It was complicated, it took up a lot of time, it made Sijen look bad and none of it really seemed worth the effort. Her evidence was really only on the border of something that really did matter. She was like an addendum, or a parenthetical point made in support of something that really did matter.

Dr Rodney Miller of Texas made all the difference. Miller remains the most important person in the case against Mark Edward Lundy, its eminent person, its godlike presence, its fabulous conjuror who held the court in thrall with his spectacular and crucial discovery of something that mattered more than anything else.

The police located tissue smeared on Lundy's shirt and worked hard to find a scientist who could identify its exact properties. 'I really don't think that it can be anything other than brain,' pathologist Dr Cynric Temple-Clamp claims he said to Detective Senior Sergeant Ross Grantham, who headed the murder inquiry. Temple-Clamp relays the conversation in his book *The Cause of Death*. Grantham asked him, 'Can you prove it?' The pathologist replied: 'No.'

Temple-Clamp takes up the story. 'How could we reach the level of scientific certainty necessary to stand up in court? We thought an international expert was needed … Our minds turned to Rod Miller, a pathologist in Texas who had been a very impressive guest lecturer at our scientific conference in Palmerston North in 2000, a short while before the murders. Rod is a brilliant scientist and an expert in using immunohistochemistry on tissue samples … We suggested to Ross that he contact Rod.'

Grantham flew to Texas. Miller tested the samples in his laboratory. He had good news: his immunochemistry (IHC) stains established that it was central nervous system tissue. Lundy was done for from that moment on.

Defence made a hash of dealing with it in both trials. In the first trial, Lundy's lawyer Mike Behrens more or less accused the police of tampering with the evidence. It was without foundation and went down like a lead balloon. Otherwise, he presented no serious challenge to the Miller findings. In the retrial, David Hislop made the tactical decision not to attempt a demolition of Miller's testing; his position was that the defence had so much evidence which exonerated Lundy that it didn't need to engage in a necessarily complicated debate. In any case Hislop's own expert witnesses agreed with Miller: the tissue was central nervous system, or brain.

And yet Miller was hardly infallible. His immunohistochemistry evidence in the Lundy case remains the only instance it's ever been used in a forensic crime investigation. And he was working on blood or tissue samples so small and so degraded – it had been 59 days before police thought to analyse the shirt, and make slides – that one expert had described Miller's test as 'useless'.

Miller claimed that once the brain tissue landed on Lundy's shirt, it was air-dried, or mummified, and could easily be tested after 59 days. He's backed up by Dr Cynric Temple-Camp, who makes grand claims about the durability of the tell-tale stain: 'The dried brain-matter was preserved within minutes of the murder and was still preserved 59 days later and will still be so 59 years from now. Once it's fixed, it is preserved pretty much forever.'

All through two trials, no one ever really attacked Miller's testing, or tried to discredit it, or even seriously question it. The first time it was attacked, discredited and seriously questioned was at the Privy Council, in London; significantly, it led to Lundy's release, and a retrial. A neuropathologist described Miller's use of IHC staining as 'a novel approach'; a professor of physiology described it 'potentially inconsistent and unreliable'.

The professor was Philip Sheard of the University of Otago. He repeated his criticism of Miller in an affidavit to the Court of Appeal. I got in touch with him and emailed him Temple-Camp's remarks that the 'dried brain-matter' would be fixed for all eternity, and asked what he thought.

He replied, 'As a neuroscientist who uses IHC to examine nerve tissue virtually every working day, I can say that air drying never has and never will be used as a means of "preserving" samples of brain tissue. Second, even where air drying is used as a means of preservation, an absolute requirement is that it must be rapid.

How long did it take for this sample to dry? We have no idea. Does it matter? Absolutely. Quality of fixation is one criterion that anyone with any experience of IHC will say is profoundly capable of having a direct influence on the outcome of the investigation ... Both failure types are catastrophic and, when they occur, render the investigation useless.'

I asked Sheard whether he regarded the use of IHC testing in a forensic context to be junk science. He replied, 'I wouldn't use the word junk. Forensic science requires robust, reproducible, reliable procedures ... to deliver a definitive outcome. IHC doesn't come close to meeting those requirements.'

In his affidavit to the appeal court, Sheard examined Miller's testing in the light of a US report, prepared by the President's Council of Advisors on Science and Technology (PCAST), which investigated the validity of forensic methods. 'Dr Miller has demonstrated the precise traits that the PCAST committee would seek to prohibit.' He concluded that Miller's evidence amounted to a 'significant failure ... to approach the desired standards for forensic scientific methods as laid out by PCAST.'

Further doubts were raised in another, damning affidavit, prepared by an attorney in Miller's own back yard. Mike Ware, the executive director of The Innocence Project in Texas, looked into the strange circumstances involving Miller's attempts to head off any criticism of the degraded tissue found on Lundy's polo shirt. After the Privy Council ordered a retrial, Miller came up with an ingenious idea. He took receipt of the fresh brain of an 84-year-old former secretary with Alzheimer's (medical report: 'She has been unaware of people for about a year') who had donated her body to science. It was given to Miller in a bucket. Miller removed a sample, smeared it on fabric, and put it aside for 59 days – thus replicating the police procedure with the Lundy stain. His IHC testing identified it as central nervous system tissue. The results were presented in Lundy's retrial and received little less than a standing ovation from experts called by both the prosecution and the defence.

I called Ware at his office in Fort Worth. He explained Lundy's legal team contacted him to see what he could find out about the so-called 'bucket brain'. He said, 'I wanted to be able to provide to Mr Lundy's attorneys how this body, and particularly the relevant body parts, had been preserved. My understanding was that it was relevant to Miller's testimony that the brain was fresh, and not artificially processed in any kind of way.'

I said, 'Specifically, that it had not been preserved in formalin.'

'Exactly,' he said. The point being made was that if the brain had been preserved in formalin, it would prevent any degradation, and make a mockery of Miller's test.

Ware made inquiries. He didn't get very far. The paperwork he received was heavily redacted. But he stumbled on something else: he discovered that Miller received the woman's brain without due permission from the University of Texas Southwestern Medical Center. It subsequently ruled that the 'removal of the brain from campus was unauthorised ... and a violation of policy and a violation of State Anatomical Board regulations'.

The redacted paperwork made brief mention of the woman's autopsy on 15 January 2014: 'The cadaver was placed into a cooler ... along with the bucket.' The bucket contained her brain. The bucket was then driven across town and given to Dr Miller. A savage and appalling double murder in Palmerston North, New Zealand, partly solved by the unauthorised exchange of a brain in a plastic bucket in Dallas, Texas.

Ware said, 'As a legal matter, none of this would have been allowed into evidence in Texas, because it [the brain] was taken in contravention of what the laws provide.'

I said, 'But the person who contravened was Dr Word, who gave the brain to Dr Miller. He didn't contravene any laws.'

He said, 'Under Texas law, that wouldn't matter. You can't break the law through an intermediary and expect a different result.'

I said, 'It's almost analogous to receiving stolen goods.'

He said, 'It's very much analogous to that. Or it's more than analogous than that. Maybe that's what it was.'

Ware's affidavit to the Court of Appeal carried a certain animus towards Miller. He noted that Miller had been given an award by the New Zealand police, and wrote of his fellow Texan, 'Miller seemed to be using the Lundy case and his perceived heroic role to market his own business as well as to aggrandize himself professionally and personally.'

Nothing that Ware said seemed to make much of an impression with the appeal court judges. 'We do not find his affidavit cogent,' they ruled. As for the ferrying of a brain in a plastic bucket, and irregularities and violations, that was all beside the point, was barking up the wrong tree. 'The steps he [Miller] took to obtain the brain tissue do not have a logical bearing on the results that Dr Miller achieved.'

I made another call to Texas during the Court of Appeal hearing. It was strange to actually talk with the legendary Dr Miller in person. That eminent person, that fabulous conjuror ... We spoke for eight minutes. He had a warm, friendly voice, until he terminated the call.

* * *

Dr Miller, my name is Steve Braunias, I work as a journalist at The New Zealand Herald *newspaper in Auckland, and I'm currently writing a story about the Mark Lundy case, which right now is being appealed. I don't know if you know that, and I would really like to ask you a few questions.*

All I will say is that I stand by my testimony, and other than that I can't really comment. I would love to. I would *love* to! I have many stories to tell. But I'm just going to have to keep my mouth shut for now.

It's not at trial right now, though.

I have been blindsided by journalists before, particularly that guy who wrote the *North & South* article. I'm sure you're aware of him. He did not allow me to comment on the other people who reviewed my work before their comments were published, and that was an extremely unfair thing to do. I'm sure you're a very fine journalist! But I don't trust them until all this is over. We'll wait and see what his appeal happens – I'm aware of the appeal, yes – and, you know, if he is successful in his appeal, then I will have done the right thing in not commenting on anything, and if he is unsuccessful in his appeal, I will not have any comment until he has exhausted all appeals. And then the floodgates will open. Ha-ha! But I really can't comment until then.

So upon that day will you then happily speak to me, Dr Miller?
Yes. Oh, yes. Yes.

In the meantime you do stand by your work? You are as confident of it as you always have been?
Yes.

In the second trial, I was expecting a rebuttal of your evidence – but no one really argued it, did they?
You don't know everything that happened behind the scenes.

That is true. But your incredibly effective duplication of the testing of the so-called bucket brain was quite vital to the trial, wasn't it?
You know – I don't know. I'm not going to comment on that.

The one question I have about that is: was that brain fixed in formalin before you made that test?
I have no comment on that. If I am … It was fresh. It was not fixed in formalin at the time I received it.

You can say that?
Yeah. Yeah. I handled it.

You have probably seen an affidavit flying around at the Court of Appeal which raises a concern about what appear to be irregularities in transporting the bucket brain to you?
I have no comment on that. There were no irregularities.

Did you fill out the proper documentation?
You know, I have no comment. I have no comment on that. I will comment if I need to.

I am wondering whether that whole thing is a red herring, and the defence are barking up the wrong tree with that?
I stand by my testimony. That's all I'll say for now.

There is one chap who is very much a fan of yours – Temple-Camp, the pathologist from Palmerston North. I don't know if you ever met him?
Yes, I have met Dr Temple-Camp.

Have you seen his book? It includes writings on the Lundy case.
I'm aware he wrote the book, but I haven't read it.

He credits you for your vital and crucial contribution to the prosecution, and one thing he does say which I find interesting, and I imagine would be your thinking also, is that he essentially counters the argument that the brain tissue was degraded, and he talks about how the dried brain matter was preserved minutes after the murder, was preserved 59 days after the murder, and will be so 59 years from now. Once it is fixed, he writes, it will be fixed pretty much forever. Is that your view too?
Like I said, I'm not going to comment on anything. Because I don't know what you're going to do with whatever I say, so I won't comment unless I'm asked to comment under oath at another retrial.

But Temple-Camp – those things he wrote are friendly fire, so to speak.
Sure it is. Sure it is. Yeah. I have – I still had, at the time of the retrial, the piece of shirt that I smeared with fresh brain. Everything was still detectable for over a year. Not 59 days; it was readily recognisable as brain after a year. And I still got it stored, and I'm thinking maybe five years from now, I'll give it another try, and see what happens.

By that time Mr Lundy may have exhausted all avenues of appeal.
Yeah. And then I'll write another paper.

It doesn't sound as though you have ever lost any sleep over this.
Not the work that I've done. Certainly not, no.

You mentioned Mike White before. You said to him, 'I can say with 100 per cent certainty that the tissue on Lundy's shirt was central nervous system tissue. Not 99.99 per cent, 100 per cent.' Do you remain as emphatic?
Yes. But don't quote me on that, okay? Like I said, I don't want any of this conversation published.

Whoa there.
If you're going to do that, my official line is no comment, other than I stand by my work. Okay?

You've said a number of things, though, before you've said that.
Okay, well, I'm asking you not to do it. Okay? Is that clear?

Yeah, you are asking me, but it's after the fact. I think the horse has bolted.
Okay. This conversation is over. If you publish it, you will be doing it against my permission. And I will testify to that in court.

Okay. I will play the recording, which—
Thank you for your call.

* * *

The day never came that Miller would happily speak to me and that 'the floodgates would open'. We texted a couple of years after our aborted phone conversation. I asked for an interview and he didn't want a bar of it: 'I remember you,' he wrote.

55

Eaton had tried to get Miller's evidence ruled inadmissible. The judges rejected the request. 'To the extent it seeks to advance an argument that IHC evidence may be bad science,' they wrote – with a rare, thrilling acknowledgement made by New Zealand law lords that the Texas staining tests might qualify as 'bad science' and subsequently collapse the case against Lundy like a tent – 'the answer that can be given is that all of those with the most relevant expertise agreed that IHC evidence had established that the tissue on the shirt worn by Mr Lundy was CNS [central nervous system] tissue.'

Well, Eaton still had the ruling that Sijens's evidence was inadmissible, and he was granted leave to appeal that single issue at the Supreme Court. It was the final thread. He duly clung to it when he appeared at the Supreme Court in Wellington.

The final court of appeal, the highest court in the land, is also the ugliest goddamned piece of state-approved junk architecture in all of New Zealand. It doesn't look so bad from the outside on Lambton Quay. It's got a shallow pool of water and a bronze lattice. Nothing outlandish, kind of neutral. But the courtroom itself is shaped like an egg, or a cocoon, a grandiose ovoid dome done out in diamond-patterned blonde wood leading to a high, distant skylight covered in what might be wire from a chicken coop – hence the egg?

The whole tasteless thing is at best viewed as a sci-fi set from a bad movie, at worst as something pompous and pretentious and really rather mocking of the poor suckers who have to sit in it, and reach sober judgment.

The poor suckers at Lundy's hearing were five in number. Three of the learned Justices didn't have a whole lot to say. Most of the talking – the interjecting, the sighing, the scorning – was done by one judge, Justice Willy Young, who took the middle seat at the

USS *Enterprise*-style bench. He made me think of a radish: his face was red, and he wore his white hair quite long at the back. He took his glasses off to read documents, which he held approximately 0.0001 millimetres from his face, all the better to study legal arguments and to try to get to grips with one of the rarest of all notions in criminal law: a proviso.

A proviso is an intricate thing of some beauty. It's a trick of the light, something conjured – now you see it, now you don't. It admits one thing and declares another. You can see I'm having trouble here defining quite what it is, but the five judges had an even more torrid time making a precise and meaningful definition at Lundy's appeal. It was the proviso from Hell.

Very well, it goes something like this. A proviso is that which admits to a failing in an argument brought against the accused by the Crown, a really quite serious failing, but is at once rendered an insignificant and irrelevant failing, a failing of no concern, a failing so small and of such little magnitude that it can barely be thought of as a failing at all, and must be overlooked, swept aside, shrugged off as just one of those crazy things that happen every once in a blue moon.

Lundy's conviction for the awful murders of his wife and daughter was that blue moon. The Court of Appeal ruled that the Sijen evidence ought to have been inadmissible. The jury ought not have heard it. It was a scientific analysis so lacking in substance that it might be referred to as junk science, as total crap. Yes, perhaps, that may be so, allowed the Crown. But so what? Who cares? Because the Crown was able to flourish that thing of beauty, that rare and delicately formed idea: the proviso.

The proviso stated that it didn't matter if the evidence was slipshod. The proviso declared that an admission of failure had no reckoning on Lundy's guilt. The proviso smiled, held up its hands, and said *que sera, sera*; it said it was a mere bagatelle; it said it made no difference, that the weight and range of the Crown case proved that Lundy slaughtered his wife and daughter as sure as night follows day.

'We have decided,' ruled the appeal court judges, 'that the proviso should be upheld and the appeal dismissed.'

'No,' said Eaton QC. 'No, you can't just turn around and say, "Don't worry about it." They [the prosecution] relied on it. They wouldn't have fought so hard to get it in if they didn't rely on it. It's all a bit rich. And it begs the question: was this a good case to apply the proviso?'

I have assembled these comments from three hours of Eaton's testimony. He seldom got to say a speech as long as that without some kind of interruption or interjection from the bench, in particular Justice Young, who stared down at Eaton with an expression of bored indifference.

Eaton stuck it to the proviso as best he could. His essential thrust was that a miscarriage of justice had occurred. His wider, awesomely nuanced thrust led to a profound conversation with the bench on the very nature of reality. Here, then, was Lundy's last chance. Forensic science has done for him. The law has done for him, over and over and over. Psychology has done for him: the public has always hated Lundy. Eaton took a deep breath, and introduced a new weapon, the final remaining act of reasoning which he hoped might work to Lundy's advantage: philosophy.

* * *

'We are dancing,' Eaton said to the five judges, 'around the pin of a head.' He corrected himself but he got it right the first time.

58

O proviso! O weird and unhummable melody under the Crimes Act. Eaton and His Honours taxed their very fine legal minds in an attempt to solve the riddle of the proviso, to capture its trick of the light in a jar, to get to the bottom of it.

'It's really a philosophical argument, isn't it?' said Eaton, and for once Justice Young, who had spent all of that first morning shaking his head to and fro at everything that came out of Eaton's mouth, actually nodded in agreement. 'Yes,' he intoned, then took his glasses off the top of his white hair – he'd been reading something – placed them between his lips, and nibbled contemplatively at the frame.

To proviso, or not to proviso? The leading test case in New Zealand law is the unpleasant case of Shane Huia Matenga. He was convicted of raping an intellectually disabled woman in 2007 after she invited him in for a cup of tea. His defence appealed, arguing that circumstantial evidence put before the jury was seriously flawed. The Court of Appeal upheld the conviction by applying the proviso: yes, the evidence was poor, but Matenga would have been found guilty in any case. It then went to the Supreme Court, which ruled against the proviso, quashed the conviction, and ordered a new trial. It was to no avail – a second jury found Matenga guilty of rape – but the legacy of the case is that it remains the classic precedent for proviso law.

The proviso, it ruled, can only be applied where guilt is considered absolute. A guilty verdict must be 'inevitable', and 'the only reasonably possible verdict based on the evidence'. The proviso 'should only be applied if there is no room for doubt about the guilt'. The proviso can over-ride any admission of a failure of evidence to meet the standard 'if the Court is sure of guilt'.

'But what,' Eaton wondered, 'does "inevitable" mean?'

The five judges stared at him.

'A philosophical approach to the proviso is required,' he continued.

The five judges stared at him a bit longer.

'What,' Eaton further wondered, 'does "sure" mean?'

Justice Young thought he could answer that. He said, 'You've got to be not just sure of guilt, but really, really sure of guilt.'

'That's a very high standard,' said Eaton.

Young made another attempt. '"Sure",' he said, 'comes down to very, very sure.'

The Court of Appeal's dismissal of Lundy's appeal was all those things and more: when it applied the proviso, it was really, really, *really* sure and very, very, *very* sure of his guilt. But, Eaton argued, was the appeal court correct to determine that Lundy received a fair trial, and that the convictions were inevitable despite the wrongful admission of evidence? Didn't the court, in essence, reach its own verdict? He put it another way: 'The proviso is saying the appeal court wears the same hat as the jury.'

'No, it doesn't,' snapped Young.

Really? In an otherwise quite boring New Zealand law article headlined 'The Role of the Court in Correcting Miscarriages of Justice', the author writes clearly and cleanly, 'Once the proviso is in play, the task of the appeal court is broadly similar to that of a jury.' The author was Justice Willy Young.

* * *

The six-week retrial at the High Court of Wellington in the summer of 2015, the week-long Court of Appeal hearing in Wellington in October 2017, the two-day Supreme Court philosophical disquisition in Wellington in July 2019 – all throughout my years of Lundy-watching in court, I've stuck to the same regime of breakfast on Masons Lane, an alleyway which turns off Lambton Quay close to the Beehive, at John's Kitchen.

It's a plain little room with a public service ambience. I love it there, and I loved being back for the Supreme Court hearing, reading the Wellington paper (a recipe for swede and beetroot casserole), and readying some change for Wellington beggars (unambiguous sign: PLEASE GIVE MONEY FOR FOOD OR FOOD) lying the length of Lambton Quay. I always order the same familiar breakfast of filter coffee and two pieces of toast. Then I trot to court and join the same familiar faces – the press, the lawyers. And the same familiar question, the only question: Did he do it? Did Mark Edward Lundy swing some kind of tomahawk with such force so many times at his wife's face as she lay in bed that it was no longer a face? Did he turn when his daughter came into the bedroom, and crack open her skull as she ran away from a monster?

Most New Zealanders will say yes to all of the above. There is a public impatience with this whole enduring business with Mark Lundy and his maintenance of innocence.

But there is another set of familiar questions which are really the only questions we can ask and expect to trust: Was it a fair conviction? Was the guilty verdict beyond reasonable doubt, did the Crown present a good and steadfast case, was the evidence accurate and correct?

We know that the first trial was absurd, a black comedy, based on evidence later found to be totally bogus – that Lundy drove at incredible speeds from Petone to Palmerston North to commit the killings in the early evening, that an eyewitness saw him run from the scene in a wig, that he tampered with the clock on the home

61

computer to hide his tracks. All of it nonsense, all of it thrown out and replaced with new theories in his retrial. There was nonsense there, too, in the shape of a jailhouse snitch who gave evidence against Lundy.

And then the revelation, via the Court of Appeal, that the theory of human brain tissue on Lundy's shirt was also a nonsense. Was it a fair conviction, was the guilty verdict beyond reasonable doubt … ? Eaton's appeal at the Supreme Court focused on the possible impact and significance of that one strand of inadmissible evidence, but now and then he found wiggle room to discuss other aspects of the case.

Of course the stain on Lundy's shirt could have come from food, he said; there was a pie wrapper in his car; there was a receipt for a $74.22 meat purchase eight days before the killings; he shopped at Pak'nSave in Petone on the night of the killings and bought a cooked chicken.

He repeated the defence argument of three impossibilities made at Lundy's trial. One, Lundy didn't have enough petrol in the car to drive to Palmerston North and back on the so-called 'killing journey'. Two, the fact that Christine and Amber's stomachs were full at the time of death suggested the killings were committed while Lundy had an alibi. Three, a neighbour noticed the Lundys' sliding door was open at a time of night when Lundy had an alibi.

Right near the end of his closing address, Eaton threw all sorts of things at the bench in a mad rush, as though he knew this was his last chance to appeal Lundy's case and he had to get it all out while he had the opportunity in the blonde cocoon of the Supreme Court. Most spectacularly, he accused a man with 'mental health problems' of being the real killer. 'He was one of the reasonable suspects,' Eaton raved, 'and believe me, he could be the offender!'

But he had been given leave to argue only the proviso. The proviso, that shimmering thread; the proviso, that strange and fragile application of the law. Eaton twitched at the thread, tested it in his fingers. For the Crown, Philip Morgan told the bench that of course the Court of Appeal was right to have applied the proviso. 'It's reasoning was impeccable.' The case against Lundy didn't rely on that one minor piece of inadmissible evidence. 'Put it aside.' Nothing to see here. 'It's wrong to argue the Crown hinged its case on this evidence ... It wasn't all that important.' In his hands, the thread of the proviso was as strong as rope, and he twisted it around Lundy's neck.

Last appeal. Last outing in the halls of justice for Mark Edward Lundy. All he had to go on was that damned proviso; I sat there and thought that it was something, but really not much, and that the outcome was inevitable. Last chance, gone.

* * *

No one thought any different, and the Supreme Court duly threw the appeal out with ill grace. Its ruling was concise. 'The approved question was whether the Court of Appeal erred in applying the proviso,' it began. 'The Supreme Court declined leave to appeal on a number of other grounds including whether the IHC evidence should have been admitted at the trial.' Miller, once again, was vindicated. And then the ruling got down to business. 'The Supreme Court has unanimously declined Mr Lundy's appeal. The Crown case at trial did not depend on the mRNA evidence. The Court was also satisfied,' it concluded, heading for the door with all due haste and apparent distaste, 'of Mr Lundy's guilt beyond reasonable doubt.'

The end. Except not quite. Within weeks of the ruling, the Criminal Cases Review Commission was officially established. It was a gleam in the eye of High Court judge Sir Thomas Thorp in 2007, when he first recommended a specialist tribunal be set up to investigate miscarriages of justice; it took only 13 years to happen, which is lightning fast for the New Zealand legislative judiciary. Thorp had said in 2007 that New Zealand's review systems were insufficient. He believed 20 people may be in jail wrongly. That figure seems a bit modest, and there will no doubt be a rush to get to the head of the review commission queue. Justice minister Andrew Little told reporters, 'New Zealand has had some significant cases where there have been miscarriages of justice and it has taken a long time for that to be detected, and for things to be put right, and ultimately for justice to be done.' All of which spells the return, once more, of Lundy.

Eaton had made that plain when he released a statement after the Supreme Court ruling: 'This is not the end of the road in Mr Lundy's fight to establish he has suffered a miscarriage of justice.' I knew exactly what that meant. I knew exactly who would be involved. When I think of Lundy, I don't actually think of Lundy: I think of a small, moustachioed man with a very direct gaze, a guy who I have come to like very much, and picture bending over a stack of papers – forensic evidence, witness statements, witness testimony – in his country house with a cup of coffee and a rolled cigarette balanced on an ashtray. 'Geoff Levick seems to be keen to fight on,' *Manawatū Standard* journalist Jono Galuszka emailed me not long after the Supreme Court's decision. 'He has been sending me all sorts of stuff about IHC ...' I thought: I bet he has. It wasn't long after that Levick sent me all sorts of stuff about petrol consumption.

Levick, always Levick, in the matter of Mark Edward Lundy. Everything comes back to Levick in the story of Lundy's bid for freedom.

Levick didn't know Lundy or anyone involved in the murder when he first started to take an interest in the case in 2003. That interest became an obsession, his life's work. He is convinced that Lundy did not commit the murders, and knows the case inside out, better than anyone – better than Lundy himself.

Levick's investigations, researches and footwork laid the foundation for a legal challenge that overturned the 2002 conviction at the Privy Council. Lundy was released and tasted freedom in the months before his retrial. Levick put him up at his home in rural Kumeu. I'd visit the house that summer and we'd sit out on the back porch of an afternoon. Lundy was intense, weepy, anxious; as for Levick, he'd just been fired by the legal defence team, who'd had a gutsful of his criticism of the way they were preparing for the trial. Levick wanted a full-on, guns-blazing attack on Miller's testing. The defence had other ideas.

'Geoff doesn't understand the trial process and the strategies you need to win a trial,' Lundy's retrial lawyer David Hislop told me in an office at the Wellington High Court, while the jury were considering their verdict. 'Perhaps after the verdict – if the verdict goes the right way – we can try to mend some of those bridges.' And then he laughed, really quite mirthlessly, and said, 'If it goes the other way, he'll probably just shoot us.'

It went the other way. I think the only thing that stopped Levick from reaching for his gun might have been that he thought a bullet was too good for Hislop. He returned to his investigations and researches, and began preparing for the inevitable appeal. I've visited him a few times since then and there are always big,

65

fat manila folders lying around, stacks of new and old paperwork, marked PETROL and STOMACH CONTENTS and, of course, MILLER.

The last time I went out to Kumeu was with the notion of looking into any documentation that might go towards answering the leading question: if not Lundy, who? Who were the other suspects? Who did the police interview, who else was on their radar? And what possible motive could lead a killer or killers unknown to inflict such violence? Was there anything, some small scrap of paper, a detail, a clue, an aside, that might qualify to make me think of the Lundy case as a murder mystery?

* * *

Levick's long-held theory is that the killings were a debt collection gone horribly wrong. On the morning of the murders, a couple of heavies turned up unannounced at the house of a man who has permanent name suppression, wanting him to settle a debt; the man was involved in a business deal with Lundy, and he and Lundy spoke for close to an hour on the phone that night. The bow being pulled here is that the heavies went to Lundy's house late that night to demand the money from him, and that it all went crazy.

Either that, or the killings were random. Police drew up a long list of deranged suspects in and around Palmerston North. They disclosed their files to Lundy's defence team. They're now stored along with about 100 cardboard boxes of Lundy material in a shed next to Levick's stables. He used to run horses on the property until a flash flood burst the river – he told an unpleasant story of one of the horses being trapped against a fence.

I spent the day in the draughty shed with a packet of biscuits and a thermos of instant coffee. I read observations made by Palmerston North police officers stationed outside the murder scene during that first week: 'Anon male stopped to say that a male Maori with long dreadlocks killed his brother with baseball bat and was acting strange before the murders, standing over people and having all-day drinking sessions at Princess Tavern.' All-day drinking sessions tend to make people act strange.

I read an anonymous letter accusing a man who no one in Christine Lundy's family had met or even heard of: 'It was common knowledge that he and Christine were secretly meeting ... He is very vain and fussy, likes fancy dress parties, fastidious in personal hygiene, terrified of pain, lazy and promiscuous, had many women during a single day, and part-owned a racehorse.' Murderers are never that interesting.

Real suspects were thin on the ground. Among the best bets were two men who lived nearby. One had only just moved to Palmerston North for job prospects – that is, to join the Mongrel Mob. His prison support worker reported he went missing for two days immediately following the murder. Police spoke with him, and he said he was in Te Awamutu, drinking.

The other man had been involved in a stabbing in 1998, committed to the Manawaroa Psychiatric Unit, and released into the care of his parents. He was on anti-psychotic medication. 'It knocks him out,' his father told police, when interviewed a fortnight after the murders. 'He spends most of his time at home, often asleep in the lounge chair or in bed ... At night he usually has tea and goes to sleep.' His mother said, 'He hasn't undergone any behavioural or mood changes in the past two weeks.' She added, 'I wish he would.'

All that was missing in this desperately vague trail of suspects was a nutter's confession. I opened the file prepared by Tim McKinnel, the private investigator hired by David Hislop, and read an email dated 8 August 2014: '[X] has confessed.' Nutter.

It was pleasant work to go through the papers, gnaw on biscuits and drink instant coffee in Levick's shed in the countryside. It was my kind of embedding. I enjoyed Levick's company, and wished I could chance across some small detail, something overlooked, that might help his cause to prove Lundy was innocent. But I had another thought in the back of my mind. What if I stumbled on some small detail, something overlooked, that leaned towards Lundy's guilt? I'd been visiting Levick for a long time, and was sympathetic to his campaign; would I turn out to be his Judas? Betrayal is the dark underground stream that runs beneath journalism. I poured another coffee, and chanced across the untold story of a Palmerston North truck driver who thought he saw Lundy near the scene of the crime on the night of the murders.

* * *

'Personally,' said Nigel Winiata, 'I think it was him.' This was the first time he'd spoken with a reporter about the Lundy murders. He was twice interviewed by police. He gave a statement about a month after the killings, and again 12 years later, before Lundy's retrial. He had seen something strange that night. It might have been nothing, just a random passerby. But Winiata is the only witness to ever come forward who could possibly tie Lundy to the murder.

Lundy had booked a room at the Foreshore Motor Lodge in Petone on the night his wife and daughter were killed. He called an escort to his room; she left at 12.48am.

In the first trial, prosecution worked on the theory that the murders occurred earlier that night, at about 7pm. Winiata told police he saw someone near Lundy's house at about 2.50am. When I spoke with him, he said, 'I seen what I saw and at the time I was told, "Nah, not possible." The cops said to me, "Nah, nah, wrong timeframe." They basically fobbed me off.'

In the second trial, police changed their mind about the time of deaths. The new hypothesis put the murders anywhere between around about 2am and when the bodies were discovered in the morning. Easy to see why Winiata was approached by police in 2014, and asked to tell his story again.

He was sitting in his beloved Scania truck in the yard at the Foodstuffs supermarket chain. He was about to drive to New Plymouth. He looked up, and saw someone walking up the Bryce Place cul-de-sac, close to Lundy's address at 30 Karamea Place.

He said, 'Cos I was working shift hours, you knew who was walking up and down the street – shift workers, there was one truck driver who used to walk to work, and I'd usually see a guy on a pushbike. Just three or four things that would regularly happen in the morning, and then when you saw something different, you'd think, "Aw, okay, what's that?"

'So this particular morning I was sitting there writing my notes up and a person started walking pretty much straight in front of me. I just had me truck there idling, and I switched the lights up on full-beam, the big 100-watt spotlights, and lit up the street like broad daylight. And I saw this guy.'

I said, 'What did he look like?'

He said, 'Big guy. Thick-set. Balding. Glasses.'

I said, 'You told the police he was carrying a bag?'

He said, 'Yep. Yep. A sky-blue sports bag with white webbing.'

I said, 'So you're able to make out that fine detail in the spotlights. How come you switched them on in the first place?'

He said, 'Aw, just because I saw something moving and I just lit it up, to see what or who it was.'

I said, 'And he was coming towards you?'

He said, 'Yep. I just thought, "A bit different", cos of the way he was dressed. A bit weird. He had on track pants and sports shoes and I'm thinking, "Well, hang on, he's got this bloody big Swanndri on over that." It was a mismatch of clothing. I thought, "Aw yeah, lots of fruitcakes walking around at three in the morning." I mean, fuck, I've been attacked in Whanganui at one in the morning by some nutter swinging machetes trying to bloody hack at me. There's all sorts out there at ungodly hours. So you're always aware of your surroundings.'

I said, 'You told police he ducked his head?'

He said, 'Yeah, he put his head down cos of the spotlights, and turned right, and disappeared ... When they arrested him [Lundy], and they showed him in the media, I thought, "Mm, okay, yeah, that looks very much like the guy I seen on the night."'

But that was much later. Lundy's arrest was made the year after the murders. I asked him, 'Do you remember reading about the murders at the time?'

He said, 'Not really. I didn't follow a lot of it. The hours I was working, I was in bed at night, and didn't see a lot of the news and stuff. But I remember the next day coming back into the yard and thinking, "What the hell's going on there?" There's cop cars on the street across from work and all that, all over the show. I didn't think much of it and then it wasn't till they were advertising in the paper looking for a white van with mags and blacked-out windows seen in the area of the night, and me flatmate said, "Aw, they're looking

70

for you", and I said, "Aw, what do you mean?", and he bought the paper, and showed me in the paper, and I thought, "Aw, shit."

'And he says, "That's you, isn't it?" And I said, "Yeah, that sounds like me", cos they're looking for a white van, and I had one that matched that description.'

I asked, 'Why were they looking for your van?'

He said, 'It was seen in the area in the early hours of the morning when I was going to work.' And then he laughed, and said, 'It cracked me up when they wanted to look at my van because I had a section that I was clearing at the time, and in the back of my van I had bloody picks, axes, shovels, I had a slasher, I had a chainsaw. They said, "Aw, can we have a look in your van?", and as soon as they opened it up, next thing you know there's eight detectives crowded around it, and I'm like, "What the fuck are you guys doing?" Unbeknownst to me, they were looking for a possible weapon.'

Who did Winiata see that night? Was it the killer? That might add up. He had the weapon and his blood-soaked clothes in the bag. He was acting suspiciously. He was making his getaway – a few minutes after the man turned a corner, Winiata saw a blue car. 'It was a big car, either a Commodore or Ford, and it shot past.' Lundy owned a blue Ford Fairmont …

But then I asked Winiata, 'You mentioned he wore glasses?'

He said, 'Aw, mate, I'm trying to think … It was so bloody long ago.'

He hadn't mentioned glasses in his two police interviews. There were a number of discrepancies between the descriptions he gave police. On 9 September 2000, he said the man was 'short', and put him at 5'8" or 5'9". He also said, 'Both of his hands were in the pockets of his jacket.' On 14 November 2014, he said, 'I believe he

71

was quite tall – maybe a little bit shorter than me. I am 6'2".' He also said, 'He carried a sports bag in his right hand.'

I asked him, 'Do you think who you saw was Mark Lundy?'

He said, 'Mate, I'd put money on it. Yep.'

But it didn't add up. There were too many inconsistencies for police to produce him as a Crown witness. 'They said if they call me up in court, I'd just get shredded, and mate I'm just not into that.' That first description, the one that would have been the most fresh in his memory, was of someone a lot smaller than Lundy. Winiata's later descriptions matched Lundy only after he'd seen him on TV and in the papers after his arrest.

So far as tying the murders to Lundy, Winiata's sighting was meaningless, without any real foundation. But one thing about it remains a fact: he saw someone. He saw someone very close to the scene of the crime, at the time of the killings, walking around late at night, scurrying away when noticed, then possibly jumping into a car and driving off, fast. It was the only instance of anyone being seen that night. In all of the police interviews, and in all of the names they had on their suspect list, no one else was ever actually reported to be in the vicinity. Just that one passersby – someone with a sports bag, in track pants and a Swanndri, walking around a Palmerston North suburb in the small hours of the night, around the corner from where Christine and Amber Lundy had been hacked to death. Maybe it was nothing, just a random guy. Maybe it was something. Maybe a truck driver shone his headlights on a short man who had just committed murder, and was making his first determined and incredibly successful attempt to get away with it.

Chapter 3

Missing: Socksay Chansy

His body was found by a gravedigger. Likely one of the last things he had ever seen, lying on damp earth near a sewer line in a grove of trees – pretty in the daytime, sunlit, with fantails hopping on low branches of flowering mānuka, but lonely and terrifying at night – was an urupā, the graveyard at Ōrākei. It has a chapel and a low white wall and a bell tower. This was all that was left of the Auckland he had come home to, the city narrowing to a graveyard, a bell, a tap for visitors to wash their hands. He had only just returned after productive years in Germany and then a kind of breakdown in Sydney. He had friends, family. There was a queue of people to offer shelter, support. But he lay down in the cold. Across the road on Tāmaki Drive, the tide swept in and shuffled out at Ōkahu Bay, sucking at the sand; and his own life ebbed away, Socksay Chansy giving up the ghost on the edge of a park right beside a village of the dead. His body lay there for a month, maybe longer.

He was 36 years old. To report on this story was to talk with other men all aged 35 or 36, a generation of guys from the same background – classmates at Auckland Grammar, friends from King's College – who had all gone to university or some other tertiary course, partied hard and perhaps unwisely, but survived the crazy years of passage to settle down and get good jobs, buy property, start young families. The more ambitious and entrepreneurial created their own line of work. Socksay Chansy was in that mould. He was part of a quite large and loyal gang of middle-class guys who valued the material life and weren't especially artistic, but nor were they white-collar straights chasing the company bonus. He was cool.

The friends remained friends. They still sometimes call each other by a sort of nickname inspired by Socksay – everyone added the '-say' in Socksay's name, pronounced 'sigh', to their own name. Duncan-say. Jamie-say. Hugh-say, and so on, an affectionate gesture in honour of their friend with the unusual name. It means 'blessed'. His parents are Laotian. There was a Buddhist ceremony at the place where he died, monks chanting in that pretty sunlit grove, a manhole marked with paint from the police crime scene. Someone had built a teepee from upright branches, and there was a more sophisticated structure, beneath a bank, of bamboo lashed together with string, next to a piece of soft foam that would make a decent pillow. How did it come to this? Even in death, Socksay Chansy didn't belong. It was one of the themes of his life; it was as though he was always on the outside, stateless.

Is that how he viewed himself? Was there some keen awareness of it that drove him away from his friends and family? He was a man on the run. He skipped town, he bailed – that was his MO when things got bad. It was always abrupt, no notice. Next thing anyone knew, he'd gone. And when he fled, he always fled alone.

There was a distant echo of it at his old school. Paul Paton, the archivist at Auckland Grammar, had photocopied Socksay's class photographs and his end-of-year results. We met in a small room tucked behind a screening room, where Socksay had probably sat and watched arthouse films in 1997, when he belonged to Grammar's film society. There wasn't much from Socksay's school career to look at. 'Date of entry to school, February 2, 1994. Father's occupation, joiner. Home address, 175 Mt Wellington Highway.' In class photographs (3G, 4C, 5D, 6J – the descent to the lower academic classes is a common enough occurrence at the school, and is known as 'the Grammar slide'), he's a tall, slim boy with a happy face and high hair. He was bottom of the class in form five, second in the class in form six. He played soccer, and was part of the victorious fifth-form side that played eight, won eight, including a 6–0 rout of St Kentigern and a 10–1 humiliation of Dilworth. Paton pointed to one of Socksay's teachers, and said, 'He went into a seminary, and became a monk.' Then he pointed to a teacher from another class, and said, 'Hm. He did, too.' Neither the report cards nor the stories of Grammar's monk exodus revealed anything about Socksay; but there was a kind of clue, something poignant, in a glass cabinet of old things in the assembly hall.

'I've got John Mulgan's cap,' Paton said. 'Would you like to see it?' It was a rugby First XV and cricket First XI cap presented in 1929 to John Mulgan, who became one of New Zealand's greatest authors. He wrote only one novel, the classic *Man Alone*, in 1939. He killed himself in Egypt in 1945; at the close of the war. Exactly why he did so remains a mystery, guessed at but unsolved even by his scrupulous biographer, Vincent O'Sullivan. In his entry in the *Dictionary of New Zealand Biography*, Mulgan is described thus: 'Those who knew John Mulgan agree on the attractive openness of his personality; he was affable, cheerful and outgoing ... But there was another side to Mulgan's character, rarely glimpsed. One of his colleagues at the Clarendon Press detected ... Mulgan's "feeling of being between two worlds".'

Two old boys from Grammar, both popular and creative, both somehow or other at odds, disconnected, both arriving at a tragic and inexplicable end. Mulgan's forlorn old cap was shoved at the back of the cabinet. What was there to look at that ever belonged to Socksay Chansy? What had he left behind?

* * *

Socksay Chansy was born in a refugee camp. Between two worlds at birth: his parents fled Vientiane in Laos during the terror of the Communist regime, slipping out of their house onto a boat that took them silently up the Mekong River. 'We leave night time,' said Socksay's father, Sam Chansy. 'You don't let anyone know. Someone know, they shoot you. We hired canoe. Eight people on canoe. One hour up the river to Thailand. Very frightening! No suitcase, nothing. Only we got money and gold. That's it. Socksay never born yet, must be eight months inside his mum. When he born, his mum stay in hospital two hours. They say, "You go now." But is okay.'

Sam was a trim man aged 65. He had a new family, including a pretty, very watchful eight-year-old daughter. We met at his big, bright home in that suburb almost exclusively made up of big, bright homes, Dannemora. Laotian refugees in New Zealand enjoyed a reputation as 'the Dutch of Asia – incredibly industrious', as recorded in David McGill's book, *The Other New Zealanders*; Sam had done well for himself, worked hard as a window-fitter. He said, 'I am lucky man. People came refugee camp and say they want a hundred people to go New Zealand.' The family arrived in

1980, and were housed for six weeks in a refugee reception centre in Māngere. Socksay's brother, Peter, was born in 1982. They lived in a plain house high up on the Mt Wellington ridge on a busy road surrounded by massive electricity pylons, each humming with 110,000 volts.

Directly across the road is one of Auckland's most arresting landmarks, the cactus farm of Coromandel Cactus sellers. And right next door to the old Chansy house was another remarkable sight in that tough, under-class suburb – a market garden, with rows of bok choy, red cabbage, broccoli and other hardy annuals on nearly a hectare of heavy clay, tended by Roy Yee, 79, these past 60 years. He said: 'I'm a refugee.' Another one, with another exciting story of getting out of Asia alive – from Taishan, China, in 1939, as the invading Japanese laid waste. 'There was a complication': his father was involved in a tribal feud which ended in a killing, and was 'spirited out of the village with a bounty on his head'. He came to New Zealand. 'But with the threat of the Japanese, our mother, who couldn't write, employed a village scribe to write to our father, and implored him to send passage.'

'Scribe', 'spirited out', 'send passage' – he used such antique terms, and said them with real pleasure. We sat together on the back of his ute. He was about to spray for white cabbage butterflies. He talked about the soil, how he and his father broke it in, in 1954. 'There's not another to generation to follow on,' he said. 'No sons. I've got a daughter, but she's too busy with her own life.' He'd simply give up the long lease with Transpower when he felt too old to want to continue. An end, perhaps, to 60 years of vegetables fighting their way out of the hard clay loam, bordered on one side by rosemary. It formed a kind of hedge beside the house where Socksay grew up. No, Roy said, he didn't know whoever lived there.

Who knows what goes on with families? What was the atmosphere inside that home, where telephone wires and pylon wires criss-crossed above the roof? Two sons and their parents in a new city. Only the boys could speak English. In the Nong Khai refugee camp where Socksay was born, there were some 20,000 Laotian refugees cooking on open fires; in the 1976 census, the total Laotian population in New Zealand was 13. Between 1979 and 1982, New Zealand took in 239 'displaced' Laotians, and scattered many throughout the country. They were an obscure community, far less in number than the so-called 'boat people' of Vietnam or the Cambodians who fled the Khmer Rouge. Their presence was low-key, near invisible.

Socksay's service was held at the combined Laotian and Thai temple, Wat Lao Buddharam, in a side street off the Great South Road in Ōtāhuhu. I went there and watched one of the monks sweep the front steps while Toulay Thaivichit, 70 ('I am, what you call it, advisor to temple'), directed a workman on the roof. 'This is Buddha tree from India,' he said, of the fat-leafed tree in the front courtyard. 'I plant myself twenty-five years ago.' Inside, lunch was ready, served on a low, round, wooden table – bowls of extremely spicy and quite delicious Laotian dishes. Another monk sat in front of shrines of the Buddha and enormous bouquets of plastic flowers, and wrapped himself in his robe.

'I knew him when he little,' Toulay said of Socksay. 'He good boy. He brainy. Learning very good. He could be doctor! But when he pass away, he got nothing. No money.' The thought of it scandalised him. 'Nothing! His mum give him five hundred dollars. But he spend it. He just walk around. He go Ōrākei. No home. Cold, hungry. No money.' He was more cross than sad. He sighed; his breath was very bad. 'But he good boy. Could be doctor.'

Socksay was never going to go down that path. Toulay simply didn't understand him. But he didn't really make it easy for anyone; there was something opaque about him – remote, hard to reach. To talk to his friends was to discover the kind of person he could be, someone gentle and kind, witty and cool. To talk to his family was to learn about the person behind the considerable charm, someone who wanted to hide from the world. He was hiding – concealed, sinking into the earth – when he died.

* * *

He was abandoned. The secret life of families: his mum and dad split when Socksay was about 10, and the boys were raised by a single parent. His cousin, Mel Wongsaene, had mentioned it during an interview at her home facing the water at Māngere Bridge.

'It was quite a hard time for Socksay,' she said. 'But he didn't say anything. With his personality type, he wasn't good at sharing the bad times.' She didn't go into any detail about the break-up. It was only while I was sitting with Socksay's father Sam Chansy in his lounge that the penny dropped that it was Socksay's mum who was the one who left her family.

'She run away. Go to Australia.'

I said, 'What?'

'His mum left me letter saying she go. I come home from work. No mum. Just letter, saying she go. It say, "Oh look after the kids, I go now. I can't handle it." '

'Can't handle what?'

'Gambling or something. She gambling, I think.'

But even if the accusation were true, it wasn't that simple. Sam later mentioned the fact that he'd actually left first, gone to Las

Vegas to start a new life, but returned home. About a week later, his wife fled. What about Socksay? How was he during all this drama? 'I think he have broken heart when mum leave him. He keep it inside. He never talk to no one about it. He read letter, go for walk.' A walk along the shabby footpath beside Mt Wellington Highway, maybe down to the volcanic crater lake of Panmure Basin ... How long was he away? 'Maybe half an hour. He come back and said: "I don't talk about her. That's it." And he didn't. If someone come to house and talk about the mum, he not say anything.'

Two clever boys and a dad in Mt Wellington. Sam said, 'But I didn't talk to kids much. Got no time. They still sleeping, I leave money and go to work. I got no time. Too busy, working and supporting the kids. Uniform, school fees. I'm by myself ...'

Well, he was and he wasn't. He made reference to other partners, other children. It was hard sometimes following Sam's stories in his broken English. Sentences would come and go, and sometimes fail to make a lick of sense. But it wasn't just the communication problem. The mess of family life is hard to understand or comprehend even when it's your own family.

After Socksay's body was found, police said that he'd been estranged from his family for a long time. In fact, he'd been living with his mother and his brother Peter in Sydney before he arrived back in New Zealand and escalated his inexplicable slide towards a private, tormented death. He was estranged only from Sam. They hadn't spoken since Socksay left home, and New Zealand, when he was 21.

Why not? What had gone wrong? Sam said it was nothing, just that he was hard to get hold of – he changed addresses, he changed phone numbers ... We tell stories to ourselves to tidy up the mess of family life, to straighten things out. 'I not stay at one

80

place. He write letter, where he send to?' Fifteen years of silence, of some cold, intense rage, reduced to the inefficiency of the postal service. The separation was Socksay's MO – cut and run, and leave the past behind – at its most severe. He removed Sam from his life.

They'd obviously been close, loving. Sam took Socksay to play soccer all over Auckland when he was little. 'Every game! Every park. He good player. Want to be number one. He always shoot the goal! Every game, he shoot the goal.'

Every park: including one in Ōrākei, near where his body was found. 'I remember that time when I take him to play there,' said Sam. His voice became softer, quieter; he drew his hand over his face. 'I think he was maybe eight or nine. I don't know. Just a kid. The game finish, and me and him walk down to the park, at Ōrākei, and he say he like the sea, and the trees, and he say, "I want to build a house here one day." Maybe this why he go there. I don't know.'

The father of a baby born in a refugee camp, weeping in his house in Dannemora. A copy of Socksay's death certificate lay on the table beside the plate of chocolate biscuits. It read: *Place of birth: Nong Khai*. And next to Socksay's name: *No fixed abode*.

* * *

He was wildly popular. 'He was like a hero,' said Jamie O'Connor. 'It was like, "Socksay's here!" He was always laughing. Big teeth, big smile. Really cool guy.'

We met at a Hell Pizza in Wairau Park on the North Shore, near where O'Connor works in IT. O'Connor was the first in the gang of 36-year-olds who I interviewed. They were all really nice guys, and they all shared one particular characteristic: gentleness. None of them was emphatic or judgmental. They existed in a state of chill; it was as though they regarded chill as a way of life, that it was part of their moral code.

They hung out with each other and looked out for each other. At school, the gang would congregate in a shed out the back of Jeremy Bailey's parents' house in Mt Eden. 'His mum was like, "Yep, cool, do whatever you like",' O'Connor said. At university, there were party flats in Gillies Avenue in Epsom, and Buchannan Street in Kingsland, where the flatmates included O'Connor and Dan Kelly, who now works as an editor at TV3. We met around the corner from the network and sat in the sunshine. He said, 'There were four of us in the flat, and it was where people would go to drink and smoke weed and play Nintendo or 64 PlayStation.

'I remember Socksay worked at Video Ezy in Ellerslie, and we'd go out there and visit of an evening sometimes, and we ended up with a Nintendo 64, a rental one which I guess we swiped, because it still had the Video Ezy stickers on it. So we'd sit and play marathon sessions – it was a wrestling game, one of the first games you could have people on at the same time. So you had to wait for your friends to come around before you could all play. And the weed would come out, and someone would bring beers … It was a party every night.'

Jamie O'Connor told a colourful story about Socksay setting up party headquarters in a downtown insurance office. He'd found work as a night cleaner and would invite friends up to raid the company's open bar and drink on the rooftop. 'So there we'd be at 2am, 3am, and he'd be like, "Have as much as you want to drink!" It was epic. It didn't happen just once; it was like weekends in a row. It was like: "Party at the insurance place!" It was great.'

But things were already unravelling. Socksay bought a black Audi, which blew everyone's mind. O'Connor said, 'We were like,

"What are you doing, bro?" Before we knew it, we were all going around in his Audi. It was fun while it lasted … But the partying wasn't working for him. And financially, I think he got into a bit of trouble. He had debts. Like he turned up to my house one time, crying and upset. He wasn't very happy with where he was at.

'All of a sudden he just picked up and bailed, you know? It was like, "Oh, Socksay's gone." It was amazing. He just left without telling anyone.'

The Audi was repossessed, and there were other debts that he couldn't settle.

'He was always a precarious individual,' said Tom Cotter. He was part of the gang and now lives in Munich, after going to Germany to complete his PhD in chemistry. 'His reputation preceded him. There were lots of stories about him. He was a contentious character, someone who inspired numerous feelings. People had a lot of opinions about him, and one was that he could be a bit of a bullshitter. But he had such a magnetic personality. He was always a lot of fun.'

Dan Kelly said, 'I never remember him being unhappy. He was always smiling, always laughing.' Yes, he said, he was Dan-say, his flatmate Jamie was Jamie-say, everyone was someone-say. The names stuck. 'When he left the country, we all remembered Socksay fondly because of that. There were all these people still carrying his memory, if you like.'

When he thought of Socksay now, what picture of him came to mind? He said, 'He's smiling. He's laughing. That slight cackle he had. And I see him with other people, with a group of friends. I don't see Socksay alone. I think of him with all my other buddies.'

* * *

'He was Filipino,' said one of his friends. 'Thai,' said another. A third said, 'His parents are from Hong Kong.' Well, at least they all agreed he was Asian. But his father Sam said, 'He not like Asia boy. He want to be like Kiwi boy. When he eating dinner, that food belong to him. He eat like Kiwi. People come to house, he say, "Mum not home. Dad not home. Come another time." Peter is different, he say, "Come in. Eat, eat." Socksay not like that. He born like that, I don't know.'

Always on the outside of things – the friends at Auckland Grammar going to school from nearby soothing suburbs (Kingsland, Epsom, Mt Eden), Socksay making the long trek by bus (about 45 minutes and 20 stops) from the pylon kingdom of Mt Wellington. And then the abrupt departure, at 21 or 22, skipping town for points unknown. It's difficult to accurately trace his whereabouts and wanderings over the next few years. He left New Zealand for Australia, and stayed with his mum. He met a girl, a German backpacker. He travelled to the US, where he stayed with his aunt in Rhode Island. That didn't go well. His cousin Arouny Wongsaene said, 'He lived there for a few months. He said he wanted to help out around the house, but he ended up just sleeping and eating, and staying in his room. "You know what?" my mum said. "You're not really helping." So she paid for his ticket to Germany, and off he went on his merry way.'

He never kept in touch with anyone – friends or family. He simply disappeared. Next thing anyone knew, he was living in Berlin, had married the backpacker, and was doing pretty well for himself as a film and video editor. No one back in New Zealand had heard from him in years, but by coincidence a group of old friends from Grammar and King's all fished up in Germany, and Socksay eventually, perhaps reluctantly, got in touch.

These were good years. Jamie O'Connor said, 'I went over and hooked up with him in Berlin. I hadn't heard from him in years, not a word, nothing! But he was just like the old Socksay. We had picnics, went on bike rides. Everything was going really well. And he was such a great host. Anything he was doing, he was like, "Come along. Come with me." Super generous.'

Hugh Smith knew Socksay at Grammar. He travelled to Berlin in 2012, and saw him for the first time in over 10 years. He works as a landscape architect now, and we met at a nice café in Parnell. He said, 'He'd got it together. I was impressed. He had a great group of friends, and he was really generous with his money. He introduced me to all these people.

'I was actually the first person from the old days who he saw. He really wanted me to stay with him. I got the feeling it was really important to him that someone he knew from Auckland was back in his life again. He was making new friends all the time, but he needed an old friend, I think. He wasn't desperate about it; it was more like he was anxious that I come and stay.

'And it was great. At first. But then I started seeing a dark side.'

* * *

He stayed in his room and heard voices – his own voice, talking to himself. 'Socksay was unravelling,' said Hugh Smith. 'Berlin has a big party scene. His partying escalated, it got out of hand, and he went on a downward spiral. He'd go out and not come back for a couple of days, and then he'd shut the door of his room, and not come out for a week.

'I'd say, "Hey man, I'm going out with some friends for dinner at their house. It's free, so no cost – come along!" And he'd say,

"No. I don't want to come out of my room." I'd hear him holding conversations. I was like, "Did you say something?" He'd say, "It's just me talking to myself." '

He stopped going into work and the money stopped coming in. His marriage had already broken up; Socksay kept their cat, but if it defecated in the corner of the apartment, he'd just leave the mess there. Meanwhile, the voices in his head. What were they saying? Demons are capable of saying anything, of bringing down the whole unstable house of cards.

'I think he was fighting against his demons for a long time,' said Pedro Deltell Colomer, a Spanish film editor who formed the Lemon Face video-editing company with Socksay. They met at an advertising agency. When the company went under, the two friends created Lemon Face. 'He was a very intelligent man, happy, a funny person. A lot of friends. But from the beginning he had a dark side.'

There it was again, the 'dark side'. Deltell Colomer said, 'He could be quiet and depressive.' Later, Socksay told Deltell Colomer about hearing voices. And this: 'He was taking medication for his illness. I don't know what kind of illness it was.' He didn't know the name of it, or the type of medication, but he knew it was to do with mental illness.

'He was showing signs of depression,' said Jeremy Bailey, an old schoolfriend who hooked up with Socksay in Germany. Bailey is part-owner of the very hip, very successful restaurant The Burger Lab, described in tourist literature as 'a kingpin of Hamburg's artisan burger craze'. Taking hamburgers to Hamburg, and knocking it out of the park. Life has been good to Bailey in Germany; when we spoke, his newborn baby was gurgling in the background. It was at his stag do where a tremendous reunion of Auckland friends took place – Jamie O'Connor was there, Hugh Smith, Socksay. That was in 2012, when life was good to Socksay, too.

'When I met him in Berlin I was surprised at how established he was,' said Tom Cotter. 'He had an apartment, and a girlfriend, and he was engaged in running a small production company. He was paying the bills and spending time with creative people. Berlin is an artist's city, and he was living the kind of life people really want to carve out for themselves over there. He had a nice place, and he took me to his studio – it was the real thing, you know, because there was always a question of whether there was anything behind what he said. But we went there and he was really doing things, and making things which were fulfilling for him.'

But the two old friends were both in Berlin for a long time before Socksay got in touch. 'I had the impression he was avoiding people from the old days, and was reluctant to get back in contact,' he said. 'Maybe he didn't because he needed to be in a good place first, didn't want to be seen as someone who was struggling or failing. I think he might have had the pathology of a manic depressive. You only saw him when he was on a high, when he was up.'

Jeremy Bailey said, 'I think that it really boils down to mental health issues which went unchecked, or properly medicated, and Socksay being stubborn and not wanting to reach out for help. Those issues just spiralled out of control.'

A strange thing kept happening during the interview with Bailey. He'd say something, sometimes at length, and then a little later he'd repeat it, verbatim. It was like having a hallucinogenic experience. It was hard to believe that it was happening.

'I don't know if there's a story here,' he said. 'I think it just boils down to mental health issues which went unchecked, or properly medicated, and Socksay being stubborn and not wanting to reach out for help …'

* * *

'He was this cool Asian dude,' said Johannes Ostertag, one of Socksay's closest friends in Berlin. 'He was very witty, a gentle person, bright, a good friend.' They worked together as film editors. For once, a date could be fixed to Socksay's whereabouts: Johannes's girlfriend at the time, Katrin Katz Kobberg, emailed her reminiscence of Socksay, and wrote, 'We all met at the video company when I was an intern in mid-2009. Socksay was always one of the hardest workers there, you know, someone to look up to, and also a very nice person to hang out with.'

She furnished another date: 2014, the year that seems to have been the beginning of the end. Johannes Osterberg sublet his apartment to Socksay. Katrin: 'I am not sure what happened exactly but I know that Socksay was a lil party animal and went wild from time to time, meaning using lots and lots of drugs. Either this destroyed his relationship [with Johannes] and led him to lose his job or other way round. I am not sure. Anyways, he couldn't pay the rent and owed Johannes lots of money, and then suddenly he left Berlin to go to his family in Sydney.

'Last time we spoke before he suddenly left he was anxious and seemed desperate. No job, no girl. And it was tense because Johannes was there and they were arguing.'

Cut and run, leave the past behind. Johannes said, 'When he left – he didn't tell me. He just left, just disappeared.'

He was like a fugitive. He travelled light, hardly left a trace. There was the cat from his marriage, a small old wooden box that he left in Johannes's apartment and which Katrin took, and keeps on her make-up table. 'It's a little reminder of him,' she emailed. 'All I can really tell you about Socksay is that he was a sweet and kind person. He had his flaws as everyone of us does, and also his personal struggles and demons he was fighting. It made me sad to see that they won.'

All the old friends from the past in Auckland were guys; it was striking to hear a woman's perspective, the tenderness which she felt for him. Slim, funny, gentle, charismatic – he was attractive to women, and there were stories about two relationships after his marriage broke up. There was a German girl: 'She was pretty kooky,' remembered Jeremy Bailey. 'An interesting character, a unique character. There were lots of arguments, it was a very emotional relationship.'

Pedro Deltell Colomer – a Spanish guy talking about a New Zealander's relationship with a German girl – met her, too. He said, 'She was a bit dark. A philosophy student. A bit depressive. But she was okay, actually; she was good for him. Arguing maybe too much. Then he meets an American girl. She was very beautiful and a bit older than him. I don't think she was bad for him exactly, but I think she was maybe a bit too exciting for him. She loved to party, you know.'

That romance faltered. Alone, broke, out of it, in debt – 'No girl, no job', as Katrin Katz Kobbert said. He was heading for a fall. His exit from Germany was like a photocopy of his departure from New Zealand. Beneath it all was depression or mental illness. Tom Cotter said, 'People who have these lives which involve a lot of movement, and get into debts or obligations which in the end they're not capable of delivering on ... There's an underlying neurological aspect to that. It's that precariousness Socksay always had.'

Jeremy Bailey talked about Socksay's descent into depression in 2014. 'We were talking about the past in New Zealand, and he said he'd made mistakes, that there were things he felt guilty about and he couldn't get over it, things like owing people money, and not doing the right things by them or whatever, but it was all in his mind. Any good friend will forgive you if you front up. It was more just that it was like a catalyst for his mental health issues.

'One of the last times we spoke I said to him, "Look, I think maybe you've got some depression issues, maybe paranoid schizophrenia or whatever," and I tried to advise him to seek help. Then he moved back to Sydney.'

Katrin Katz Kobbert: 'The last thing I heard from him was a short Facebook conversation when he was in Australia. He said he was sad that he left without paying Johannes and to ruin their friendship. I tried to calm him down and told him they will be friends again.'

He got in touch with Johannes from Australia, and wired him the money. 'I said, "Well, thank you, Socksay, that's great." And we had a nice talk. He seemed okay,' said Johannes. 'Actually I travelled to Australia in 2013, and visited his mum and family. They were really nice people and just had a normal life. When I heard he left Germany to go there, I thought, "That's good! They will make things alright." '

* * *

'He stayed in his room for a couple of years,' said his cousin Mel Wongsaene.

She was bottle-feeding her baby on the couch; her daughter was born the day before Socksay's funeral. Mel and Socksay were close as kids. Their mums are sisters, and came to New Zealand a year apart. 'We were like brother and sister,' she said. 'Tree climbing, jumping off roofs. He had a calm personality, and I was quite bossy and loud, but we never really had fights. We made make-believe TV ads! He was always really creative. I always thought he'd do really well. Later he talked about wanting to go and live in Berlin, and he did it.'

The note of pride in her voice fell away as she puzzled over what led him to die alone, in the cold, at the edge of a park. 'We've talked about it, and no one really has got a conclusion about what happened,' she said. 'I don't want to say it's depression or mental illness because I'm not 100 per cent. But towards the end of last year my mother kept in close touch with Socksay's mum, and she was very concerned for him – sleeping all day, not working, talking to himself in his room. She was concerned with his mental health. But he refused to see anyone.'

When he first arrived in Sydney towards the end of 2014 to stay with his mum and his brother, though, he was hopeful about picking himself up and finding work. He Skyped another cousin, Mel's sister Arouny Wongsaene. She said, 'He sounded really positive. He said his next step was to go to Melbourne, that he had quite a number of contacts there. He was up about life in general and asked how the kids were, and he spoke about coming back to New Zealand and visiting us, and meeting his nephews and nieces.'

It was Socksay's last stand. The call marked the final time he felt confident about the future or made plans. 2015 was his lost year. He went into his room, and shut the door.

'That Skype call was when he last spoke to me,' said Arouny. 'I hadn't heard from him for a few months, so I Facebooked him. He didn't reply, but that was just how he was. He never needed to keep in constant touch with you. He'd go and do his own thing, and come back when he wanted to.

'Then my auntie [Socksay's mum] called me, and said he wasn't doing well. Whatever prospects he had in Melbourne must have fallen through, and she said he was spiralling into depression. She said, "It's really bad." I said, "Oh, you know he how he is, he'll get over it, and he'll find something, you know, to get him back on his feet."

'In the past, like at my mum's house that time, when he slept all day and only came out to eat – I don't know, I just thought it was part of his, I guess, creative process. I didn't think there was anything different. I kept reassuring her, telling her he'll come out of it.'

'You can see on his Facebook that he stopped talking to people from the end of 2014,' said Mel. 'He didn't make any contact with me or anyone.' Arouny said he didn't respond to her messages on Facebook. 'I'd call, and they'd say, "He's in his room." He was like a recluse. He'd come out to eat, and go back to his room.'

He was falling to pieces, the pieces getting smaller and smaller. He was disappearing. He was hiding. He was sick, and he wasn't taking any medication. If he was in Hell then he was surely dragging everyone else down with him; it must have been intolerable to have to live with him while he stayed stuck in his room, talking to himself – worse, listening to himself. What gloom he must have created, what anxiety and distress. If the walls were closing in on Socksay, then they were surely closing in on his family, too. They were living with a kind of monster, a creature in depression's black lagoon.

It was always going to come to a head. It duly exploded, and afterwards it left everyone in an agony of guilt. But no one was to blame. It was just a sick person forcing his way out.

According to Arouny, the fight began when Socksay started yelling at his mum, and then yelling at Peter's fiancée so aggressively and frighteningly that she locked herself in the room and called Peter. He raced home and there was another massive argument. It ended when his mum paid for Socksay's ticket to Auckland, and gave him $500.

Yes, said Mel, a fight was inevitable. 'It was going to happen. And when it did, that's when his mum decided to buy his ticket. It all happened in the heat of the moment, and he said something to her like she wasn't ever going to see him again.'

Families carry their secrets and their various assorted shames, and bundle them out of sight. We try and make an accommodation with unpleasantness. We make things comfortable, reach a compromise which involves silence and a tacit understanding that lids are best sealed tight. Arouny said, 'I guess it just runs in the family where nobody ever really says anything until it comes to a head and it all spills out and what is said is said.'

He entered a happy home, and broke it. Peter had reunited with his mum. He'd got engaged, and there was a wedding to plan. The idea was that when Sam Chansy came to Australia for the wedding, he'd fly home with Socksay. 'He really wanted to come back to Auckland,' said Mel. 'It was his thing, that he kept asking to come back to Auckland, and he'd secure a job. The plan was for his dad to help him and Socksay was very open to that.'

He had his ticket. He had $500. He must have calmed down, and at least said goodbye properly, because Arouny said, 'He told his mum he would get in contact. He reassured her that he's got friends there, he's got family, and the worst-case scenario was he'd be taken care of by the system and go on unemployment benefit.'

Was there ever any job prospects in Melbourne? Did he ever intend to get in touch with people who loved him and would have taken care of him in Auckland? It's possible. He'd been badgering to come back to New Zealand; it must have signalled a fresh start, an opportunity to get his shit together. He'd had a lot of good times in Auckland before things got too much. He'd been happy there. It was his city, he knew it intimately. He could renew old friendships, straighten himself out. He was only 36.

* * *

He was depressed, and the depressed person lay down and died. A gravedigger had gone into the bush to look for ferns. There was a tangi scheduled that day, on Saturday afternoon, at the Ōrākei urupā. A cold wind blew in off Ōkahu Bay. It had been raining heavily that week, and the ground had turned to bog. The body had been in an advanced state of decomposition, and even the gender wasn't immediately apparent. Socksay's old friend Hugh Smith, who knew him during good times in Auckland and later in Berlin, went for a jog along Tāmaki Drive and saw the crime scene – the yellow tape, the forensic team in blue paper overalls.

Socksay hadn't called anyone. Not his father, not his friends. He didn't let anyone know he was back. He roamed around the city with just the clothes on his back as autumn turned to winter, and he lasted less than a hundred days, possibly not even a month. He was always on the run from dates, they revealed his whereabouts, but they finally caught up with him and pinned him down – he arrived on or about 1 April, he was spoken to by police on 25 April, his body was found on 23 July. The coroner's report was equally vague: it put his date of death between 16 May and 30 June.

Sam Chansy got a phone call from the police a few days after Socksay arrived. He'd been in the police force himself, in Vientiane, as a sergeant. 'Policeman say, "I got something to ask you, Mr Chansy." Then they come to house, show me photo, and say, "Is that your son?" But I'm not quite sure. I cannot identify him. I'm 65, my memory's not much good. I never seen him in long time. So I phone up the mum straightaway.'

What misery it was for him to sit and talk about the death of his son who he didn't recognise. And part of the wretchedness of it was that it could have been prevented, that there were at least three occasions after Socksay arrived in New Zealand when he could have been saved from himself. He managed to slip through each time.

There was the case of the unread email. When he left Sydney, his mum emailed Sam to tell him that Socksay was on his way and to pick him up at the airport. But he didn't check his emails until after the flight had arrived.

Well, that could have happened to anyone. It was just bad timing. But there was another, stranger incident when Socksay was put into a kind of protective custody – and still slipped out of reach. It was at the airport. Police later told Sam that he attracted suspicion. 'Police there, immigration peoples, they say he doesn't look like he has nowhere to go. He just walk around and around.'

Was he looking for his father? 'I don't know,' said Sam.

'Police hold him and check him and see if he have a drug. They say, "Are you alright, do you need help?" He say, "I am alright." They bring him to the hospital for two days. They check him, and ask if someone can help him, but he say he is alright. He got my business card.

'They say, "Well, he still got some money." The mum, she gave him $500. He still got $407. He got money, he is thirty-six years old, he's a man, he not harm anyone, they can't hold him.'

What was all that about? A guy shows up in New Zealand after 15 years, with a little over $400 to his name, no one there to meet him at the airport, wandering around, and he's apprehended, questioned, taken to hospital, given a bed – the apparatus of the state appears in good working order, and acting responsibly, even vigilantly, but someone who was surely showing evident signs of instability still manages to leg it, to just walk out. He was like some kind of escape artist. Nothing could hold him.

The corner's report records his escape act in full and exasperating detail:

> Airport security staff told Police that when they first spoke with Mr Chansy he had told them he was a full-blooded Maori and he owned the Air New Zealand hangar nearby. Police spoke with Mr Chansy, who gave them several names which did not result in an identification.
>
> Mr Chansy told Police he had just arrived back in New Zealand and he was waiting for his wife to pick him up. He could not provide them with her contact number. Police noticed Mr Chansy's demeanour became erratic and 'paranoid' while speaking to him, and he told Police that he was a Homeland Security operative . . .
>
> Police took Mr Chansy into custody, where he told them he was Columbian and spoke German and Spanish fluently and had numerous passports for his classified work purposes. Whilst in the police custody suite at Manukau he was seen by a nurse from Counties Manukau DHB mental health intake service. Mr Chansy

refused to speak to her. She described him as neatly groomed, well dressed and polite and that he stated very clearly that he had no wish to speak to her. He had been quiet and polite whilst in custody. The nurse assessed that there were no immediate indications that Mr Chansy had any significant mental disorder from either his presentation or subsequent behaviours and there was no known history. No contact details were available to obtain any collateral information. She considered that he did not appear to be a risk to himself. She did not consider that compulsory assessment was indicated at that point. Mr Chansy was released by Police that day.

The aliases, the dramatic fictions – did he even know who he was? For his father, the issue was *where* he was. Sam went looking for him, the whole family were anxious and worried. 'I drive up to that place where they collect the food. You know? Hobson Street. Yes, the City Mission. There. I stop the car and see if he come out or not.' He parked outside backpacker hostels, he drove around and around downtown.

Where was he, what did he do after he arrived back in Auckland? The trail goes cold, and then it's picked up again on 25 April, when a third opportunity presented itself to stop Socksay from his descent into a dangerous and ultimately fatal madness. The police caught him committing a crime. He'd broken into a house. He hadn't taken anything, he was just using it for shelter. They took his photograph, they questioned him – and let him go.

The coroner's report tells the story in full.

Police were called to a property in Parnell. A member of the public who was house sitting the property had found Mr Chansy in the

97

backyard asleep. When woken, Mr Chansy told Police that he was the owner of the house and he was waiting to be let in by his wife or children. Police told him that he was not the owner and asked for his name. He told them his name was Adam Atreides. On examining some bank cards in his wallet, Police found the name Socksay Chansy. Mr Chansy told Police he had arrived in New Zealand a few days ago. Due to his odd behaviour he was detained pursuant to section 109 of the Mental Health (Compulsory Assessment and Treatment) Act 1992 and taken to Auckland City Hospital for mental health assessment. Police noted he seemed quite disorientated.

At Auckland City Hospital Mr Chansy was assessed by a member of liaison psychiatry team, registrar Dr Griner. He explained to Dr Griner that after being released from police custody, he walked around Kohimarama during the day and went to Parnell and found the house where he believed his wife lived. He rang the bell and when he found no one home, exhausted, he jumped the fence and went to sleep in the backyard thinking his wife would find him and wake him up.

Mr Chansy told Dr Griner about his life and living in Berlin working in films and that he had been employed for many years by NATO and the New Zealand arm of Homeland Security, which he said is the SAS. Dr Griner said that Mr Chansy described an elaborate delusional system wherein it was difficult to determine which aspects were factual and which were not. Although Mr Chansy told Dr Griner that he felt low due to missing his family, Dr Griner said that he had no signs of depression or thoughts of self-harm and had reasonable energy levels. Mr Chansy denied any previous or current manic symptoms, as well as any significant anxiety. He told Dr Griner his plan was to rent a room in a hotel or hostel and begin making attempts to contact his wife and friends.

Dr Griner's impression was that Mr Chansy had a delusional disorder of unclear duration with no other psychotic symptoms evident on assessment. He did not consider that he was at acute risk to himself or others and that he had 'reasonable plans for near future with regard to self-care.' Dr Griner was unable to determine a principal diagnosis but noted Mr Chansy had delusional ideas he was acting on. He considered that Mr Chansy did not meet the threshold to be detained for compulsory treatment – specifically that although he had an abnormal state of mind he did not meet the 'second limb' of the definition of mental disorder in the Mental Health Act (that requires that the abnormal state of mind give rise to serious danger to self or to others, or a seriously diminished capacity for self-care).

Dr Griner offered Mr Chansy voluntary admission to hospital with a trial of antipsychotic medication. Mr Chansy declined this. He said that he was open to being contacted by mental health staff by email and would provide a contact number by email once he had a New Zealand telephone number.

Mr Chansy left the hospital – declining a ride by the Police. That is the last time his whereabouts are known until he was found dead.

* * *

His friend Jeremy Bailey said from Hamburg: 'I wouldn't blame anyone or place criticism on the system, but there seems to me like there were some small opportunities there for someone to realise this guy has some issues and needs help. It's a massive shame. It's frustrating for everyone, because he had so many good friends who would have done anything for him.

'He had his problems and everything, but he was a good person. He meant well. He screwed up with money and things sometimes, but he was just a – he was a good guy, and people would have helped him out.' And then Bailey's strange habit of repeating himself word-for-word kicked in again; it was as though he pressed play on a tape recorder: 'I don't know if there's a story here. I think it just boils down to mental health issues which went unchecked ...'

The incident with police was Socksay's last chance at salvation. He didn't want it. He wanted darkness, he needed rest.

He chose Ōrākei, out in the pleasant east, around by Kelly Tarlton's Sea Life Aquarium on the beautiful waterfront of Tāmaki Drive, beneath Bastion Point and the wonderful views from the Michael Savage Memorial. Strange that he kept to that side of town, unless he really was drawn to the memory of a happy, innocent day in childhood, when he told his father that this was the paradise where he wanted to build a house. He made his final bed in bush beside a park overlooked by the magnificent homes along Paratai Drive. To meet his friends, that generation of 36-year-olds from Grammar and King's such as Brody Nelson and Duncan Greive – homeowners and talented entrepreneurs, both with young families – was to see the life that Socksay could have enjoyed, too. He was just as clever, just as chill.

But he was suffering. Maybe what he managed to achieve is more remarkable than the extreme circumstances of his death; he overcame his illness to carve out an awesome life for himself in Berlin, he helped create a successful film-editing company, he got married, he made new friends, he remained the same sweet, kind, funny, generous guy. All of that was a triumph. To do as well as he did for as long as he did, despite whatever profound and ultimately tragic disturbance, might be something to marvel at.

But he was too vulnerable, too far gone. When the body was discovered, word went around the immediate neighbourhood that it was probably the crazy old lady who lived rough and could be seen most days outside the local bakery, feeding seagulls and pigeons. The ex-Grammar boy was mistaken for a homeless woman. Police ruled out foul play. The coroner's report ruled that the cause of death was the effects of toluene inhalation: huffing.

> Toluene is a common constituent of aerosolised cans and can be found in the blood of people who undertake huffing. It may cause euphoria and hallucinations. It may also cause respiratory depression or an abnormal heart rhythm and thus death. Dr Stables stated that the presence of toluene strongly suggested that this caused his death. However, he noted that no bags or aerosol cans were observed in close proximity to Mr Chansy that may have indicated huffing.

Friends and family are left to contemplate the horror of Socksay huffing aerosol and dying on the wet ground at the edge of a reserve. One call or Facebook message would have changed everything. A bed, a meal, friendship – it was all there waiting for him, all over Auckland. But as Tom Cotter wondered, hadn't he always been too afraid to show signs of failure? The thought of asking for help must have been horrifying.

Jamie O'Connor said, 'How could someone die like that? What were they doing there? It's – I mean – it's – it's unspeakable.'

Tom Cotter said, 'That such a miserable thing should happen to someone who had such a genuine spirit, if not the most straightforward of characters, to come to such an end – it's pretty awful. It's a tragedy.'

Auckland friends held a wake at Galbraith's Alehouse in Mt Eden. They sat around in a state of shock and tried to make sense of it. It was a very New Zealand send-off – beers, low voices. In expressive Berlin, about a hundred people who knew Socksay on the party scene assembled one night at Görlitzer Park to light paper lanterns and say goodbye to Socksay as the pretty lanterns drifted, glowing, into the sky.

The family have the worst of it. Sam Chansy wept in his home in Dannemora, and said, 'I don't know why this happen. I got a good house, I got spare room for him, he be comfortable. I prepare a job for him; I ask my boss, he said he can start anytime.'

He went to the spot where his son died. 'I think he lie down there and not have energy to get up,' he said. 'Too cold. Just not get up.'

Peter Chansy initially agreed to an interview. He emailed, 'We are still shocked and devastated about it all but I will answer what I can.' We arranged a time to talk on the phone. But the call went unanswered, and he didn't reply to messages or emails.

His cousin Arouny talked about the Buddhist service held for Socksay at the temple in Ōtāhuhu. All the family were there. She said, 'Peter told me he'd written a eulogy but couldn't bear to get up and say it. He hasn't found peace yet. He said when he was in New Zealand [for the funeral], every night when he closed his eyes, he'd see his brother, and thought about how his brother was lying there in the cold. He was scared to close his eyes because he'd see him, and he'd imagine Socksay in the cold.'

Sam's lovely eight-year-old daughter watched and listened as the brother she never knew was being farewelled. She said to her mother a few days after the funeral, 'Do people really go to Heaven when they die?'

'Yes.'

'Good,' said the little girl. 'Because that's where Socksay is now. He's not cold anymore. He's warm.'

* * *

Socksay talked with someone not long before he died, very likely the last person he spoke to, not far from where he lay down in the cold. 'He made a profound impact on me,' said Neil Mahi.

We met at the Savage Memorial. Tourists from China bent forward against the wind that tore around the grassy point. Neil was a big man, with a thoughtful, open manner. 'Let's walk,' he said, and we strode down a hill towards Tāmaki Drive. The water was choppy, and boats rose up and down. 'I met him there.' He pointed to a concrete gun emplacement that clung to the side of the bank; the roots of a tree twisted around the roof in a kind of embrace.

Neil is security manager at the nearby Ōrākei marae. He patrols the grounds most afternoons. It attracts vandals, drug users, vagrants; he asks them to respect his ancestral land, and to move on. He'd been told about a guy who was sleeping in the emplacement. He went there, and found Socksay.

The emplacement is a snug kind of place. It's an ideal spot for someone sleeping rough and needing shelter. It has a roof. There's a small window where a shaft of light creeps in. There's a kind of gutter in the middle of the floor where rainwater collects. Neil found Socksay lying on a black plastic rubbish bag.

'What struck me straightaway was that he had almost nothing on him. Nothing substantial. A little backpack, and the plastic bag – that was his bed. That was him. He had a supermarket bag with a few supplies in it. He had light clothing on, and it was obvious there wasn't much in his backpack. He looked like he was out for a stroll.'

The two of them went outside, and sat on the grassy bank and talked for maybe quarter of an hour. Socksay told him he'd been out of New Zealand, and had got back not long ago. Neil said, 'Where are your family?' Socksay didn't say anything. Instead, he opened his hands and moved them apart, in the gesture that says: don't know. 'I didn't push it,' said Mahi. 'How could he not be where he was without a heartbreaking story behind him? If he wanted to volunteer it, I'd have listened. But I'm not going to flush it out.'

Neil asked where he'd been staying since he arrived back, and Socksay said in the city, but that he thought it'd be better to get out of there and come out to Ōrākei. Perhaps Sam had come close to finding him on those night drives around the city, searching for his son.

'I said, "Are you hungry, bro? Do you want some lunch?" He declined. He said, "No, I'm fine." I told him he was on Māori land. He didn't realise. He said, "Oh, I'm really sorry." He was really understanding. He offered to give me some money as an offering. I said, "No, you keep your money, bro."

'He really was the nicest guy. Quietly spoken, polite, courteous, respectful. But his body language was all closed. He sat there huddled, with his head down. No eye contact. He was holding something within himself.

'He really made an impression on me. I went home and I was in such conflict about asking him to leave. There's always been a level of conflict that I've felt, but none like this before, and it was because he was such a sweet guy.

'"Bugger it," I thought, and I filled a container from my dinner – we'd had a chicken meal – and my old army thermal mat. I thought, "He'll have come back." So I went there but he was gone.

'I went inside the emplacement and there was $2.40 in coins that he'd left on the black plastic mat as a koha. That broke my heart.'

Socksay's last act was to honour an debt. Unpaid debts always meant a lot to him; they were a torment, a sign of bad faith, of letting people down. He couldn't bear that. The coins might have been the last of his money, and he spent it on paying a debt he didn't actually owe.

Neil Mahi kept an eye out for Socksay over the next couple of weeks, looked at other gun emplacements at Bastion Point, all around. 'But there was no sign of him.' The reserve where he died wasn't far away.

He picked up the *Herald* about a month later, and recognised Socksay in the photograph that police had taken of him when they caught him breaking and entering.

'I come back here sometimes,' Neil said. 'I had my own ceremony for him. I have a Buddhist faith, so his passing resonated with me on that level, too.' We looked out towards the water, and North Head. 'He was such a nice guy. Gentle.'

When we'd first walked inside the emplacement, and we were looking around that small, damp tomb, Neil pointed to a coin on the floor. 'I think that was Socksay's,' he said. We stared at it. It was a 20-cent piece. We weren't in there very long. It was too sad. He said, 'Let's get out of here.'

Chapter 4

An old con: Malcolm Rewa

Now and then I studied Malcolm Rewa during his retrial for the murder of Susan Burdett and wondered whether it was within reason to view him sympathetically as just another pitiable old con. He turned 66 on the day of the verdict. His back and shoulders were hunched over when he walked. If you took away his cane, he'd have fallen to the ground like a sack. There was more of him when I last saw Rewa, just over 20 years earlier, at his first trial. Back then he wore his thick black hair in a mullet and raised his head high in the witness box. Back then he was a tough sonofabitch, 45, strong, mobile, alert, and it was well within reason to view him with as much fear as loathing. He had big hands, a long, watchful, ugly face.

Rewa beat Susan Burdett to death one night in March 1992 and got away with it for 27 years. He only got away with it as far as his bad hip was able to take him within the walls of Paremoremo prison. The cops busted Rewa as a serial rapist in 1996. The brutality of those crimes, and their sheer prolific extent, made him one of the most repulsive offenders in New Zealand criminal history, a man without any redeeming qualities, a suburban terrorist acting as a one-man trauma squad. But he escaped the murder charge, until February 2019, when justice caught up with him, finally, at last. 'Guilty,' said the jury, and that long, watchful, ugly face took on a familiar expression: a sourness, a spite. He was just another remorseless old con.

'I walk,' he told the jury, 'the Christian walk.' It's not a very straight walk. He was revealed in court as a nasty piece of work, and not just in his 1990s pomp as a rapist who terrorised women across the Auckland isthmus. It took a special and enduring nastiness to stick to his story that he and 'Susan' were lovers. The old crocodile searched for some tears. 'She wasn't just Susan Burdett to me,' he said, impersonating a lovelorn ex. 'She was my friend.'

'Susan', 'my friend' – Rewa's rape victims told police that his typical form of address was to say to them, 'Shut up, bitch, or I'll kill you.' After he raped Burdett, Rewa's DNA was detected in a vaginal swab. His defence was that they had fun sex on the night of her death. They were high on the Ecstasy he shared with her. He spoke of his generous nature: 'It was a freebie. The expense was on me.' He was asked in court when he first started supplying drugs to her. 'Maybe … two to three weeks before she passed? It wasn't long before her passing.' Before she 'passed', before her 'passing': the dainty little respectful words to describe the fast and violent death he brought to Burdett late on a Monday night, fracturing her skull with a blunt weapon. There were deep lacerations. 'Brain matter,' Crown prosecutor Gareth Kayes put it, 'was oozing out.'

The date was 23 March 1992. She was getting ready for bed. Her routine every Monday night was to come home from work, clean her unit in Pah Road, Papatoetoe, make dinner, and bake sweets to take with her when she went out to play 10-pin bowls at Manukau Super Strike. Her team, Ratbags, won their game. She drove home and left a plate of left-over fudge on the passenger seat to take to work the next day. Her neighbour in the next unit heard her slam the door inside the garage. The neighbour couldn't sleep; she usually went out to singing practice on Monday nights and got home late, but not this evening, and wasn't used to sitting at home twiddling her thumbs and counting sheep. At about 11.40pm she heard a loud bang through the walls. Gareth Kayes said, 'It's possible to kill a person in a blameworthy or not blameworthy way. But we are not talking here about an accident.' The neighbour said, 'Then there were other bangs, softer, and closer together. One after another.'

The jury were shown a 28-minute crime scene video. It was a silent movie filmed on a shaky hand-held camera. Burdett's body was discovered on a Wednesday morning. The film was made that afternoon: the clock on her kitchen wall reads 2.10pm.

It opens outside her house. There's a really close-up view of the tarseal on Pah Road. The anonymous film-maker seemed to love that road; their camera lingers on that road for quite some time. And then it pans to a crime scene tape in front of a long hedge. There's a power pylon in the distance. The houses are small, there are broken fences, a rubbish bin on its side: South Auckland noir.

It filmed a single tea towel on the clothesline. It filmed a moth in the back yard. It filmed in and around her house, slowly taking in a tea cosy in the kitchen and teacups on hooks, then out the back, to deckchairs on a patio, and bright hibiscus in late summer bloom.

It filmed Burdett's bedroom. There was a floral pattern on the wallpaper and a row of soft toys – a white cat, a blue teddy bear – on a bedside table. Her slippers were by the door and her feet were next to a pillow dropped on the floor. Her body sank a little into the mattress – this was New Zealand in 1992, peak times for a waterbed. All of this was filmed in silence, and all of this was viewed in silence, too.

The killer had crossed one of her legs over the other. What sort of staging was that supposed to represent? Concern for her modesty? Shame? Better still, disgust, for what he had done to her? Burdett's softball bat lay on top of the bed. It was left in a tidy, straight line, exactly parallel to the body. Forensic investigations failed to provide any physical evidence linking the bat to the fatal assault. It cannot properly be labelled the murder weapon. The fact that it was kept in the bedroom for Burdett's protection, and would have been seen by her killer, might be just one of those things. The fact that it corresponded to the kind of blunt object that struck and killed Burdett might be just another of those things. The fact that it was left next to the body, tossed aside like a kind of calling card, might be just one after another of those things.

But the police contrived to follow the demented logic that it really was just all of those things, because it didn't fit their case against another suspect, a kind of living ghost who had haunted Rewa's trial these past two weeks: Teina Pora.

* * *

The miscarriage of justice, the epic disgrace of it – which saw Pora serve 20 years in jail for Burdett's murder, a crime he did not commit on account of such various assorted facts as never having been in her house or knowing where she lived – gave Rewa's trial an importance and significance that Justice Geoffrey Venning acknowledged in his welcoming remarks to the jury. 'You may make a connection in this case,' he said, 'with Teina Pora.' Pora, who made a false confession to the police that he murdered Burdett in the company of two men from the Mongrel Mob; Pora, duly found guilty in 1994, and again at his retrial in 2000; Pora, finally cleared by the Privy Council, ruling in 2015 that he had been wrongfully convicted.

Two juries found an innocent man guilty. Two juries, in 1998, were unable to reach a verdict when Rewa was charged with Burdett's murder. One of the central problems was Pora. It was a Catch-22. An innocent man found guilty meant that a guilty man got away with it. Crown lawyers tried very hard to persuade the 1998 juries that Pora and Rewa were in cahoots, but it was an insane prosecution and of course it didn't make a lick of sense. Pora didn't know who Rewa was. Rewa always operated as a lone wolf; in part, the Privy Council heard, because he had problems getting it up and wouldn't have welcomed another man witnessing his humiliation.

The shocking story of Pora's false convictions was investigated at great length and in great detail by *Herald* reporter Phil Taylor. I fully expected to see him at the trial. All reporters are obsessed with being a witness to history, and Rewa's appearance was a historic event. But all or some reporters are also human, and Phil was on leave.

However, there was a brief visit from Tim McKinnel. The private detective, also hired to uncover evidence in the Lundy retrial, initiated and stuck at the long campaign to prove Pora's innocence. We ran into each other in the shade of the giant magnolia outside court. He cut a spruce figure in a black suit, but I resisted the temptation to insult him by saying he looked like a lawyer. He was actually at the High Court on other business, but a meeting had been cancelled. I urged him to come into Courtroom 7 and have a

110

look, saying, 'The prosecution are about to call the guy who found Susan's body.' Tim said, 'Steven Dawson.' He knows all the names, all the secrets, but came in and sat at the back of the court for a little while, listening to evidence he has pored over many, many times.

Many of us wish to reserve a special place in Hell for defence lawyers who appear to manipulate the law to release murderers and rapists. Too few of us want a hotter circle of Hell set aside for prosecution lawyers who go after innocent people accused of murder and rape. These days Justice Paul Davison sits in wise judgment at the bench. In 1994, Davison was a thin and monotonal QC who acted for the Crown in Pora's first trial. He told the jury that Susan Burdett was stalked by three men, including Pora. They spied on her through her window while she watched TV. They broke in, and two men raped her while Pora held her down. Then they killed her with their baseball bat, wiped the blood off, and threw it in a drain in Boundary Road ... All of it a travesty, but it worked like a magic spell, and it took five trials to finally break it and reveal that Rewa, and only Rewa, was Susan Burdett's killer.

It was all about Rewa at his fortnight-long trial in February 2019. Rewa and his comb-over, Rewa and his wretched Christian walk, Rewa and his walking stick, which he gripped tighter and tighter and tighter while his lies were exposed during cross-examination – he sat very close to the only physical exhibit in Courtroom 7, Burdett's dark brown softball bat, 82 centimetres in length with four small nicks taken out of the wood to test for blood, and the thought most certainly occurred that he had once held that very tightly, too.

His defence lawyer Paul Chambers tried talking about Pora. He didn't get very far. Justice Geoffrey Venning closed him down.

111

It concerned the bat. Chambers wanted to ask former detective Neil Grimstone about a softball bat that Pora knew about in a drain on Boundary Road. 'I'm not suggesting it had anything to do with Mr Pora,' he said, but the only relevance of the bat found in a drain on Boundary Road was its connection with Pora. Venning ruled there would henceforth be no more talk, ever, of the bat found in a drain on Boundary Road.

Chambers is a strange fellow. Sometimes I wondered whether he was just some guy with white whiskers and a big mole on the side of his head who had walked in off the street and got handed a black gown. 'Ask the witness a question,' Justice Venning was compelled to tell him, a number of times. And: 'No, no, Mr Chambers. No, no, no, no.' Also, more succinctly: 'No.' The screensaver on Chambers' laptop was an illustration of actor Leo McKern playing his great character Rumpole of the Bailey. Chambers was more rumpled than Rumpole; there were days he scrubbed up well, and other days when he wore scuffed shoes and a loose, sagging suit. In any case, the jury plainly had a gutsful of his Rumpole screensaver. They asked the judge to please tell Chambers to turn his laptop away from them so they didn't have to look at it.

'Paul,' Rewa would whisper, usually once or twice a day, to attract his attention. 'Paul!' Chambers would turn to face his client, who'd lean forward in the dock to hand over a handwritten note. One day, Rewa added: 'It's crucial!' Chambers may or may not have put any of the many scraps of paper to any use, but he remained very attentive to his client, always bounding over to talk to him at the end of each session. He felt a particular need to discuss something with Rewa one day, but the guards had already taken Rewa out of the courtroom, to take him to the downstairs cells, and were in no mood to cease the journey. 'But,' said Chambers, indignantly, 'I need to speak to my lawyer! I mean, my client!'

He tried pinning the murder on Dallas McKay, Burdett's son. Chambers said McKay had driven from his home in Kamo in the Far North to Auckland and bashed her to death. The motive was a life insurance windfall. But McKay was at the pub in Kamo that night, playing darts (his team won), until he went home at about 11pm. He was next seen at work at about quarter to seven in the morning. Chambers put to him that he made the return six-hour trip to Auckland to kill his mother and then showed up for a day's work.

'You killed your mother!' Chambers said.

'Nah, mate,' said the son. I think it was the best denial I ever heard in a courtroom. You can't fault the honesty and integrity of a Kiwi joker who talks as casually as that.

At least Chambers tried. He went in hard, he looked for inconsistencies, his manner was grave, severe, determined. His cross-exam was his finest hour in court, but really that's not saying much. His closing address was rambling and weird. How rambling and weird? So rambling and weird that I got a shout-out. He talked about a witness who had suffered post-traumatic stress disorder. Chambers could empathise. 'I've suffered a traumatic incident in the past, which I don't need to go into,' he told the jury. 'I don't want to give Mr Braunias palpitations.' I suppose it might have been a fair comment on my reporting of the trial. My daily reports were perhaps exercises in amateur psychology based on close observation of meaningless details, such as noticing that Chambers appears to have missing teeth.

Still, it's always nice to be read. I just didn't expect it to be acknowledged in the closing address of an important and historically significant murder trial, and I really didn't expect it to be acknowledged by a jury. Jurors operate under strict guidelines which include ignoring media coverage and generally treating the media like they don't exist. I guess it was okay when a juror at Rewa's trial made a passing remark to me outside court about one of my reports mentioning his shirt. A brief conversation about a shirt isn't likely to pervert the course of justice. That was in the first week of the trial. A few days later, the *Herald* published my report on Rewa's performance as a witness. It wouldn't be stretching things to describe the story as sarcastic or even withering or actually downright contemptuous. A juror made a passing remark about it outside court later that morning. 'Thank goodness,' she said, 'for your writing.'

God bless her, but it was a shock to be spoken to about court proceedings during a murder trial by a juror. Mr Braunias had palpitations.

* * *

The trial drew a large crowd. They included former Crown prosecutor Ross Burns, who divides his time between Mount Maunganui and Spain. There was another visitor from Tauranga, who approached me one day. He was evidently a true-crime fan: he'd come to watch Judge Paul Mabey QC and myself talk about murder trials a few years ago when we appeared onstage at the Tauranga arts festival. 'I'm on holiday,' he said, 'so I thought I'd come here for the day.' He made it sound like a pleasant outing.

Well, even a historic event, and the usual horror of a murder trial, can veer into low farce and parrot sketches.

One day in court was taken up with a learned conversation between the judge, a witness and the prosecution on how best to describe one of Susan Burdett's ear-rings, a silver-coloured sleeper. Crown prosecutor Gareth Kayes asked former police detective sergeant Michelle Moore what a sleeper looked like. She said it looked like a ring or a circle. Kayes asked if it had a hole in the middle and Moore confirmed it did, because that was the essential nature of rings and circles, but Justice Venning burst in, and said, 'Sorry, I might be missing something. Is it just to keep the holes in the ears open, or is it something else?' Moore did her best to illuminate His Honour, and so did Kayes, who asked her whether she agreed that a sleeper is a hooped, circular ear-ring. 'Yes,' she said. Justice Venning nodded sagely, and said, 'That's good. I always like to learn something every day.'

Then there was the parrot sketch. It began when the jury asked a question of Justice Venning. It's not unusual for juries to seek clarification. The expectation at Rewa's trial was that it would involve some complex forensic detail – DNA, blood spatter, something in that range – but in fact it briefly transformed the trial into the case of the missing bird.

The issue that exercised the jury concerned the photo booklet of the crime scene. A police photographer recorded the rooms in Susan Burdett's house. It showed a toaster, a hanging fern, slippers on the floor, a washing basket, a birdcage … The jury asked: 'Photo 33 has a cockatiel in a cage but not in photos 32 and 37. Was it removed at some point?'

Justice Venning looks rather a lot like John Key. He has the same pink, good-humoured face. He told the jury in one of the most high-profile murder trials in recent New Zealand criminal history: 'It's fair to say I don't think anyone else has addressed their mind to this issue. Mr Kayes has indicated to the court he'll make inquiries of the police to see if we can clarify that for you. I'm sure the fate of the cockatiel was looked after. I'm sure it was alright. But please put that to one side, and don't think about it again.'

But who could think of anything else? I was compelled to make my own inquiries about the fate of the cockatiel, and can confirm that Justice Venning's guess was correct: the bird was looked after. The purity of a crime scene requires that all pets are removed from the property. Police gave the cockatiel to a friend of Susan Burdett.

* * *

I dedicated my first true-crime book to May Mackey. She was 95 when we met at her apartment in Parnell. She brought out custard squares to have with our tea. I wanted to talk to her about a tragedy in 1963, when a maniac in Bethells Beach shot and killed his neighbour and two police officers. May was married to Detective Inspector Wally Chalmers. He was 42 when Victor Wasmuth ended his life. I asked May what her feelings were about the man who killed her husband, and she said, 'From the beginning, I wanted to see him. To talk to him. I always had that yen to see him. Because I never had nothing against him. Not at all. It wasn't my attitude towards people. And that's why, for thirty years, I've been visiting prisons.' Then she talked about visiting Paremoremo Prison and becoming close friends with Malcolm Rewa.

Rewa talked about May at some length when he gave evidence. He spoke quietly, and with affection, respect and gratitude. He had become a Christian in prison, he said. 'It's thanks to the Christian people who came to see me. One in particular, Whāea May. She was a woman in her late seventies then, and she had an aura about her … May came to see me last Saturday. She's ninety-nine now, and thank God she's still with us. She treats me like her son. That's the way she sees me.'

Dear May. I dedicated my book *The Scene of the Crime* to her because she had such a long, close experience of violent crime in New Zealand – the widow of a police officer killed in the line of duty, and now friends with serious offenders, including Rewa ('Malcolm') and William Bell ('Willie'), who murdered three people at the Panmure RSA in 2001 – but had remained a gentle soul who believed in kindness and redemption. 'I never ask about their crimes,' she said. 'We just talk.' The Rewa she knows is warm, decent, good.

It was that Rewa who I tried to see in court. May is no fool, and I was loathe to think that Rewa had played her for one. Murderers and rapists become murderers and rapists through their actions, but no one is any one thing; even the evil are unable to sustain being evil every minute of the day; of course a Rewa or a Bell or a Brenton Tarrant is capable of goodness or just getting on with the errands and chores of daily life. When he gave evidence, Rewa talked about taking his son to a particular dairy because it sold the boy's favourite ice cream, Rocky Road. That same boy featured in a strange story that I heard outside court one day. It concerned Pora. The police took Pora to Burdett's house and filmed him on Pah Road; the video was shown at both his trials. A boy walks past at one point, bouncing a ball. According to the story I was told, it was Rewa's son.

Rewa sat in court day after day with his head bowed, wearing a pair of glasses, and writing in a 3B1 notebook, and I sat nearby day after day with my head bowed, wearing a pair of glasses, and writing in a 3B1 notebook. We'd raise our heads, and look at each other. He saw just another journalist. I didn't see, or was unwilling to see, what May saw.

117

In cross-examination, Rewa presented himself as someone devious, pathetic, enraged. His walking stick operated like the needle on a lie detector. It jumped and jerked all over the place. His problem was that he introduced a whole new set of lies never previously heard at his two earlier trials, but they felt improvised, made up on the spot. He claimed he had sex with Burdett in his truck. Under cross-examination, he admitted he didn't own his truck until two years after Burdett's death. Wildly, he claimed he'd never broken in through a window at any of the rapes he committed. Under cross-examination, he admitted the time he broke in through a bedroom window, and a kitchen window, and a toilet window, and a window by the back door, and a ventilation window …

Things were getting away from him. Things weren't going according to whatever haphazard plan he'd cooked up for his appearance in the witness box. He tried to avoid answering Gareth Kayes's questions; he wanted to make a speech. He screeched: 'I'm going to say my piece!' Justice Venning closed him down. Where could he turn to, what did he have left?

All he had left were his own lies. The new ones probably struck him as exciting and fresh. Sex in a truck that didn't exist! Sex, too, beneath the trig station on Māngere Mountain! As ever, Rewa chose stories that established his virility. I remember at his first trial, in 1998, when he said in court, 'She said I had the kind of physique that would turn women on.' Kayes listened to the Māngere Mountain revelation with interest. Why was it, he wondered, that Rewa only shared the location of this tryst now, at his third trial? Rewa gripped his walking stick very tight. He answered: 'No one ever asked before.'

Kayes is a smooth-faced man with dark hair and soft hands. He has a gentle, patient manner, and has always struck me as a sensitive and artistic soul. His hands shook when he cross-examined Rewa, but he held his nerve. Kayes told Rewa that he broke in through Susan Burdett's window, like he did with many of his other victims, hit her, like he did with many of his other victims, and placed her legs over the side of the bed when he raped her, like he did with many of his other victims. 'I never climbed through any windows,' Rewa repeated; but Kayes took him patiently through the cases where he climbed through the windows of his rape victims.

There was a 19-year-old in Panmure; Rewa placed a pillow over her face, and said, 'Don't fight or I'll kill you.' There was a 24-year-old in Manurewa; Rewa tied her hands and feet, and placed a duvet over her head. There was a 23-year-old in Ōtāhuhu; Rewa blindfolded her, punched her in the jaw, smashed her face into the carpet.

Rewa listened and held onto his walking stick. He held onto it tighter and tighter as the agreed facts of his past crimes were read out. He throttled it, he twisted it in his hands; I kept looking at the stick, expecting it to splinter and snap. But it was Rewa who was splintering. His lies were smashed apart, tossed onto a scrapheap that grew higher and higher with the accumulated rubbish of his past lies.

He was running out of ideas, running out of angles. Chambers approached myself and my *Herald* colleague Sam Hurley outside court just after the trial had begun, and said that he hoped that 'the tenor' of our reporting would reflect the person Rewa was, not just a black-and-white stereotype. But who was Rewa as he appeared in court? Damaged, plainly and profoundly; vain, writing Burdett's script to cast himself as the romantic lead; reckless, inventing lies that could easily be exposed; afraid, an old con backed into a corner, twisting his walking stick in his hands, coming out with sudden announcements: 'There's other people involved!'

What other people? Who? Not Pora. Pora was a ghost. Rewa was by himself, the culprit, the rapist and murderer, caught out after 27 years. In 1996, police kicked down his door at 37 Mayflower Close in Māngere at 11.15pm. He ran for it, but was brought down by police dogs. It put an end to his CV (1987–1996) as a serial rapist who hit many of his victims, who raped one woman who was pregnant, who raped another woman in front of her two-year-old – a police detective said the name of his last victim out loud when we spoke in private during the trial, a 15-year-old girl who he attacked on the street in Epsom, breaking her jaw while attempting to abduct her in broad daylight, but her screams attracted her father and Rewa ran for it, too slowly, the girl's father taking a note of the license number of Rewa's car. The detective said her name with real feeling. She was responsible for taking Rewa off the streets. He had been a skilled and effective hunter, but his hunting days were over.

The hunt began to convict Rewa as Burdett's killer. It was long and demented and caused untold suffering, but finally came to an end on a Friday in February 2019. The jury – the one who wore a T-shirt proclaiming *ONLY GOD CAN JUDGE ME NOW*, the one who spent a lot of time ogling pretty journalists – were told a straight story. They replied with a straight answer. Case closed: Rewa, the end, at last: but not quite. He lodged an appeal. Dragging it out one more time ('I'm going to say my piece!'), dragging God into it ('I walk the Christian walk'), dragging up the past ('There's other people involved!'). But it had all been told before, wordlessly. That 28-minute silent film played in court – Burdett's house, Burdett's body – ended with an abrupt edit. It went back to the bedroom. Her body had been removed. All we saw was the bed where she was killed, the scene of Rewa's crime.

Chapter 5

Take my hand: Simonne Butler

We sat in her little cottage in an enchanted wood, and Simonne Butler said, 'I've been to Hell and I know the way out. So take my hand and come with me.' But which hand? The left hand that was chopped off at the wrist, or the right hand, which was sliced apart vertically through the palm? It's always rude to stare, and I hoped that I was being covert, but really I found it hard to take my eyes off her hands. Each scar held the memory of their violent and famous damage, when Tony Dixon went berserk with his Samurai sword on a summer's afternoon in 2003; they also told the story of their spectacular bionic reattachment. They were strange and powerful exhibits, objects of horror and pity and awe, although actually they were just body parts that belonged to a woman who goes about her life, and the hands go along for the ride.

Dixon was her ex. He had smoked tremendous amounts of P when he attacked Butler, and his new girlfriend, Renee Gunbie. He left them for dead in a house in flat, rural Pipiroa near Thames, and sped off, to Hamilton for a gun, then to Auckland to shoot a stranger dead, to open fire on police, to announce his intention to go down in a blaze of glory, to finally give himself up and live a few more years as New Zealand's weirdest killer. He died in prison, a suicide.

Such is a journalist's précis of events; Butler takes up the story with a rather more direct style: 'Dead and gone, yay. Nicest thing he ever did for me. If nobody ever asked me a question about him again, that'd be sweet. I don't think about him. He doesn't even pop into my mind. He's just like some random dude I used to know.'

More or less all I did for a couple of hours in her house in west Auckland was ask questions about Dixon. He's one of two very strong, quite vivid characters who appear in her memoir, *Double-Edged Sword*, a compelling and unusually well-written survivor's story. As literature, the Louise Nicholas book *My Story* is a dull read, one cliché after another; Butler's book, ghosted and as such beautifully shaped by Andra Jenkin, is artful, intense, actually quite funny sometimes. It's true crime. It's got a lot of good, hard-boiled sentences: 'He was a freelance thug.' And: 'I was the soldier and Tony was the war.' Also: 'He wanted me to bow down, to kneel, so that when he chopped my head off it would land in the washing basket, because he didn't want a mess.'

Dixon, eventually, recedes in the telling, and Butler emerges as the most interesting character. No small feat to overshadow that sonofabitch. True, he wasn't a bad father to at least some of his kids, and a woman fell in love with him after he went to prison for the murder and the sword attacks; no one is a complete monster who is better off dead, but Dixon came close. As for Butler, who has beautiful eyes, a sensual manner, and a loud, enormously happy laugh, she now operates in the unseen world sort of thing. Mumbo doesn't get much more jumbo than her role as a shaman whose medicine name is Moonstone Phoenix.

There were lots of short brown bottles of flower remedy in her cottage, and also the collected works of Jackie Collins. I asked, 'What is a shaman?'

She said, 'A shaman is somebody who walks between the worlds of the unseen reality and the seen reality, and their job is to create order and balance in the universe. So, yeah. Pretty much that's it.'

Good; and she also offers spiritual counselling and flower essence therapy. 'I specialise in trauma recovery, eliminating depression and anxiety. I help people move past trauma and be able to live a joyous and empowered live again.'

She was describing her own life. She knew about trauma; she knew the way out. I said, 'How are you now?'

She said, 'I have to pace myself. I have to be careful about where I'm spending my energy and who I'm spending it on – there are times when people suck the life out of you, like an energy vampire … I have to sleep sometimes for four days. I hit the wall and not only do I get tired, I end up in pain.'

'Where do you feel the pain?'

'In my hands.'

'Always the hands,' I said, looking at her hands.

'Yeah,' she said. 'Always the hands.'

* * *

Her book is a love story gone bad, very bad, and it's also a very Auckland story. 'It was in Clevedon that I was hit with a ratchet.'

123

And: 'I was at work when Tony was arrested in the St Lukes Mall carpark.' There's the first date in Penrose (Coke and tinned salmon), making love five times a day in Beachlands, burgers from Al & Pete's, oh and the time he was up in the trees at Judges Bay spying on her with his night goggles when she met friends for dinner at Mikano.

Love and sex, weed and acid, and violence. Dixon beat her without warning, regularly, during their two-year relationship. She said, 'When I counted it up, there were twelve times when I was actually knocked unconscious. There's probably only five or six in the book. Like I didn't mention the time I got hit in the knees with a four-by-four. There were lots of different implements.

'He'd plan it all day. We had conversations about this; he told me he'd start getting angry, and then think about hurting me, and that would make him happy for the day, and then I would come home and he'd hurt me.'

I said, 'But other times you were just really happy.'

She said, 'Certainly there were times I was so ridiculously happy and I didn't think life could ever get even better. I mean everyone thinks he was violent and angry all the time, but he wasn't. What it was, was we would have a day, a week, a month of amazingness and then three minutes of psycho craziness. It was like a train that just whizzed by. He wouldn't wake up angry and be grumpy all day. He was more of a clown. If I was angry, he would spend the entire day trying to make me laugh.'

I said, 'You were in love.'

She said, 'By the time I was twenty-two I was absolutely madly in love. Yeah. And a lot of the reason for that was that he was so needy and so into me. And then he started doing things that made me think he was amazing, like driving really fast.'

Like driving from Wellington to South Auckland in four and a half hours in a stolen car while Butler was on Ecstasy. Like driving at night in the middle of the road at 180 kilometres per hour with the lights off. Dixon loved Commodores, also Holdens; all his cars were black; he vacuumed them, polished them, stripped them, and now and then put them back together.

'His passion was souping up a V8 to get extra power and extra speed,' she said. 'It might be that it needed longer extractors for the exhaust, or a six-speed gearbox instead of an automatic, but you can usually soup up your power by twenty-five per cent by changing the exhaust … I spent a lot of time sitting in exhaust shops rolling joints and passing tools.'

I thought she was describing a kind of bogan nirvana, but the first time I ever heard from Butler was when she got in touch to say how much she hated my classification of Dixon in my book *The Scene of the Crime* as 'a bogan ninja'. So not true, she protested; it was as though I had violated the codes of the bogan by assuming Dixon was one of their number. She explained, 'I'm not a bogan; I'm a westie – we're higher class! A bogan is black jeans, black T-shirts, mullet, greasy hair, doesn't wash much, listens to metal.

'Tony was no bogan and no westie, either. He loved Kylie Minogue! He was constantly stealing my Kylie CD. He was an east Auckland boy; they tend to have a nicer dress sense. He liked to wear Barker's trackpants and Adidas. If he saw a new pair of Adidas that he loved but didn't fit him, he'd buy them in my size because he had to have them in the house. His image was really important to him. He spent more time in front of the mirror than I did. So vain, and so insecure.'

I said, 'Was he handsome?'

She said, 'I was never into him physically. His lips were too thin and his eyes were too close together.'

Correction, then: he was a thin-lipped ninja in Adidas and Barker's, his eyes too close together as he picked up his ornamental Samurai sword and started swinging.

* * *

She said that she can play the attack like a movie. It opens with Dixon locking the door behind her when she called at the house in Pipiroa; it ends with Dixon bending down beside her as she lay on the floor, her blood sticking to the knees of his pants, and saying to her: 'I'll see you in Hell later.'

Those last few seconds after he locked the door and before the blade struck, and struck again, and again, and again, were the last that she remained whole. Dixon tore her asunder. He separated her. He divided her, and I asked her whether she thought of herself as two different people – the Simonne Butler who walked into that house, and the Simonne Butler who was airlifted out, minutes away from death, about to have her hands reattached in 27 continuous hours of surgery.

She said, 'For many years it was like my life completely stopped then. There was before and after, and it segregated my life completely. Now there doesn't seem to be a disconnect. Now I'm just me.'

I said, 'The violence of the attack – it was so insane, so one of a kind, that people like myself are still fixated with how shattering it was. We think of the sword and what it did. But you don't.'

She said, 'Trauma can be an opportunity to put ourselves back together stronger and better and newer. Most people get lost in the shattering. But when everything falls apart, we only lose the things we don't need.'

'What would have happened to your life if you hadn't been attacked?'

She said, 'I was always going to find this path. This is what I was born to do. I have a really deep understanding of the human capacity to heal on all levels. But this fast-tracked me. It was absolutely horrible, it was the worst thing in the world, but I learned how strong I am, and I learned how to heal effectively, and I now have a platform to go out and help people.'

The very least compliment you could give Butler is that she's staunch; she has another, stronger quality as well – serenity. New Age westie, born 1975, full of good humour with an appetite for life, who survived to tell the tale, and tell it skilfully, of the time she was chopped apart and left for dead by a wretch. Fear haunts the book; laughter jumps out when you least expect it. She said: 'They took my dishes! They took my cutlery!' She could only laugh at the opportunist monstrousness of thieves who went to the crime scene – the house in Pipiroa – to loot it. 'All of my jewellery and all of my make-up and all of my perfumes. My mum rescued my bathmats, bless her. Pink bathmats with yellow hearts.'

I said, 'Did you ever go back to the house?'

She said, 'I had to, to sell it. I spent months preparing myself to go back. I really prepared myself hard-out for it and I walked in, and – nothing. I got to where it all happened, and there were no blood stains, not even a mark where it had been.'

'Do you revisit the attack? Or does it revisit you, in sleep?'

'Never,' she said. 'I've had nightmares not of the attack, but about Tony turning up at my door – not to hurt me, just turning

127

up, like nothing had happened, and trying to get back in my life again.

'The things that freaked me out when I got home from hospital wasn't the violence but having to live in the world again. There were years when I couldn't leave my house. There were five places I could go to, and, anything other than that, I'd be a blithering mess. If I needed to go to the dairy for something, I'd have to prime myself up for three hours.

'And I thought I was being followed. Tony's reach was so far, and so I never knew whether I was or I wasn't. There were still so many people on his side. It was like he was a cult leader. So many people were at his bidding. He has this charismatic patter. He makes friends so easily. He gets what he wants.'

Strange the way she slipped into the present tense, as though he were still alive, a 48-year-old man roaming around, knowing how to make people like him. But he died in 2010. The anniversary is next Friday: 25 November. It won't register with the woman he loved and wanted to decapitate. She talked about feeling so scared after she got out of hospital, so frightened at the prospect that one of Dixon's goons might come after her, that she slept with a hammer under her bed for about eight months.

'A very big hammer,' she said, and then she laughed and laughed and laughed. 'It was so big I couldn't have picked it up!' Not with those hands, that claw up in winter, and she has to soak them in a basin of hot water when she gets out of bed in the morning. After that, they're good to go.

Chapter 6

Missing: Nigel Peterson

Nigel is going to make a run for it. Nigel is going to break out. Nigel is going to— A tūī rushes overhead, noisily beating its wings. A pair roost in the branches of an enormous gum tree further along the road. He can see it from the passenger seat, but he's not really looking, he has other things on his mind, he has one thing on his mind. The driver told him that everyone – there were five guys who lived there – had to move out of the house. The hot-water cylinder burst that morning, and flooded. It was going to be a job to fix it. They had to find somewhere else to stay. He receives the information, and a single, brilliant impulse takes hold of his mind, seizes it, but he doesn't let on, he doesn't say anything. For a secret to exist, it must be concealed. The car turns into a steep driveway, and stops at the top outside a house. It's not his house. It's not where he lives, not anymore. He swings open the car door, leaps out, and walks fast, very fast, back down the driveway before anyone even has the chance to react. Nigel is making a run for it. Nigel is breaking out. Nigel is going to fly.

Nigel Peterson was 33 years old when he disappeared on a sweateringly hot afternoon in Rotorua on 17 November in 2017.

He was last positively identified in broad daylight on a busy street. He was alone, lost, mentally unstable. His family got together on his thirty-fourth birthday in his honour. When he turned 33, they took him to Valentines on Fenton Street in Rotorua; the boy loved his meat, and loaded up on chicken wings.

Chris Peterson, 61, is a vet. He remarried and has two daughters, 12 and 9; their artwork was on the walls, including one of a dancing giraffe. His ex-wife Eileen Goldsmith, 58, works with her second husband at PGG Wrightson. Nigel's younger sister Michelle, 32, teaches secondary school in Whanganui. On Nigel's birthday after he disappeared, she drove north to Whakatāne, to her dad's property, with its chickens and goats out the back, and the sleep-out where Nigel would stay at Easter and Christmas. It's now filled with the things from his home in Rotorua – mattress, suitcases, model tanks. Geneva Healthcare, which provided Nigel with an independent living programme and 24-hour care, asked the family to empty his room a few weeks after he vanished.

It was a vanishing act so complete and so baffling that to look for him was to look for a ghost. Rotorua constable John Fredericksen, 44, who led the police search, described it as working in a kind of void. 'It's relatively easy, getting information,' he said. 'But I would say this case has had the least amount of information. It was a whole lot of nothing. Everything was just nothing. Just nothing.'

Nigel lived in his own world. He drew the search party into it, crossing over from their world, with its fixed expectations and defined behaviour, as they tried to guess his movements and whereabouts. What would Nigel have done? But not even Nigel knew. His own world was in constant uproar. Of course there are probabilities, likely scenarios, sound theories, and the best of them may well be a patient, beautifully thought-out analytical deduction, reached by the police behavioural science unit, and that is that the end came quickly, maybe even the same afternoon he went missing.

His parents separated when Nigel was a teenager, and his life began to spiral and fall into a Hell of mental illness; Chris and Eileen laughed that Nigel put them together a lot, together looking for their boy. A two-hour interview, which it would be fair to describe as often pretty harrowing, was held around the dining room at Chris's house in Whakatāne. They wept, they fell silent; they were in an agony of unknowing. Where did their boy go? Eileen wore her powder-blue PGG Wrightson workshirt. There were lines on Chris's face which got there and formed deep grooves from years of worry. They sat next to each other, and were asked that if Nigel's life ended quickly, if at least he didn't endure days or weeks of being lost and afraid, was there any comfort in that, was that a good thing to think?

Eileen said, 'But we don't know what's happened.'

Chris said, 'If it had happened, then we could think that. But we don't know.'

Eileen said, 'We have no idea.'

No one knows what happened. But what did they think happened?

'Aaah,' Chris sighed. 'In the early days, what I was always putting my hope on is that he could survive. Now I think he has come to some misadventure and succumbed. And whether that was the first night, or in the first week, I don't know. There's certainly a real possibility that it was very quick. But it could have been longer. But I think that's the only sort of credible option, that he's come to a misadventure. How that exactly happened and where and what timeframe,' he said, 'we'd dearly love to know.'

He disappeared on a Friday afternoon. The last absolutely reliable and verified sighting of him was at 3pm, outside 385 Old Taupō Road, when one of his caregivers saw him from her rear-vision mirror; he was walking fast, very fast, on the side of the road, heading towards downtown Rotorua. Old Taupō Road runs more or less parallel to the main drag of Fenton Street. Nigel was at the south end of town, near the famous tourist attractions of Whakarewarewa and Te Puia. The geysers are spectacular to behold and always worth the price of admission, but you can see burning, bubbling infernos all throughout Rotorua, free of charge, steaming out of the side of the road and from streams and mudpools in parks; to vanish into thin air in Rotorua is to vanish into mist.

* * *

His whole life was a kind of mystery. He was born Nigel Jeffrey Peterson, on 16 August 1984, 8 pounds 15 ounces, in Ōpotiki maternity hospital. 'They had to call the anaesthetist from his squash tournament,' said Eileen. Nigel was taken home to their beautiful spread on the estuary where they farmed beef cattle. 'He was perfectly healthy from a baby, and then …' Eileen cried for the first time, but by no means the last, during the next two hours. She continued, 'He had an illness at eight months old, which left him with a brain injury and like a stroke victim.'

What happened?

'We have no idea really what happened,' she said. She meant they had no idea how, exactly, he caught a virus – the virus that resulted in encephalitis, inflammation of the brain. 'We don't know for sure. Everyone's got ideas. But we can't be certain.

'It was totally sudden. The day that it started happening, he had a wee bit of a runny nose, the snuffles, and then he had a fit. He started to get a temperature that morning, and fitted, and from that time on, he kept on fitting. We took him to Ōpotiki [hospital], where he kept fitting there and turned blue, then an ambulance to Whakatāne, fitting there – couldn't control the fitting. That was pretty terrible.'

'Mmm,' said Chris.

'And then to the hospital in Auckland, and on the tenth day it stopped as quickly as it started. But he'd been left like a stroke victim. One side of him was paralysed, and there was quite a lot of different damage in his brain, so he had a lot of learning disabilities … It's a complicated case.'

When he went missing, and the first, anxious stories appeared in the Rotorua *Daily Post*, Nigel was described as 'autistic'. Eileen: 'We said that because that's the easiest way for everyone to understand his behaviour.'

Was he autistic?

Chris: 'Nigel displays a lot of autistic characteristics.'

Eileen: 'If he hadn't had that illness as a child, you wouldn't know how autistic he would have been.'

If at all?

Chris: 'If at all, yeah. I can't believe that it's not related to his illness; it *has* to be. And then he also became psychotic at about sixteen …' The accurate label for Nigel, he said, was brain-injured with psychosis.

The encephalitis came and left as mysteriously as Nigel himself left without a trace 33 years later, in a swirl of the same confusion – 'No idea', 'We can't be certain', 'We don't know what happened.' But there was something else about his strange exit that afternoon which reached back to his infancy. Nigel survived the encephalitis, and the constant, convulsive fitting, and even the paralysis – his right side would always be weak, but he regained mobility; it certainly didn't hold him back when he shot through the streets of Rotorua and raced towards some oblivion – and there was the conviction that he would also survive being lost, whether it was on unfamiliar streets or on the edge of a black forest. A lot of that belief was based on a quality Nigel had in spades: courage.

'Brave as brave, tough as tough,' said Chris, with a fierce pride. His son couldn't catch a ball and was no good at athletics, but he excelled at horse-riding: 'That was his sport.' Eileen brought out photo albums of Nigel winning ribbons at shows, sitting confidently on ponies, looking relaxed, happy. Chris said, 'He rode real loose and real kind.' He found a photo of Nigel on a horse called Thunderbolt. 'See?' he said. 'He's not tense, his body's not reacting – horses love that. He had a real affinity with horses. He'd kick 'em down to a fence and they'd go for him. He was fearless like that.'

'He had his own style, all his reins flapping. Gung-ho,' said Michelle, who grew up as his adored and adoring baby sister, younger by 18 months. They played for hours at a secluded spot on the estuary that they called the hot pools. 'He was always the one looking after me,' she said. It was a happy childhood, years and years of it suspended in a New Zealand bliss of family, animals, tides, the farm, golden weather. Chris said, in a voice that started off soft and got more and more faraway, 'He was a lovely little boy.'

He did well at school. Eileen found some old report cards; he got good marks in Year 12 for English, physics, chemistry, biology. There was talk of becoming a scientist, maybe a helicopter pilot. But psychosis stormed in and took Nigel away. He heard voices. Eileen: 'It's like he didn't know what he was doing. Uncontrollable.'

There were hallucinations. Chris: 'It started to unravel for him.' He had psychotic episodes. Eileen: 'It was like a breakdown.' The marriage ended around this time, and it was just Chris on the farm with his son, losing the ability to function, not coping, essentially going mad. 'They were heartbreaking times,' said Chris.

He never gave up hope. Chris arranged for Nigel to pre-train a neighbour's racehorse. Nigel fed it, rode it for hours every day. Chris: 'It was a real difficult horse to handle, it'd try and bite and all sorts of things, but Nigel had such a lovely, calm way with it. I said, "You've got this role with animals, you could work with this." But he had to be taken away, and he never rode a horse again.'

* * *

Nigel is flying. Nigel is out of the car, down the driveway, past the three letterboxes and a pink camellia bush, and turns left onto Otonga Road. It's ten to three on a hot, beautiful afternoon – looking straight ahead, there are sheep on a distant hill, the grass bright and smooth in the sunshine. Smoke reaches up into the sky from Whakarewarewa and Te Puia. He walks past a vast magnolia, a trailer balanced on top of a barrel marked POISON, a garden statue of Pania of the Reef. He's on his own, he's not stopping for anybody. When he's in the mood, no one can catch him. He's a slim man, tall (180cm, or 5'11"), very fit. He covers 400 metres in less than five minutes, and comes to the intersection of Otonga and Springfield Roads. The easiest thing to do is turn left. Nigel turns left. He's on a mission, he's executed it perfectly, and has no need to consider the question: where to?

If he'd turned right at the end of the Otonga Road driveway, he'd have gone towards the house where he lived. It's possible he would have recognised something, got a handle on his whereabouts – only two hours earlier, in fact, he'd called in at the Super Lucky Takeaway on the corner and bought fish and chips. It was the exact same distance from the driveway, 400 metres. Super Lucky owes its name to the amazing circumstances of the previous owner of the site, Leo Gao, who ran the BP station and was mistakenly given a $10 million overdraft by Westpac in 2009; he took the money and ran. Another getaway on Otonga Rd. Gao, though, was caught, sentenced, jailed. Nigel had him beat: he even managed to slip past CCTV cameras without being seen.

Raj Kumar, 50, runs the Springfield Superette on the corner of Otonga and Springfield. He still has a 'missing' poster for Nigel taped on the wall behind the counter. He gave the shop's CCTV tapes to police in case it might help; the cameras were bound to have caught Nigel on the other side of the street, before he turned left onto Springfield.

Constable John Fredericksen studied the tapes. 'I can confirm,' he said, 'that there is no CCTV footage of Nigel.'

None? What about from Raj Kumar's dairy?

'You get a shape, and it's more than likely human.' Nothing more. Same with CCTV film taken an hour later at nearby Te Puia on Old Taupō Road. 'I'm satisfied,' he said, 'that it's a person.' Nothing else. A whole lot of nothing.

In any case, it's a known fact that Nigel turned left into Springfield Road, opposite Raj's dairy, because one of Geneva's caregivers drove after Nigel and saw him leg it around the corner. She caught up with him on Springfield Road, and drove alongside, trying to talk him into getting in the car, but he wasn't having a bar of it. He turned left onto Old Taupō Road, heading north, and she kept at it, telling him it was all going to be okay, and then she got out of the car and talked to him. This time he stopped. For a moment, maybe longer, he considered getting in the car. But the moment passed, and he pushed past her. The caregiver decided she needed help. She didn't have her cellphone on her, and drove back to the house on Otonga Road. She and another caregiver got in their cars and went back to where she'd last seen him – but it's at this point that Nigel becomes the man who wasn't there.

Constable Fredericksen collected four credible but unconfirmed sightings in the next week, and they were all further south along Old Taupō Road. The theory is that Nigel turned around as soon as the caregiver drove off, maybe lost his bravado now that he was suddenly alone, and retraced his steps, intending to get back to Otonga Road. But he missed the Springfield Road turn-off and just kept walking south on Old Taupō Road, past the Hemo Gorge roundabout, past Te Puia, then downhill on State Highway 5 towards Taupō, with deep, dark forests on either side of the road.

There are two sightings of a man who may or may not have been Nigel on State Highway 5 that afternoon. A woman returning to Rotorua with her partner reports seeing someone just past the Hemo Gorge roundabout at about 4.10pm. Another motorist identifies a man a little further south at 6.30pm, near a display of daffodils on the side of the road, placed in memory of a woman who was killed in a car accident. Both sightings seem to be a good match for Nigel – what he was wearing, and the unsteady, shambling way he walked.

Two more sightings come in during the week. A woman sees someone on the Monday, at about midday. She'd driven from Napier and was on her way to Rotorua to see her father before he went into surgery. 'She used to live here,' said Fredericksen, 'so when she sees someone she thinks is drunk walking down State

Highway 5, she thinks to herself, "Here we go. Rotorua special." But she said to me, "When I thought about it, it actually struck me as someone who'd had a stroke." So some really good detail there.

'And then a woman going into town to buy cigarettes on the Wednesday says she sees someone directly opposite the Tamaki Māori Village, which was the previous sighting, again at midday.

'Okay. How to explain the two days between sightings? He's hiding. He's avoiding people. The profile for Nigel was we expected him to try and seclude himself, remove himself from the public eye.'

Police conducted massive searches near the four sightings. Nigel's family, and their friends, searched even wider and more intensively, for weeks, all through summer. His grandfather Ian Jeffrey, 84, hit the road on his bicycle, never gave up. 'Nigel wasn't going to stay where they wanted him to stay,' he said. 'You can't change his mind easily. Once he gets an idea in his head … But I don't know what the idea was. We just don't know.' The search included the Redwood Forest, Lake Rotomahana and Lake Rerewhakaaitu, at Kāingaroa, behind Rainbow Mountain, at an abandoned sawmill on State Highway 38 – a notice in an empty office advertises a job vacancy for a general hand in 2007, there are couches and office desks and a bicycle and crates of fungicide inside vast, dry, spooky sheds. They were looking for a ghost in a kind of ghost town.

There was thought he might have seen a road sign for Whakatāne, and followed the arrows. There was thought he never got very far at all, and the very last police search, in May 2018, concentrated on the golf course right beside the Hemo Gorge roundabout. A tree has fallen over a golf course fence on Old Taupō Road. It's easy to step over it and into thick, low mānuka; right behind it are three steaming pools, spitting out mud, devouring the end of another tree that has snapped and sunk into the boiling pit.

Chris said, 'You can't have no hope. But I'm a rational, science-based person, so I go on evidence, and the evidence ain't giving me any hope. But we're still his parents. What can we do? We miss him. You can look back and say, "We did everything we could possibly do." We pursued everything. When a new sighting came in, bang, we'd be down there like a flash ... But we never came up with anything.'

Eileen had come and gone from the room quite a few times. She returned when Chris was talking, and when he finished, she said, 'I just think that Nigel was on his own journey.'

Chris said, 'He wrote his own agenda. You'd have to say that. All the way through, Nigel did things his own way.'

* * *

Dominic Gielen had never spoken to a reporter about Nigel. He was a caregiver at Geneva, and privacy laws prevented him from talking as an employee. But he left, burned out with the stress of working in mental health; Nigel's disappearance, too, hit him hard. They were close, had a bond. Nigel's parents mentioned his name with tremendous warmth, and gratitude for everything he'd done for Nigel.

He lives on Otonga Road – it was his Pania of the Reef statue that Nigel sped past that afternoon last August. He is a tall man, extremely handsome, 58 years old, with the ghost of a stutter, and he speaks with intensity.

He said, 'Nige was highly intelligent. Loved the outdoors – I'm a keen walker, but Nige was something else. Loved birds. I felt

139

birds represented freedom for him. Because Nige was aware of his situation, and that led to his frustration.

'When he was elevated – yelling, screaming, people talking to him in his head, he'd go, "No! No! Don't say that anymore!" Those messages would drive him absolutely bananas.

'So you'd give him a drug to try and curb it, and I'd take him away somewhere quiet. And then he'd come down and sleep. I remember one time him saying things like, "I don't want to be Nigel."

'I knew exactly what he was saying. He'd had enough … When he got his chance to run, all I thought was – I said to the police when they interviewed me, "Do you think you'll find him?" They said, "Oh yes. Yes." I thought, "Hm. They're not Nigel, though, are they?" '

Meaning?

'Meaning: "You're not going to find me. I'm not going to be sitting under a culvert, or hiding behind a hedge, or behind someone's garage. I'm out of here."

'He would have felt, "They're taking me out of my home. This is it. I've had enough." Because Nige had had enough anyway. We used to walk further and further and further. It was like once Nigel gained his confidence, he was, "I don't need you anymore. Nigel can do this on his own."

'I noticed towards the end, the last six months, Nigel would say, "Nigel can look after Nigel. Nigel doesn't need anybody."'

But Nigel can't do this on his own. He needs his medication, he needs Dominic, he needs his family. 'He'd switch off a lot,' said Michelle. 'Almost impossible to have a conversation with him. But he'd still want to hug you, and be with you. Nige was very loving.' That morning, he bought a bottle of Coke Zero and a packet of

Eclipse Chewy Mints at a dairy on the city end of Old Taupō Road; but now Nigel is stranded at the other end of town. 'When he was at primary school, the kids all loved him,' said Ian Jeffrey, his grandfather. 'Kids can be cruel, especially with someone like him, but they loved him. I remember he did a cross-country race, and the teacher decided to show him a shortcut. Well, he came in first! The whole school cheered him when they saw him coming in. That's one of the things I'll always remember.'

Nigel doesn't know where he is.

'He'd watch animal programmes for hours,' said Chris. 'The funny thing is I've still got – and I can't delete them – all the dinosaur documentaries I recorded for him on SKY. He'd sit down with my older girl, who's 12, and she'd watch them for the fifteenth time … She just loved him.' The sun is beating down, and the air is heavily scented with the sharp, fresh tang of thermal smoke. 'Michelle got married in June last year, and Nigel came down and was absolutely perfect,' said Eileen. 'Dom looked after him. There's a little murky clip of Nigel dancing. They were good times.'

Nigel's world is closing in. Nigel – sometime, somewhere, somehow – finds a way out. Nigel is free.

Chapter 7

World's end: Kim Dotcom

This is the way the world ends: in a candy store. When I asked the amazing Kim Dotcom for his address in Queenstown so I could sit with him a while and interview him about his views on how to survive the coming apocalypse, he replied that he would send someone to collect me on a Thursday at 4pm at the Remarkables Sweet Shop on the main street in nearby Arrowtown. I got there early. It was a cold, fresh winter's day, with black ice and low snow, and birds shivered in the trees above the pretty Arrow River. Tourists filled the candy store. I stood there lurking among the trays of Aniseed Twists and Cola Fizzballs. As soon as I stepped onto the pavement, a big black Mercedes pulled up. It was four o'clock on the dot.

The rendezvous had come about because Dotcom got in touch after reading a story I wrote for *The New Zealand Herald* about preparing for Doomsday. 'The end of the world as we know it is coming,' he emailed. 'We are close, I think.' I thought so, too. I wrote a year-long series of stories about end days; the subject occupied my mind day and night, I was sleepless, worried, a wreck, but I fancied that I was also practical and methodical, and kept busy by laying down provisions and supplies to protect my family when the world spiralled towards Hell in a fiery and terrifying hat.

The particular story that Dotcom had read was based on a far-sighted study commissioned by the government in 1987. It looked at ways New Zealand would – and wouldn't – survive a nuclear war. He asked for a copy. I got a PDF made of the 342-page report and sent it his way in exchange for an interview. And so to the rendezvous in a sweet shop, where I took the opportunity to lay down a few more provisions for Doomsday – who wouldn't be grateful to suck on a tin of Pac-Man Ghost Sours as eternal night closes in?

The drive to Chez Dotcom took about 10 minutes. It was at the end of a long, straight road on a tussock flat. The mountains of Coronet Peak loomed to the north, the mountains of the Remarkables loomed to the south. There was a lot of looming going on, and there was more to come as we drew up to the house on a small rise: Kim Dotcom suddenly appeared, vast, mountainous, loomsome.

It was immediately apparent that there was even more of him than the last time we met. That was in 2016, in an Auckland court, during his extradition hearing. A special leather chair was brought into the courtroom to support Dotcom's bulk during the weeks that his legal team argued against the full, awesome might of the law agencies of the United States of America, which sought to ship Dotcom to American soil so he can rot in an American jail. Dotcom, as the former head of Megaupload, was accused of copyright infringement, racketeering, money laundering and fraud. He waited over two years for the Court of Appeal to decide his fate. Like a raven of doom, I flew into Queenstown on the very morning that the appeal court finally made its ruling.

'Sorry,' I said.

'Yeah,' he said.

* * *

'Never feel sorry,' Anthony Hopkins's millionaire character says in that great movie *The Edge*, 'for a man who owns a plane.'

Dotcom's wealth was beyond anything I could even imagine. The FBI had seized something in the region of $60 million in its worldwide raid of his businesses. He was still able to operate in superb luxury. But when I met him in Queenstown, I saw him as a tragic figure, marooned and under constant threat of imprisonment, and felt ashamed that I'd routinely seen him for so long as merely a ridiculous figure. Yes, I always felt the case against Dotcom was a shocking disgrace and a black mark on New Zealand constitutional law, that we were the willing dupes of the US law enforcement military complex, that the US law enforcement military complex was itself the willing dupe of Washington via Hollywood and the income it lost to Dotcom's home entertainment site which allowed users to watch movies for free; and that all of it conspired to deprive Dotcom of his basic human rights. This was the guy whose house was invaded by gun-toting goons, for God's sake. A black-ops Special Tactics Group burst in on his Coatesville mansion at dawn and hauled Dotcom's ass to jail. He'd been spied on, raided, royally shafted.

Equally, though, I found it hard to care. By the time of his extradition hearing it felt like Dotcom had worked hard and very successfully to make himself look silly. He repelled widespread sympathy and support when he financed a weird, terrible political party, and staged the infamous Moment of Truth rally at the Auckland Town Hall during the 2014 election campaign. He promised it would reveal Key as a crook. It didn't. The only thing I can remember from that night was an appearance made by Julian Assange via Skype at the Ecuadorian Embassy in London – not because of anything Assange said, but because just as he began his monologue a cleaner from the embassy arrived and did the vacuuming behind him.

It was around about then that Dotcom was lumped with just about the worst term of abuse that a visitor to New Zealand can suffer: overstayer. People wanted shot of him. They tired of his antics. He complained, he was a bore, he talked about the deep state and held to conspiracy theories. In my newspaper despatches from the extradition hearing, I regularly and snickeringly referred to him as Fritz. It was as bad as calling someone Sambo. Fritz was large, *ja!* And – tee-hee – German! Naturally, I referred to his car (the big black Mercedes G55 V8 Kompressor in which a driver chauffeured him to court in downtown Auckland each morning for his extradition hearing) as the Fritzmobile.

Poor show. But who could take Dotcom seriously, apart from Dotcom, who took himself very seriously? On the opening day of his 2016 hearing, passersby outside the courtroom took selfies in front of the V8 Kompressor. You don't see a V8 Kompressor every day, but what tipped them off that it might possibly belong to Dotcom was the license plate, which read KIM.COM. Not only was its vastness required to accommodate the enormous German, it was also needed to transport an incredible big black custom-made leather swivel throne, which was taken up the escalator and into a courtroom for Dotcom to park himself in during the hearing. He sat on it like some sort of stateless or deposed king in his familiar uniform of black tunics and black vests and black fleeces. His skin was very pale.

The hearing was billed as the largest copyright case in history. Dotcom was represented by the ubiquitous Ron Mansfield, and also his American lawyer, the talkative Ira P. Rothken. There were three co-defendants, former employees of Megaupload, including two prime specimens of Eurogeek, the computer programmers Bram van der Kolk and Mathias Ortmann. A third man, Finn Batato, defended himself. He sat in another row, marooned and lonely.

The hearing dragged on for two months. One of the highlights included The Case of the Missing Papers.

They were very important papers. They were copies of a particular series of affidavits. They were crucial to Dotcom's defence. But where were they?

'Your Honour,' said Mansfield, 'they cannot be located.'

Judge Nevin Dawson looked down upon Mansfield with something that may or may not have resembled a cold fury. His jaw was firm. The line of his mouth was severe. He did not part that line; he said nothing. His silence was concise. It spoke paragraphs. It demanded that Mansfield step into the void and fill the silence. Mansfield tried his best. 'It's due to their size,' he gabbled.

And still Dawson said nothing. Mansfield swallowed, and talked about the importance of the papers. He loved those papers. He loved them like them they were his family. He couldn't proceed without them; their absence was inexplicable, the Devil's work.

'Registry can't find the files,' he said. 'I'm not trying to attribute blame, but ...' He looked at court officials. His eyes were attributing blame.

Finally, Dawson spoke. He had a deep, thrilling voice, with a mahogany timbre. It was the voice of authority. But when addressing the conundrum of the missing affidavits, it became the voice of hope and optimism. He attempted a smile, and said, 'It's possible they're out there somewhere.'

It bucked Mansfield's spirits. He took heart. Now that he thought about it, there was every chance the papers were in a box in a storeroom at the end of a hall in a building on the North Shore. The building could be located. So could the hall, and the storeroom. But which box? 'We just need to check through the boxes,' he said.

The judge sighed. It was an audible, very expressive sigh. It was a sigh from the heart. Here he was, 64 years old, appointed to the bench in 2003, now presiding over a complex and difficult case which involved the FBI, Hollywood, politics in Washington and Wellington, armed raids, allegations of money laundering and fraud, in a hearing conducted before the narrow-eyed squint of national and international media interest – and the whole damned thing had ground to a halt because some papers went missing.

His gaze shifted from the square-shouldered Mansfield to Grant Illingworth QC, who sported a pair of socks with the happy message BEST DAD. Illingworth represented the co-accused, van der Kolk and Ortmann. The judge's eyes roamed to the prosecutor, Christine Gordon QC, resplendent in purple skirt and jacket. And then to Dotcom, wiping his brow with a black cloth. And then to – just who was that gentleman at the back of the court, rather more than merely resplendent in an outrageous suit done out in bright candy stripes? No one was quite sure. He wore an array of vivid outfits and threatened to model his pièce de résistance: a suit patterned with bananas.

The judge closed his eyes. So much was on the table. There was Julian Assange on National Radio that week, comparing his weird exile to Dotcom's situation, saying they were both victims of

147

US security laws gone rogue. There were also issues of safe harbour, of extradition law, of civil law versus criminal law, of treaty agreements between the US and New Zealand, of frozen funds of hundreds of millions of dollars. The judge had been around; five years ago, stationed in Vanuatu, he had faced down death threats by a senior thug in a paramilitary unit; but the Dotcom case was huge. It demanded intense concentration. It required stamina. It kind of like really needed all the paperwork.

Dawson ordered an adjournment for counsel to sort it out. When he left the room, lawyers and court officials faced off. There were loaded questions, recriminations, tensions.

'Don't look at *me*. *I* don't know where they are.'

'But you had them …'

'I'm not lying!'

'No one's accusing you of that. Let's not get carried away.'

'Well, when something's gone missing …'

'Is it in the front office? Could it have gone there?'

'*No.* I've *checked.*'

* * *

The hearing spluttered through three weeks of such stops and starts. Mansfield remained preoccupied with presenting an argument for a stay of application – to pause or halt the entire proceeding – based on the US refusal to allow Dotcom to release his funds to pay expert witnesses. It would cost, Mansfield estimated, about $500,000. He continually made the point that, without these experts, the defence had its hands tied.

As for the prosecution, Christine Gordon spent a long time reading out loud from Agent Postin's greatest hits. FBI agent

Michael Postin, who led the investigation against Dotcom and his Mega empire, was the author of a massive document which detailed every single film and TV show that Megaupload users had downloaded from Dotcom's site. It proved that they watched a hell of a lot of junk.

Gordon also read out choice snippets of email chat between van der Kolk and Ortmann. Their cheerful comments about piracy were presented as incriminating evidence of their alleged conspiracy to commit fraud and engage in copyright violation. How they chatted and shot the breeze in all those emails; their exchange suggested a warm friendship. They spoke the same language, shared the same sense of humour. In court, they looked like the same person – they wore seemingly identical black suits and white shirts with no ties. They were like some kind of act, a duo.

An out-of-work duo. Mansfield to Ortmann, in the witness box: 'What do you do?'

Ortmann: 'I'm unemployed.'

Mansfield to van der Kolk: 'Do you work?'

Van der Kolk: 'Not at the moment.'

In cross-examination, prosecutor Mike Ruffin asked Ortmann why he didn't attempt to use his own money to pay for the experts. He said he didn't have the cash. Ortmann had 21,750 shares in Mega; before the raid on the company, they were worth an estimated $210 million. And now? 'There is no market for these shares,' he said. 'No offers.' All he had to his name was about $43,000 in his ASB account.

Like Ortmann, van der Kolk was paid for his Mega work in shares. He had a parcel of 8700, which he gave to his wife. She sold them last year for $US1 million. Well, said Ruffin, why didn't he didn't attempt to use his own money to pay for the experts? He said he didn't have the cash … Where had all the money gone? Oh, he said, on legal bills, various debts, tax, 'and a credit agency was chasing me'. How much was left? About $100,000.

Dotcom's attorney, Ira P. Rothken, was also called to the stand. He was born in New York, and now lives in Marin County, California. A man of east coast and west coast, of sea to shining sea, Rothken was all-American, which is to say he had the not uncommon American characteristic of seemingly being madly in love with the sound of his own voice.

'It would be of great service to the court,' said Judge Dawson, with an edge to that thrilling voice, 'if you just answered the questions with yes or no.' But he couldn't. Rothken was born to preamble. He answered yes or no only after delivering a Gettysburg address. Mansfield objected, too, even though Rothken was on his team. 'It's like having to watch a movie to find out what happens in the end,' he moaned.

By and by, Rothken detailed the kind of expert witnesses that were needed to defend Dotcom. They included a 'technical interface expert', and experts in various points of law. One such expert was running for the US presidency – Professor Larry Lessig, from Harvard. Lessig volunteered his expert services for free. But a problem remained. Crime reporter Rob Kidd's droll passage in the *Herald* put it very well: 'His attempts to replace Barack Obama at the helm of the most powerful country in the world might make his appearance before a New Zealand court difficult, Mr Mansfield said.'

* * *

Six weeks into the hearing, Dotcom's legal team began its defence of their excitable client. 'Big day today,' Dotcom advised his 468,000

Twitter followers that morning. 'Let's go!' He added, 'I wish you could all be at my court hearing ... It's going to be good.'

But the public gallery was empty, and the press bench was down to three. Dotcom looked a bit glum. Ron Mansfield looked even worse. The poor devil was struck down with a killer head cold. His great moment had arrived; here, at last, was his chance to denounce the US in loud, ringing tones; but he felt like he had sheep running around inside of his head.

He played the sympathy card with Judge Dawson. 'Your Honour will be aware I'm not recognised for being an orator,' Mansfield said. 'I struggle with words beyond one syllable.' Dawson stared at him. His implacable face sent a message spelled out in words which only required one syllable: get on with it.

He got on with it. Mansfield's submission – volume one, 300 pages – was wide-ranging and powerful. In essence, he said the US case was woeful, pathetic, lame. Worse, it was political. He said it was driven by Hollywood, which demanded that the White House crack down on Dotcom's Megaupload file-sharing empire. 'This is not a conspiracy theory. Hollywood threatened the Democrats and Republicans that they would lose their massive financial support.'

And then he played a Megaupload promotional video. It starred Kim Kardashian and Kanye West. They chanted: 'We love Megaupload!' Kim and Kanye in a New Zealand court – history was being made, but Judge Dawson saw no good reason for history to be made, and demanded that Mansfield put a stop to it.

Mansfield explored one of the key tenets of his argument: that the prosecution had failed to meet the extradition standard of criminal activity. Dotcom's activities were a civil matter, he argued. Copyright infringement cannot be prosecuted under the Crimes Act. Mansfield said, 'The highest court of the United States, the

Supreme Court in *Dowling* has unequivocally held that allegations of copyright infringement can be prosecuted only under copyright-specific legislation.'

The case of Paul Dowling dates back to 1982. The feds busted him for making and distributing Elvis bootleg albums. The charges included mail fraud. His appeal was upheld by the US Supreme Court, which ruled that the actual bootleg records, as objects, qualified as issues of copyright infringement, but not as matters of criminal fraud. 'Interference with copyright does not easily equate with theft, conversion or fraud'.

The same principle, said Mansfield, applied to the electronic files stored by Megaupload. 'There is no case to answer under US law … It's fatal to the extradition attempt … It's the end of the story, really.'

It wasn't anywhere near the end of the story. Later that week, Mansfield invoked the case of Jonathan Dixon, the Queenstown bouncer who got busted in 2011 for trying to flog intimate CCTV footage of England rugby player Mike Tindall to the UK tabloids. The point of law was whether the digital files which Dixon downloaded to his USB stick could be defined as an 'object', or 'property', which could then be 'possessed'.

The Supreme Court in New Zealand ruled that Dixon's file was, in fact, 'property'. It was tangible; it existed. But only sort of. From Mansfield's submission: 'Even if a digital file can … constitute property, it cannot constitute property which is capable of being possessed.' Possession is ninth-tenths of breaking the law, after all; and, as Mansfield argued, 'They [Dotcom and the co-accused] did not possess the files which their users uploaded … No offence can be made out.'

Curiously, after a lengthy submission regarding *Dixon's* precedent, Mansfield was suddenly interrupted by the judge. 'Are you,' said Dawson, in his deep, beautiful voice, 'aware of the Supreme Court case of *Dixon*?'

Mansfield blinked. The sheep in his head bleated. 'Ye-es,' he answered. 'I've dealt with that today, in fact, Your Honour. Quite rigorously, sir.'

'Thank you,' said Dawson, as though nothing had happened. Had he switched off? Had he been dreaming? Had he let his mind wander to other, more pleasant territories than the largest copyright case in history? Mansfield continued standing, and looked at Dawson, open-mouthed and baffled.

Dawson later ruled that Dotcom was eligible for extradition.

* * *

And so to Queenstown, where Dotcom had moved to with his wife, his children from a previous marriage, and his constant worries of extradition and imprisonment. He appealed Dawson's ruling, and went to the Court of Appeal. He appealed that ruling, too, and went to the Supreme Court. When we met, he'd been instructed not to talk about that. 'But I'm happy,' he said, showing me inside his gracious home, 'to talk about end of days.'

We sat at a large, round table and talked for over two hours. I liked him a lot. I thought he was a sad person. As ever, he wore black everything – boots, pants, zip-up top, scarf, with five black hand-towels at his side. He's long been crazy about little plastic bottles of Fiji mineral water, and crates of the stuff had followed him to Queenstown. The new house was neither as large nor as preposterous as the Coatesville mansion, made famous by the security-camera film of his dawn raid on 19 January 2012, when attack dogs and 72 cops armed with assault rifles arrived to begin the process of ruining his life.

He had spent the past six years in limbo, fighting against extradition, and meanwhile trapped in New Zealand. 'I am actually here for ten years,' he said. 'My first visit to New Zealand was ten years ago. I was looking for a home where I could raise a family that I had planned but I didn't have, and I was thinking, "What is the best place in the world to allow my kids to survive, and comfortably live, after World War Three?"

'New Zealand was going to be a bolthole, a bunker. I never had a plan to live here permanently until we are close to the event, just like many other entrepreneurs who are setting themselves up here. I may have accelerated it, because I told my friends in the Silicon Valley, and I'm very well-connected.'

Everything about Dotcom is on the grand scale – his build, his wealth, his boasts ('I'm very well-connected'), his rise and fall. He estimated his legal bill was $40 million. He argued that his extradition was a political conspiracy led by Barack Obama and the former US President's servile caddy, John Key. 'My main base was in Hong Kong,' he said, continuing his narrative of how he came to New Zealand. 'My plan was to remain there. I had a beautiful set-up in Hong Kong. You know? A hundred square metre penthouse on top of the Grand Hyatt Hotel, with the full service of a five-star hotel.'

I said, 'But the Grand Hyatt has a grand disadvantage.'

He said, mystified at the prospect of a flaw, 'What?'

I said, 'You wouldn't want to be stuck in a penthouse at the top of a hotel tower when it's end days.'

'That's right,' he said. 'That's why I was looking for a place. And I thought that if I had somewhere in the South Island, shielded by mountain ranges on both sides, I would install a really sophisticated solar power plant. I was thinking if I had something like that, you could survive. New Zealand strategically is the safest spot in the world. It has everything that is required to sit it out and start again.'

I said, 'Do you really think the planet is doomed?'

'Eventually, one hundred per cent,' he said. 'No doubt about it … I don't know if you know my background. I used to be a hacker. I have a very analytical mind; I love statistics, I love numbers. I programme these analytic tools, and just punch in some numbers and see what happens in the simulation, and in my mind it's pretty clear that humanity is heading to a large mass casualty event simply because of the increase in population and the pressures on resources, and the political pressure that causes.'

He gave a lengthy disquisition on international politics, and spoke without pause, until he said, 'You have the situation in Syria continuing to … What's the word? … Uh … sorry, my English is not that good …'

We sat in silence. The afternoon light fell grey and soft outside the window. There was a very big framed colour photograph leaning against the wall; it showed Dotcom standing on the shore at Cape Kidnappers in bright sunshine. It was obviously taken many years ago. He not only looked much smaller – almost petite compared to the large German fellow right now concentrating hard on locating the right English word – he looked much happier, not a sign of woe or distress on his smooth millionaire's face.

'Escalates!' he said, triumphantly. 'The situation in Syria will continue to *escalate*.' He spoke of the political situation in the Middle East, and Russia, and China, and said: 'There are so many different scenarios how we can get into World War Three, it's frightening. I think World War Three is the most likely scenario that is going to create the biggest mass casualty in human history, other than the comet that might potentially strike.'

Such annihilation, such waste; and then he said, almost singing, 'Hi, baby!'

His wife, Liz, came into the room. She was very thin and very pretty. They kissed, and he asked her, 'How'd it go? Did you think you found some good stuff?'

'I think so,' she said, and he gave her a high-five.

* * *

All preppers – people who are preparing for end days, shoring up their defences, making cogent or crazy plans to survive – are preoccupied with keeping their loved ones from harm. Dotcom has five children. He shares custody with their mother, his ex-wife Mona. There was a stack of his children's watercolour paintings on the far side of the table; he spoke of the kids with a fierce devotion.

I said, 'How will you keep them safe?'

Long before the raid, he picked out the ideal spot: a lodge on the shores of Lake Wakatipu. 'I identified that as the spot where I wanted to set up my family,' he said. 'But my assets were seized, and I'm still fighting my legal battles, so unfortunately I have been distracted from building the infrastructure and having things in place that I would have had by now.

'I can tell you exactly what I would have done. I'd have created a large underground area under the lodge – it's big enough to have maybe even two levels under the ground, and the good thing is you are surrounded by solid rock. You basically create a shelter surrounded by solid rock walls.

'After a nuclear war, there will be a time of fall-out, of stuff you don't want to be exposed to much – yeah, nuclear winter. You can go up and do a few things, but you want to have the right suit, and you want to do it no more than an hour, and come back and shower yourself off and be in a safe, radiation-free environment. You know? That's the ideal scenario.'

It didn't sound all that ideal – stuck underground, limited time only above ground, life as we know it made extinct by an airborne toxic event. But his vision of the future got much, much worse. He took things to a dark place.

I said, 'You'd need a supply of water.'

He said, 'I'd have a facility that allows you to recycle any kind of fluid waste into drinking water again. These technologies are quite advanced. They basically turn your own pooh and your own pee back into drinking water.'

With an answer like that, I wasn't going to ask about food. I quizzed him about power, and he said the plan was to have a network of solar panels and high-storage batteries that would supply enough energy to sustain a compound of 30–40 people.

'I'd have built all that now,' he said.

I said, 'Well, what can you do now?'

'Well,' he said, 'not much.' This was the first time in our interview that he said something uncertain, that didn't deal with impressive numbers and grand scales. The moment passed. 'I am of course still an entrepreneur,' he said. 'I built Mega, raised over forty million dollars for that business, over twenty million dollars went to a family trust, and even after the raid, when they destroyed my entire business, I was still able to make a lot of money for my family. And I have created a new business which is about to launch.'

He planned to venture into the brave new world of cryptocurrency. Without irony or shame, he said the name of his new currency will be called KimCoin. 'I believe it's going to be big, and that it will allow my family to have assets again that might be someday be utilised for this idea.'

He was a man with two visions. One, the fear of rotting in jail, a creature in captivity; two, the idea of hiding in an underground bunker.

* * *

All preppers, sooner or later, talk about the right to bear arms. The post-nuclear landscape is always imagined as lawless, a state of anarchy, the Wild West. I asked Dotcom what kind of security he had in mind for his fortress of the future.

'I talked about thirty to forty people earlier, right. I am going to surround myself with … with friends,' he said, but his pause made him sound like a man who wasn't entirely sure about the concept of friendship. 'Some of them will be employees. Some of them will be helping out the family … I have a lot of people interested in coming to join me. I've been talking about this for a long time, I've dreamed about it, and there are many people who agree with me.

'You read that report,' he said, meaning the 1987 government document about New Zealand after nuclear war. 'I think you know that what I'm talking about isn't crazy. I think it's good to be prepared. If I have the ability to create enough wealth to create something like that, great, but I hope I will never have to use it. I hope it will just sit there idle. That would be the best outcome. Don't think that because I'm a pessimist when it comes to the future of the world, that I'm not hoping I am completely wrong.'

I didn't think what he was talking about was crazy. I regarded Dotcom as a shrewd operator with a brilliant mind. But I still didn't know what he meant by security. I said, 'If a major event did come to pass, there would be civil unrest, traditional forms of law and order would be threatened – this is why I am asking you about security. You have to protect yourself, right?'

He said, 'You want to surround yourself of course with people and guns, with people who know how to fight, who know how to defend, and that's a necessity in a post-World War Three environment.'

So there it was: an armed militia, Dotcom's own private army.

'Everyone needs to understand there might be a requirement to defend yourself against attacks,' he said. That included Peter Thiel and other billionaires who are supposedly buying up remote fortresses in the South Island. Dotcom scorned them as naïve. 'Because it's just not enough to have a nice piece of land. You're a fool if you think your beautiful property isn't one of the first that's going to be taken over by a stronger group.

'If you think you can arrive here in your private jet with four or five people, if you don't have the right people around you, the defence mechanisms, you are just going to be rolled over. You know? I don't think any of them have really spent time thinking what it actually means to survive in a post-World War Three environment.

'People are going to be looking for food, people are going to kill for food. They will not be knocking on the door and asking politely for food, they will shoot you in the head and take it. That's the reality.

'You look at Auckland, or other big cities – you will have warlords, you will have gangs forming, you will see the Hells Angels all of a sudden being the most powerful force in New Zealand, or the Mongrel Mob will take over … It will be complete chaos. How do you think it's going to be in a world where police and everything that provides law and order has completely collapsed?'

But there would still be a form of law and order in a post-nuclear society: martial law, and Dotcom's orders, in his lodge on the lake. I asked him, 'What's your position in this underground bunker?'

He said, 'What do you mean, my position?'

I asked, 'Are you the friendly local despot at the head of it?'

He said, 'That's a good question. I would say … the PC thing to say would be, you know, "We'll all work together." But I don't think that's realistic. I think in an environment like that, leadership qualities will become more important than ever, and you need people that can think strategically, that can problem-solve instantly, you can't have long debates over important decisions that need to be made in a heartbeat. There has to be a leader. I would say if I am building that community, and I'm providing for everybody in that community, I should at least have a direction. You know? I should be able to decide what's best for the community to sustain it. So I think it's fair to say in that community,' he said, merrily reaching an inevitable conclusion, 'I would call the shots.'

King Kim, ruler of a future society with its armed guard and its regime of having to drink pooh. God almighty. It sounded so supremely joyless. But then Dotcom chuckled, and said, 'But here's the thing. This would probably be the best opportunity for me to get some serious weight loss underway. Unfortunately, when you live in an environment like me, dealing with a case like this, and making sure my family can survive this process, it's not easy to shed weight. I've actually gained quite a bit since this happened six and a half years ago. The stress, you know?'

I stole a glimpse of the younger Dotcom in the photograph at Cape Kidnappers. It looked like a different person.

'Well,' I said. 'Anyway. You need to make haste.'

He said, 'What is haste?'

'You need to hurry,' I explained. 'You need to make money from KimCoin, you need to prepare for the end of the world. When's it going to happen, do you think?'

He said, 'I can't predict. But when you look at world affairs, and where things are heading, it could be anywhere between now and the next twenty, maybe thirty years. Not much more than that.'

Night had fallen. I could make out illuminated ski-lifts going up and down the glowing white slopes of Coronet Peak. It was very beautiful. Dotcom didn't turn to look at the view; he was contemplating something else. He said, 'If I ever do get extradited, I'll probably die in a US jail, and the last thing I'll hear is going to be on the news how it's all blowing up now. You know?' The ski-lifts shone like lanterns.

Chapter 8

Half the man he used to be: Colin Craig

In spite of everything – and everything was a lot in the strange case of Colin Craig, who could be seen as deranged at the very least and at worst quite despicable – I always liked him and found myself drawn to him. He tied up the courts for years in an incredible series of widely reported libel actions, and never seemed bothered that the deep and lasting public impression of his legal campaign was that he was essentially defaming himself. He became an object of ridicule and loathing. No one took him seriously. No one ever did, except for a brief, very peculiar time in New Zealand politics – someone wrote a book about it; may I recommend my 2014 analysis, *Madmen: Inside the weirdest election campaign ever* – when Craig came thrillingly close to winning a seat in Parliament as leader of the Conservative Party.

His failure put an end to his political ambitions and his delusions of grandeur – he once told me that he entertained thoughts of being elected prime minister – but the nature and circumstances of his failure were constantly relived as the subject of his many and varied courtroom litigations. It became the longest death in New Zealand political history. Everyone else had moved on, but for Craig it was forever the election campaign of 2014 and its background story of an illicit love gone wrong.

He fell for his press secretary Rachel MacGregor. He kissed her. He wrote her poems. He wanted to possess her and be the man in her life, and in a terrible sense he achieved exactly that: she couldn't get rid of him, because he hounded her for years in the courts. MacGregor had quit 48 hours before election night. She accused Craig of sexual harassment. Craig disputed it. He described it as 'an emotional affair', and claimed that she welcomed his advances. Their relationship was the central issue of all Craig's endless visits to court.

Two members of the Conservative Party spread MacGregor's version, and a blogger made mischief of it. Craig took them all to court for libel. In turn, they all filed counter-suits. Jordan Williams was awarded the fabulous sum of $1.27 million, only for the Supreme Court to later quash the verdict and the costs. Williams issued an apology.

Each of the various proceedings were widely reported, partly because Craig was a public figure, but also because of the timing. As the most profound hashtag of the 2010s decade, #MeToo exploded just as Craig blundered into view as a boss who was accused of hitting on and hitting on and hitting on a blonde younger employee. Abuse of power, all that. Much of their argument in court degenerated into the familiar hopeless territory of alleged sexual offending – he said, she said – and made it hard to define what really happened between Craig and MacGregor. Private lives, private distresses. His insistence on dragging her into court, over and over and over, was like another form of harassment, in plain view.

It was thought during his years as leader of the Conservative Party that Craig was a religious fanatic. But his condition was more specific than that. He was his own rare and singular loose goose, with his own unique set of psychological disturbances and personal convictions. The strangest thing about him was that he was a poet. I think that's why I warmed to him. It wasn't a case of literary appreciation, because his poems were quite bad. But he had a poetic sensibility, an innocence and a sensitivity. He came across as a grossly misunderstood artist, and suffered like one, too. Even there he set himself apart: he made others suffer for it.

I attended a number of his libel cases at the High Court of Auckland. I saw him put MacGregor on the witness stand and make her talk about their time together. It was the last thing she wanted to do, and the experience was deeply painful for her. I didn't like Craig one bit during his cross-examinations. But I found it impossible to really care about the other people who he faced in court, and in any case it was somewhat overlooked in public debate that Craig had a valid point. 'It's a matter,' he told judges, 'of principle.' He felt wronged. He believed he had been libelled. It was ruled, now and then, that he had been libelled. One of his opponents was a legendary right-wing agitator who went by the name of Whaleoil, and who was proud and even boastful of his status as a bad guy. But Craig was never seen as the good guy. He didn't have that status, he didn't have that virtue.

He has always had the look of a hermit about him – gaunt, unworldly. There were days in court when I pictured him picking his way along some wild shore, deafened by the hiss and crash of the surf, collecting driftwood washed up in a storm. I closed my eyes to get a better view. Yes, I fancied, there he is, with his sunken eyes and long limbs, his pants held up by a length of twine. He is barefoot. He looks out to sea; he has visions, he is in receipt of a message from God. He heads back to his dark and quiet cave. The whites of his eyes shine like torches. He plots his next move ... I was probably wishing he really was alone on that deserted shore, anywhere except in public, in court, exposing himself. So much of the defamation proceedings were unseemly and pathetic. 'Please,' emailed one of our most cherished broadcasters when I mentioned to her how I was spending my days, 'make it stop.'

Two judges granted her dearest wish. 'This must be brought to an end,' said Justice Kit Toogood. 'Enough is enough,' said Justice Matthew Palmer. He added: 'I consider it would be an abuse of the High Court's processes for the claim to continue.'

The problem wasn't that Craig wanted his day in court. The problem was that there were so many days, so many libel and counter-libel suits, so many separate and overlapping proceedings that no one could tell apart and felt like one long crazy mess. His foes included John Stringer, a former board member of the Conservative Party. I sat in on their case and heard Stringer tell the court: 'It sits within a battery of more than a dozen parallel proceedings linked to Mr Craig, mainly in defamation.' It felt closer to more than a thousand.

Very often I reported the proceedings as comedies. They weren't at all like the kind of trials that I usually attended elsewhere in the High Court: no one had got killed. Craig was strange, weird, a poet; I viewed his court appearances as light relief. But it wasn't actually like that a lot of the time. A lot of the time it was dismal and sad. His court appearances transformed the courtrooms into the foul rag-and-bone shop of the heart.

Still, it was easy to laugh at all the old and meaningless political memoirs on show. Nothing dates as quickly as politics. The 2014 election campaign was old news by Christmas that year; Craig's court proceedings in 2016, 2017, 2018 and 2019, which all existed to argue things said and done in 2014, made it feel as ancient as Pompeii. Everything was covered in the ash of history. Craig himself was a smoking ruin, a leader brought down by ordinary lust; and there, too, was another ghost from the past – Cameron Slater, also known as Whaleoil.

Craig claimed Slater libelled him on his Whaleoil blog. Slater counter-claimed Craig libelled him in *Dirty Politics and Hidden Agendas*, a piece of fulminating junkmail delivered to 1,623,402 letterboxes. Their argument was heard before Justice Toogood during a four-week, judge-alone trial in 2017. It was more or less Slater's last stand in public. His once-infamous Whaleoil blog collapsed in 2019. The previous year, it was reported that Slater had suffered a stroke.

He went out bragging. 'I have a legion of followers,' he told the court. 'My blog is better than every other blog … In a few short months my figures will skyrocket. They will double … I break a lot of stories … I'm respected for my political views.'

But they were empty brags, no longer accurate or true. Craig and Slater were both shadows of their former selves; 2014, the setting of much of what was said in court, was when both were key players in New Zealand politics, but that time had passed. Slater was brought low by the wrecking ball of Nicky Hager's book *Dirty Politics: How attack politics is poisoning New Zealand's political environment*. The subtitle was an ode to Slater's tactics in association with the National Party. It was a very effective partnership, but the Hager revelations put an end to it, and Slater had only one place to go after that: oblivion. He pretended not to notice and maintained the illusion of power and influence in his long aria to the court. 'I know what most politicians are up to. There's plenty of them playing around … They can't keep secrets … I get things right … I talk to parties across the political spectrum … I told someone from John Key's office to get stuffed once.' One of his best quips was, 'I'm the same as any other media organisation. But in many respects, I'm better.'

All of it was little more than an exercise in nostalgia. Craig, too, was stuck in the traffic of memory lane. '2014,' they both chanted throughout the trial, wailing like ghosts.

They hadn't moved on. Slater said the same things in court that he'd been saying for years. 'Politics is the best game in town. There are no rules', etc. At one point he said, 'Most MPs I know use the same cab driver all the time because they know they can trust them.' His misanthropic philosophy was that everybody's got something to hide. Craig had existed as a politician *manqué* (everybody's got something to hide, including a *manqué*) and was considered fair game by Slater. Craig, in his closing address, complained about Slater's campaign to force him out of politics. Justice Toogood leapt in, and said, 'Does it matter that Mr Slater has a personal view? He wears his heart on his sleeve; it's crazy to expect him to be balanced. He was simply engendering public debate … What's wrong with that? This is important, Mr Craig. It seems to me to be something you have to confront.'

In essence, Craig claimed that allegations written on Slater's blog were irresponsible, inaccurate and damaging. Justice Toogood agreed. He ruled Slater defamed Craig with the untrue statements that Craig had placed MacGregor under financial pressure to sleep with him, and had sexually harassed at least one victim other than MacGregor.

Craig could claim victory, but so could Slater: the judge refused to award costs to Craig. Justice Toogood ruled: 'I have also held that the reputational damage which Mr Craig suffered ... resulted almost entirely from his own actions. I conclude, therefore, that Mr Craig is not entitled to an award of general damages to compensate him further for such damage.'

The court case was the last time I ever saw Slater. I'd always been fond of him as a person – I claim no wise judgement of character – and one time when I was out of work I held talks with Slater about working for his blog. He shouted me a cup of tea and an Afghan biscuit one morning at QC's, the High Court café. It was very generous considering his legal expenses. Slater was represented by Brian Henry. In his closing address, Henry mentioned in passing the matter of costs; his client, he said, was seeking $450,000, and then there was his own fees, which were $12,000 for every day of the trial.

Well, there were times when he had to work hard for his miserly 12 grand per diem. One day he poked the bear. We know this because Justice Toogood said to him, 'You poked the bear.' He meant Henry's cross-examination of Bev Adair-Beets, who replaced MacGregor as Craig's press secretary.

She made an immediate impression. She was the lady in red. She wore a red watchstrap and red nail polish, and carried a red purse, a red laptop cover, and inside her red handbag was a ball of red wool.

Henry had asked her about MacGregor's personal view of Craig. Slater's blog posts had cast Craig as an obsessive, grubby sex pest; Craig maintained that MacGregor and he shared a beautiful but forbidden love.

Henry to Adair-Beets: 'What do you have to say about Rachel MacGregor's tweet in which she wrote, "Craig is trying to frame me as a mistress"?'

Adair-Beets, quietly: 'I'm sorry she said that.'

Henry, loudly: 'Well, maybe she said that because it's her side of the story, but maybe you're so beholden and besotted with Mr Craig that you think it can't be right.'

Adair-Beets, alarmed: 'How can you use a word like that! What sort of statement is that! How could you—'

Henry is a tiny man, a kind of tall dwarf – you should see him next to his close friend Winston Peters; easy to spot which one is Grumpy. He waved his small paws at Adair-Beers, and attempted to interrupt her. 'No, you can't—'

But Henry was in turn interrupted by Justice Toogood. 'No, Mr Henry. You poked the bear. Let her speak.'

Adair-Beets, very loudly and also shakily, spoke. 'Besotted! Good grief! If you knew anything about me and my background of abuse, you wouldn't throw words like that around!'

Her eyes were red behind her red-framed glasses.

* * *

Colin Craig, always Colin Craig, as much a fixture of the High Court of Auckland as the downstairs cells, the payphone in an alcove, the magnolia tree in the courtyard. He must have got to know the place better than his house. He should have brought pyjamas, a kettle, a dog. There was a kind of domestic arrangement to proceedings. Things started coming out of the woodwork – wētā, driven inside after the court building was waterblasted. I found one in a Styrofoam coffee cup in a corridor, and showed it to everyone.

'Golly,' said Craig.

'Whopper,' said Slater.

Year after year, the long days of the same old arguments, the steady tumble of court documents in the photocopy machine. The steady stream of unusual people taking the oath. There was Orewa lawyer Madeleine Flannagan. Craig introduced her as a witness. Henry opposed it. Justice Toogood ruled in Craig's favour. His decision allowed the court to hear a really quite amazing story. Henry later said in his closing address, 'In my forty-two years in the law, I've never seen anything like it.'

Flannagan said she was engaged in 2014 as the family lawyer for Craig and his wife, Helen. They were looking to adopt a child. Things became complicated when Rachel MacGregor accused Craig of sexual harassment. Worse, rumours started surfacing that Slater had possession of a dossier that contained even more damaging information about Craig. By coincidence, Flannagan was friends with Slater, and blithely said to the court, 'I considered I knew Cameron well enough to call him.'

She phoned, and asked for the contents of the dossier on behalf of a client. She said, 'He assumed my client was another victim of sexual harassment. I tried to dissuade him from that idea. I had to pitch my words quite carefully.'

The words she pitched collapsed like a tent in a gale. Slater, she said, told her that he had 'reasonable grounds' to believe Flannagan was, in fact, acting for 'another victim'.

Flannagan described how her call had quickly led to an ethical minefield. The last thing she intended was to deceive a friend. She said, 'I felt quite torn.' She began to weep. The registrar fetched a box of tissues. She pulled herself together, repeated that at no point did she tell Slater that she was acting for 'another victim', and then she said: 'I was telling Cameron the truth.' A bark of laughter erupted from the public gallery. I turned around, but I didn't really have to: the only person in the public gallery that day was Cameron Slater.

Slater later took the witness stand, and said to Henry: 'I'm lost for words at the betrayal of someone who I considered a friend.' Judas, c/– Orewa.

Then there was Laurence Day of Hamilton. He was called to give evidence, and said that he donated \$675,000 to the Conservative Party for the 2014 election campaign. He talked about a conversation he had with Jordan Williams, who claimed to have documents confirming the sordid nature of Craig's feelings towards MacGregor. 'He had a file an inch thick,' said Day. They included his notes of a sext Craig had sent to his press secretary: 'I wish I was lying between your naked legs.' But Williams later told Day he got that wrong, and it actually read something like 'I wish I was lying on your naked legs.'

What? Who does that? Is it a *Kama Sutra* thing? Isn't the preferred position between, not on? As Day sat in court and discussed Craig's conduct with MacGregor – the poems, the cards, the sitting upon naked legs – he surely heard the sound of his generous donation of \$675,000 gurgling down the drain.

Then there was John Stringer. He took Craig to court in 2018. I went along, almost out of habit by that stage. Stringer is an interesting cove, possessed by an antic spirit. His legal folders were decorated with photographs of British bulldogs wearing powdered wigs. He owns two of these beasts. 'They're stubborn,' he said to me, admiringly, as we waited for proceedings to begin. 'Resilient.'

I asked, 'Are they stupid?'

He claimed they weren't.

Stringer's opening address compared his case with the historic Oscar Wilde trial of 1895. There were so many parallels, he said. Such as? 'Wilde, famously, wrote poems. Mr Craig and I do, too, but rather less famously.'

Craig's cross-examination of Stringer centred around 19 June 2015, when Craig announced he was stepping down as party leader. Stringer immediately raced off and gave an interview on the subject.

Craig: 'Do you agree you breached confidentiality by speaking without approval?'

Stringer: 'No. The party had melted down by then.'

'Do you accept you weren't a designated spokesman for the party?'

'We didn't have any, because you didn't allow them.'

Political losers, squabbling in a court. Old politics. Old blogs. Old, ruined Whale. Ghosts and shadows, tumbleweeds and yesterday's news. Litigation and re-litigation ... Behind it all, at the core of it, ran the faint echo of some kind of love. Except it never resembled love as the awful saga of Craig and MacGregor played out in court. 'This is a record of hate,' as Graham Greene wrote in his great novel *The End of the Affair*, 'far more than of love.'

* * *

There was a problem when MacGregor appeared in the witness box to begin her evidence in the *Craig v Slater* trial. She stood and took the oath, and was asked to please be seated. But there was no seat.

'I can stand,' she said.

172

'No, no,' said the registrar, and sprang to his feet, in search of a chair.

'It's important that you be comfortable,' said Toogood.

The registrar looked hither and yon for a seat. There was no seat to be had in the courtroom. He disappeared, and a silence settled on the court. The press sat and waited. The judge sat and waited. Craig, Slater and Henry sat and waited. MacGregor stood and waited, until the registrar appeared with two things: a happy smile on his face, and a seat.

It was important that MacGregor could be comfortable while she was tortured. It was bad enough when she talked about her relationship with Craig to Brian Henry, who was gentle, cautious, supportive; by the time Craig got to her, in cross-examination, her contempt was thorough, constant, absolute.

'A dork.' That, she said, was her first impression of Craig. She was hired as his press secretary in 2011, just as Craig was making his first attempt to get into Parliament. It sounded like a memorable job interview. 'He seemed a jovial chap,' she expanded. 'Badly dressed. Yeah. I don't know. Yeah. He was a little bit odd, he had his pants sort of pulled up high. Yeah.'

Beware of men with their pants sort of pulled up high. For two long days on the witness stand, MacGregor described him thus: 'weird … ridiculous … awful … dodgy … weird … untrustworthy … disgusting … ridiculous … horrendous … dodgy … deluded … weird.'

She was also essentially describing a kind of tyranny of sexual harassment. He sent her poems, he tried to kiss her, he touched her breast, he looked down her top. As well, according to MacGregor, he insisted they drive rather than fly to Whanganui so they could spend more time together; he routinely made her stay late, took off his shoes, and asked her to rub his back.; he put up curtains in her office, and closed them when they were together; he bought her a necklace, and told her to get rid of her dog.

She said she resisted his advances, was sickened by them, and advised him to listen to a recording of *The Lure of Infidelity*. Henry wanted to know more about that, and said to her, 'Now, Miss MacGregor, you've mentioned a song.'

She said, 'Where did I mention a song?'

He said, 'It was in your evidence that you said you gave him a song. Some music?'

She said, 'I don't know what you're talking about.'

The court transcript was seized. 'Here', said Henry, pointing at her reference to *The Lure of Infidelity*.

She said, 'That's not a song. It's a recorded talk.'

'Oh,' said Henry.

He dropped the subject. It was merely an awkward moment, and soon enough MacGregor was once again taking about how much Craig repulsed her. Words were not enough; her entire body, the core of her being, expressed her repulsion from the moment she was forced to engage with Craig when he began his cross-examination, and the hostilities commenced. It was fairly horrible to watch, and Justice Toogood ordered a day off for MacGregor to recover. She returned to the witness box when court resumed on a Friday, and finally it was over, Craig asked his last question, and the weekend swung open like a prison door. And yet there she was again on Monday morning, sitting outside the court, by herself, no sign of a support person, unlike the previous week; when court began, her presence was explained when Craig, incredibly, attempted to recall MacGregor to the witness stand. Justice Toogood heard him out, which is to say he heard him out for about, oh, say 90 seconds before snapping at him that the request was denied. He asked Henry's associate lawyer Charlotte Foster to go outside and tell MacGregor she was excused from any further obligation to the trial. It's within the realms of possibility to imagine that this came as a relief.

Justice Toogood's ruling pretty much stuck it to Craig. He wrote: 'Mr Craig did not demonstrate, at any point in his evidence in this proceeding, any understanding of the difficulties created for an employee by an employer's expression of intense feelings of emotional engagement and sexual longing … He never acknowledged the possibility that Ms MacGregor may have felt she could not protest about, and was obliged to tolerate, sexually charged language and conduct for fear of losing her employment or failing to meet her employer's expectations.'

He divided their relationship into before and after the election night of 2011. 'The election night incident,' Craig put it. 'The election night event,' Henry put it. Same difference; Craig and MacGregor kissed, there was something resembling mutual affection. Justice Toogood: 'I am not satisfied that Mr Craig's behaviour was unwanted by Ms MacGregor at that time.' After that time, though, he was satisfied that Craig was 'guilty of moderately serious sexual harassment'.

But, Justice Toogood also wrote, he accepted Craig 'did not know' he had sexually harassed MacGregor 'largely to his oblivious and self-involved perception of their professional and personal relationship'.

Oblivious and self-involved: thin as a stick, rattling around somewhere inside the same blue suit from The Italian Shop and long winter coat from Rodd & Gunn that MacGregor advised he buy several years ago to smarten up his image, Craig took every

175

opportunity to tell the court that MacGregor desired him, wanted him, found him sexually attractive.

'We had fallen short of our Christian values,' he said, describing their election night kiss in 2011. They agreed not to let it go any further than that, he told Justice Toogood.

His Honour nodded, and said, 'And by that, do you mean actually having a physical sexual relationship?'

Craig said, 'Correct.' He added, 'If we were both free to do so, I think we would have had a sexual relationship.' They were chaste, he said, but suggested their sexual longing for each other was epic. It was, Craig stressed, a story of forbidden love.

'It's a figment of his imagination,' said Henry. 'He's weird,' said MacGregor, over and over.

She was sickened by his advances, she said. Gossip at the time was otherwise. Press gallery journalist Barry Soper gave evidence, and talked about the widespread rumour that Craig and MacGregor were having an affair.

Craig: 'What was your impression?'

Soper: 'I didn't form one.'

Craig: 'Did you form *any* impression?'

Soper: 'I thought the relationship was a very familiar one.'

I was with Craig and MacGregor three days before the 2014 election day – that is, the day before her shock resignation – in Albany. He'd been standing on the side of the road and waving at motorists. And then MacGregor came bearing incredible news: an opinion poll put the Conservatives on 4.9 per cent.

Only another 0.1 per cent and they would cross the MMP threshold. Craig and MacGregor left to discuss the good news in private, sitting together in the front of a beat-up Honda Edix. I watched on, and described it in my campaign diary *Madmen*: 'There were coathangers in the back seat, an open packet of Vocalzone throat lozenges in the glovebox. They put their heads together and talked in low voices …'

'I did not sexually harass Miss MacGregor,' Craig declared, repeatedly, in his closing address. He was stating things for the record, but sometimes it felt as though he was talking to himself. 'Ours was an affectionate, mutually appreciative relationship … Myself and Miss MacGregor took part in a workplace romance … At the very least, Miss MacGregor had feelings for me.'

He read out her emojis that were produced as exhibits. 'Hug, hug, hug,' he quoted. 'Smiley face … Hug, hug.'

On the last morning of the trial, before court opened, Craig sat by himself in QC's Café with two pots of tea and worked on his closing address. Slater, his wife and his father sat at a nearby table with Brian Henry and Charlotte Foster, everyone laughing and chatting.

The registrar unlocked Courtroom 14. Craig took his seat next to his McKenzie friend, Tom Cleary. No doubt some McKenzie friends are more loquacious than others, but I never saw Cleary so much as move his lips.

A tall, elderly gentleman appeared in the public gallery. He had long hair which almost looked to be blond, not white with age. It was Craig's father. He didn't go over and talk to his son.

Craig's wife, Helen, had said from the witness box, 'It is, and continues to be, a wonderful marriage.' She didn't return to the courtroom after that.

The final minutes of the trial dragged towards the finish line. 'Affectionate,' droned Craig. 'Close.' MacGregor had left the building. It wasn't 2014 anymore, with its high passions; it was a Thursday in the autumn of 2017, with wētā coming out of the woodwork. 'Please make it stop,' begged Kim Hill; 'Enough is enough,' said one judge; 'This must be brought to an end,' said another; Craig held on as long as he could. No family, no friends other than a mute McKenzie. It was just Craig, seeing it out by himself, seeing it through, raking over the cold, dry ashes of something he thought of as 'a workplace romance', mooning over old emojis ('Hug, hug, hug … Smiley face'), alone.

Craig wrote a poem for MacGregor. It read:

There is only one of me it's true
But I wish this were not the case
Because I wish that I could have you
If instead one man, I was two
That would be one for all the others
And one of me, for you.

Terrible, I suppose, but sincere. It was a poem of the divided self. One of his selves had died: the one he set aside for MacGregor, the one he loved. All he had left was the self 'for all the others'. The one that kept haunting the High Court, the only place where he could be in the same room as MacGregor, and where he could speak freely, at length, of love.

Chapter 9

The neighbourhood:
Te Atatū

1

You know you've found the place you're looking for when the householder slams the door in your face. This was on a Wednesday morning at a home on the Te Atatū peninsula in west Auckland, when a rather ferocious-looking matron with her hair in a bun said one word to the visitor on her doorstep – 'Goodbye' – before closing the door, locking it, and pulling back the curtains.

Another set of curtains were open in the lounge, allowing a view of an uncommon sight in Te Atatū – a bookcase. In fact, the homeowner, who was about return to his house after a long absence, is a published author. His 1984 book, *This is Vanuatu: People, customs and art*, is a kind of souvenir of his 20 years on the Pacific island, where he curated a museum, was a founding member of the Kiwanis, and was introduced to the Queen and Prince Philip.

He raised his daughter, Tanjas, on Vanuatu after his marriage broke up. 'I was father and mother to a little girl,' he once wrote from prison, with delicate, even quite beautiful penmanship, 'who I cared about a great deal and totally spoiled.'

Ron Van der Plaat was found guilty in 2000 of appalling sex crimes against his daughter. She said the abuse started when she was nine years old. It continued for over 20 years. After they moved to Auckland in 1982, his sadism escalated, becoming manic and routine; there was bondage, role play (she was a prostitute, he was the client who paid her money but took it back afterwards), and that old favourite, urophilia, the joy of being urinated on.

There was more and worse, but Judge Tony Randerson covered it off quite nicely in his sentencing remarks, when he said, 'It was not ordinary sexual abuse but was bizarre in the extreme and can only be described as depraved.'

Van der Plaat has always maintained his innocence. (So has his first wife, and Tanjas's mother, Charlotte Stravers, who paid for his legal defence, and is listed in a property search as having a third-party caveat on the house in Te Atatū. The woman who slammed the door that Wednesday matched her description.) Prison letter: 'All allegations against me are a conspiracy for revenge and to obtain my possessions and money.'

Police found hundreds of photographs he'd taken of his daughter nude and *déshabillé* from the age of nine until about thirty. 'It had become a habit,' he said with bland indifference. The hobbies of sex: when a journalist visited the Te Atatū house not long after he was sentenced, Van der Plaat's Chinese wife cheerfully pointed out the hooks above the door frame, used to secure pulleys and harnesses for the happy couple to act out sex games. 'It's very normal.'

The terms of his release ordered him to have full-time GPS monitoring, a curfew, and a ban on contact with anyone under 16. A report from the Community Probation Service said that he 'remains an undue risk to community safety'.

In essence, the entire report described Van der Plaat as a hopeless case. It recorded a psychological assessment, which concluded that the risk of his reoffending was 'medium high'. The assessment tested him on that handy measure of insanity, the psychopathy check list. It's actually quite hard to fail the psychopathy check list, but he failed with flying colours. It's at once a simple and very thorough index, and if you fail it then you can have no real argument at being thought of as a psychopath – although the key to it is lack of remorse, and how can you show remorse for something you say you've not done? Even psychopathy has a riddle.

He scored particularly low marks for something called 'interpersonal and attentive deficits'. The assessment puts it more simply: 'That is,' it writes, 'superficiality, grandiosity, lack of remorse, deceitfulness etcetera contributed to his elevated score.'

You have to wonder about that what constitutes that casual 'etcetera'.

The assessment concluded: 'It is the view of the psychologist that Mr Van der Plaat's progressive ageing, possible cognitive decline, consistent denial of sexual deviancy and lack of insight regarding his risk, combined with collusive social supports, hinders relapse prevention planning.' In English: hopeless.

But Van der Plaat had served his time, and his release was statutory. He was an old Dutch jailbird, 82 years old, returning to a quiet street and the comforts of home. There was a lemon tree out back, and a spectacular avocado tree. 'We had more avocadoes than we knew what to do with,' said a woman who rented the house after Van der Plaat was jailed. She met her husband there, and they now have three children.

There were large posts freshly dug into the front lawn. It appeared that a very high fence was about to be built. Neighbours also reported new lace curtains, a lick of fresh paint here and there, and the guttering was recently cleared and cleaned. Welcome home.

* * *

I live a few streets away. I walked from my house on the day I had his door slammed in my face. The flat, watery peninsula of Te Atatū (Māori for 'the dawn'; it offers excellent views of the sunrise over the Waitematā harbour), is fringed with mangroves and sluiced down the middle by Henderson Creek. A lot of streets end in riverbank cul-de-sacs and a lot of the houses are two-storey with home living above a garage and rumpus room. The light is made pale and wan by the harbour. Tides shuffle in and out over mudflats. Shorebirds crowd the water's edge. Houses prices have soared according to the dictates of Auckland life in the twenty-first century, but it remains a modest, average-decile suburb tending towards low-income and flat-out poverty. There are three \$2 Shops, four barbershops, five laundromats. It's peaceful, friendly, a good place to raise kids. As such, it has the classic New Zealand blend of fear and resentment just beneath the surface.

Van der Plaat's return brought that to the surface. I had an interesting few hours talking to his neighbours. Things were tense, things were not exactly on a knife's edge, but there was an explicit sense that they weren't going to take it lying down. There were 21 houses on the cul-de-sac where he lived. Nearby streets shared a jaunty nautical theme – Fathom Place, Spinnaker Drive, Bosun

Place. Everyone mentioned that one of the homeowners, a parent of three daughters, was behind the opposition to Van der Plaat being released back into the community, which is to say the community where she lived. I reached out to her, but she avoided me like the plague.

The woman had hosted a neighbourhood meeting where a Corrections officer discussed the terms of Van der Plaat's release. 'It was in case any of us parents had any questions,' said one of her neighbours, Petra Rangi. There was a Lakers basketball hoop in the front yard; she had a five-year-old son. 'It's a bit scary, him coming back. But as long as he sticks to himself, I'm not going to harass him. I don't reckon anyone would want to go near him. We'll all be staying clear.'

'I really can't say anything,' said a woman who didn't wish to be named. She had her hands full with a bunch of lively preschoolers. 'Go put your helmet on if you want to ride your bike,' she said to a little boy. The last thing she wanted was publicity about a paedophile and rapist: she operates a daycare centre on the street.

Tuakeu Grover, 19, was sitting around at home with his shirt off, and answered questions while leaning out of his window. 'My mate told me about him,' he said. 'He said, "It's pretty bad, bro." I said, "I bet I've seen worse." I've lived in Avondale and Rānui.'

I said, 'What sort of things?'

He said, 'Aw just, you know, people being killed. But this guy … My mate said he tied her up like they do in America. I mean, what the fuck? That's sick. I better not see him with any little kid.'

A woman came to the door of another house with her hair in a towel. She didn't wish to be named. She's a long-time resident, and remembers Van der Plaat and Tanjas before the police made their arrest. 'They never talked to anyone,' she said. 'He always dressed quite smart, although sometimes he went to the letterbox just wearing a little pair of underwear. I saw her sometimes weeding the garden, when she'd wear a nightie. She had beautiful long hair.

'I can't believe he was living there so many years and doing so many crimes and no one knew. That poor girl.' The woman began to cry. 'What he did to her … it's … you know … it's just … He never should get out of the prison for what he did.'

She said the neighbour who held the meeting with a Corrections officer also hosted a similar meeting when Van der Plaat was first released, in 2010. Locals were outraged, but there was nothing they could do. The woman said, 'I saw him at Countdown. He looked very good; he was a lot older, but he hadn't changed much.'

He was sent back to prison in 2012 for parole violations. A neighbour (had they followed him?) saw Van der Plaat holding a four-year-old girl's hand at Auckland Museum. He'd become friends with the girl's mother. It doesn't sound much; but as the parole board noted, there was also the issue of Van der Plaat 'making an intimate visual recording'. Van der Plaat and his photos of naked girls; Van der Plaat and his lusts, his compelling habits.

His daughter wrote a book about her ordeal. There are a few scattered references to Auckland life – visiting someone in an office in Windsor House on Fort Lane, working for a little while at Royal Road School in Massey, and wanting nothing more than to die alone in bush out west in the Waitākere Ranges. 'I'd ring a taxi,' she wrote of her daydreams, 'and go out to Huia. From there I'd walk into the bush and find a place where I'd never be found. I didn't want my father taking photos of my dead body.'

There are no references in her book to Te Atatū or the plain house (613 square metres, CV $665,000) on the street with a jaunty nautical name. It was incredible to look at only with the knowledge that Van der Plaat was returning to the very home where the crimes were committed. The closed curtains weren't just concealing the occupants; they were concealing the layout of a depraved past.

His daughter left New Zealand a long time ago. Returning for the trial was traumatic; she'd got married, but that had since ended. I tracked down one of her friends. She said, 'I don't know where she is right now. She moves around a lot.'

Asked to describe Tanjas, she said, 'Intelligent. Damaged – there's a surprise. Yeah. But fun! A very unusual woman. She's extraordinarily … she's so admirable. She triumphed.'

'If you meet him,' Tanjas said about her father in an interview in 2000, 'he's the nicest man imaginable. He's the perfect gentleman.'

She also said, 'He will hunt me until the end of his days.'

The hunter became the hunted, or at least the hounded, until the end of his days. That sense of fear and resentment from neighbours simmered and escalated over the next few years. Residents phoned police whenever they were concerned about his 'behaviour'. By the time of his release, Van der Plaat had advanced dementia. The *Herald* reported, 'One person who lives on his street said he had been seen in various places where they believe he is not supposed to be.' Numerous residents sought or obtained trespass orders to keep him away from their homes and children. There was an incident when a mob targeted Van der Plaat's house – they threw eggs at it and graffitied the fence – after one of the neighbours posted his address on Facebook. But they posted the wrong address.

He appealed his extended supervision order – the GPS, the curfew – and was photographed outside court in 2019. Old, stooped, with an expression on his face of a man who was anxious

185

about his next footstep, he wore a blue shirt buttoned to the neck ,
and he looked like he had swallowed his teeth. Eventually he was
more or less driven out. Van der Plaat was ordered to live in a secure
facility to 'protect the community', but was allowed to return home
on day visits. The *Herald* reported, 'His neighbours are furious and
say it is "unacceptable" that he is allowed back near their kids … A
neighbour said, "All residents of the street, particularly those of us
with children, are once again on high alert." '

High alert for an ex-con, weak and old, gone ga-ga with
dementia. I thought back to the day I went to his house. I was
able to look over his back fence by placing the tips of my toes on
a small rung, hoisting myself up, and clinging onto the top of my
fence with my hands. Yes, the things a journalist does, and insists
that the trade is dignified. I noted that there were two tea towels
on the line. One red, one blue; both gingham. The lawn needed a
haircut. There was an upturned pot plant on the grass. But there
was also something remarkable: a statue, a giant wooden carving of
some kind of Pacific bird-god – Van der Plaat collected Polynesian
artefacts, and was described as a 'well-known' buyer at Webb's
auction house. Like all bird-gods, it had a cross and menacing
expression. The beak looked like a sharp, hacking weapon. Was
it meant to attack, or protect? The community spirit of Te Atatū,
that friendly place with the sunrise shimmering on the harbour,
crouched in the shadows.

2

We rally around. We look out for each other. We're good like
that … There it was again, the community spirit of Te Atatū, once
more reaching out in times of crisis, on another cul-de-sac, this one

just around the corner from where I live – I go drinking sometimes with a real nice guy who has a house on the street. He was shaken at what happened. Everybody was, even before the gruesome details were known. A couple of days afterwards he was cutting back the laterals on his tomato plants and heard, as he put it, employing a word too seldom heard, 'a hubbub'. He poked his head around the corner of his house and saw that maybe 200 people were gathered outside his house. They were there to stage a candlelit vigil, walking in a procession to a nearby Baptist church. Labour MP Phil Twyford was there. National candidate Alfred Ngaro was there. A couple of minor celebrities were there. TV was there, as well as reporters from radio and newspapers collecting testimony from the sad and the angry. My mate went back to his tomatoes.

A year later I walked past the bakery which sells elongated sugar doughnuts, past the battered and collapsing wooden house that looks like a shipwreck, past the pātaka kai box where food is left for those in need, to the cul-de-sac and the scene of the crime. 'That's it,' said 75-year-old Errol Shute, getting to his feet and pointing through one of the windows of his sitting room. He meant the house next door where 69-year-old Cunxiu Tian was sexually violated and killed with stupendous violence on a hot Friday morning in the summer of 2016.

The curtains to an upstairs bedroom were open and there was a green motor-mower out front. The house had stood empty since the murder. Errol used to see her now and then at the letterbox, a shy, sweet woman who evidently didn't speak much English. Pretty much her only other public appearance was when neighbours saw her cutting back the hedge that ran beside the long paved driveway to her front door. A couple of clumps of lovely white lilies were in blossom, their flowers leaning out of the hedge.

A young Māori guy walked down that driveway and stood by the letterbox around the time of Cunxiu Tian's murder. He stood there long enough for a woman who lived nearby to notice him and wonder about the fact a stranger was just standing at the end of the driveway that belonged to an elderly Chinese woman. She later gave police a description of someone tall and thin, wearing a green and white tracksuit. It matched the description of a 19-year-old called Jaden Stroobant.

His murder trial at the High Court of Auckland had been set down for four weeks. It lasted 18 minutes. Stroobant had a handsome and alert face, and held his head up high. His expression read: FUCK YOU. He wore a black-and-white check shirt, and his hairstyle featured a braided rat's tail coming out the back of his head. Three tormented-looking women, including his mother, sat directly behind him. 'Guilty,' he said, to the charge of murder; 'Guilty,' he said, when the registrar read out two charges of sexual violation. The language of the charges was very precise. The horror they described was something that ought to have been beyond belief.

The rest of the brief appearance was taken up by an attempt from Stroobant's lawyer, Emma Priest, to suppress certain explicit details of what had happened. It was a matter, she said, of his personal safety in prison. Justice Lang, a shaggy-haired fellow with a deep tan, seemed a little vexed by the plea to suppress, and said that it was up to the prison authorities to manage his physical safety. Well, yes, said Priest, but there was also the issue of Stroobant's mental state; it'd be better, she argued, to wait until a psychological assessment could be made. Justice Lang sighed, and upheld the suppression.

The summary of facts was released to media afterwards, and you had to wonder what difference it made to suppress certain

188

explicit details, because the rest of it was bad enough. To read the document was to scarcely believe it, with its catalogue of wanton cruelty and sadistic impulse. Worse, he seemed to take his time.

The police reconstruction of the crime begins with Stroobant entering his victim's property on the morning of Friday, 15 January 2016. 'As was typical of any week day her daughter and son-in-law left home at around 9am to work in the city. The victim began her usual gardening tasks around the house. The defendant [Stroobant] was at his home address next door.'

He was living in a somewhat battered wooden rental property across the road from Rutherford College and Rutherford Primary School. There are two houses side-by-side, divided into four flats. A few householders were around when I visited to ask about Stroobant.

'The people he was with, they've shot through, eh?' said a cheerful Māori woman whose grandchildren came to the door licking the jam off their toast. 'I don't know nothing about it,' said a rather stern woman at another flat. She was wearing a dressing gown and slippers, and sucking hard on a cigarette. 'And don't bother talking to them next door. They've got phobias.' What kind of phobias? 'They never answer the door or open the curtains.'

Something loomed over the ugly back fence of the two houses: Cunxiu Tian's townhouse. It's a big place and it takes up a lot of room. It's really the only thing to look at when you're in the back section. The lawn is bare, no trees, no garden, just an iron clothesline, and the top storey of the townhouse kind of looks like a cruise ship, a luxury liner, clean and white.

* * *

189

Summary of facts: 'He struck the victim about her head with sufficient force to knock her to the floor. He struck the victim about the head numerous times when she was on the ground. During the assault he stood up and stomped on her face and head. This caused the fatal head injuries that eventually killed her.' The post-mortem recorded extensive bruising to the head and face, blood clots on her brain, and multiple broken bones including one in her neck. 'At the time of the sexual violations the victim was alive, unconscious and dying from the injuries inflicted.'

What punishment and degradation might he have suffered to inspire him to inflict such levels of punishment and degradation on a complete stranger? The question is too broad and essentially meaningless because it cannot be answered. But a general picture of Stroobant's life emerged at his sentencing, and there was nothing surprising about it. It was written all over his face, which continued to read FUCK YOU. 'Without doubt you had a disadvantaged and dysfunctional upbringing,' said Justice Lang, and made an almost perfunctory comment that he was 'disturbed from a young age'. He left school at 13. He slept on the streets. He was sent to prison four times after he turned 17. He'd been released from prison 38 days before the murder.

Yes, said Errol Shute, the man who lived next door to Cunxiu Tian, he'd known numerous killers in his time. He worked as a prison guard at Mt Eden from 1974 to 1984. He was in sole charge of the old Eastern Block, and something called The Pound, 'where they locked up mentally ill and dangerous prisoners'. What did he make of lunatics and psychopaths as people? 'I've got no time for them at all,' he said. 'You can't rehabilitate bred-in bloody traits. A lot of it's handed down from father to son. It's a sad fact of our society, an indictment of it, really.'

How did he regard the killing of his neighbour? 'That's straight-out low-life carry-on,' he said.

Shute had led a colourful life; there were the years as a professional wrestler and boxer (his opponents included Dwayne 'The Rock' Johnson's father), when he was billed as 'The Battling Blacksmith' on account of his long practice of shoeing horses. As for his prison experience, he said he gained a lot of respect from inmates after the time another guard slapped him for not wearing the regulation tie and cap, and Shute gave him a boxing lesson: 'I laid him out as cold as a maggot.' The reason he never wore a tie or cap, he explained, was for protection. 'The least you had on the better, because it was the least something people could grab. It was a threat to your safety, really.'

He was providing a small glimpse into the kind of world Stroobant will inhabit at least until he's almost twice the age he was when he killed the blameless and vulnerable Cunxiu Tian. Justice Lang sentenced him to life with a minimum non-parole period of 17 years. The fact he'd belatedly entered a guilty plea failed to qualify as a mitigating factor of any significance. Police were going to call 21 witnesses, including the woman who saw a man that day who matched Stroobant's description at the time of the killing. I spoke with her on her doorstep. She said, 'I have an autistic son, and he's always looking out the window at things. He was doing that on that morning, and I said, "What's out there today?" That's when I saw the guy.'

In fact it may not have been Stroobant at all. The man seen lingering at the end of the driveway was likely just some random dude; police think Stroobant climbed back over the fence to his house, a teenage killer who made off with things he stolen from that big white ship – an iPad, a gold watch, and $370 in Chinese yuan.

To disguise his movements, he later rode in the boot of a friend's car. It was too little, too lame. Good, quick police work established him as the prime suspect. Stroobant had form as a burglar. His mother was immediately door-knocked and questioned by police. An arrest was made within days.

I love living in Te Atatū. It's really pretty – the tides, the light, the beauty within its wonderland of mangroves along the shore of the harbour and the banks of the creek. My daughter rides her bike along wide, empty streets towards the library. I dress from head to foot from Te Atatu Menswear, run by Mal Buscomb, and his father before him, when it opened in 1962. It's got good schools, and the annual mud-run – a tremendously difficult marathon, attempted waist-deep in thick, sucking mud – is a highlight on the social calendar. It feels more like a town than a suburb, something separate and distinctive. It feels like home, anyway.

Now and then I meet my mate from the cul-de-sac for a drink. We decided to go to the Te Atatu Tavern one Friday night. A band played Credence Clearwater Revival covers and it was all very boozy. When it got too loud, we sat outside with the smokers. We joined a table of people we didn't know and got to talking. Some of them recognised me from my byline photograph in the *Herald*. 'Aw yeah,' said one of the women. 'I'm Jaden's mum.' She seemed like a good sort.

Chapter 10

The pamper party murder: Anna Browne

Something very mysterious and strangely alluring made a rare visit to the criminal courts during the murder trial of Anna Browne. One of the central arguments of her plea of not guilty at the High Court of Auckland was the obscure defence of automatism. To witness it in action was like catching sight of a griffin or a white tiger, or to hear tell of an idea so original and striking that you don't know whether to burst out laughing or regard it in silence and awe. Automatism is seldom raised as a defence, and is one of the most ingenious possibilities to mitigate guilt. It describes a trance-like state. It strays into dark corners of the human brain. It doesn't make any sense, and that's the point of automatism – it's a senseless act, something performed by the body without any control of the mind. But almost as soon as it was held up for inspection at the trial, it disappeared, and it made no difference to the verdict. Browne was found guilty of the murder of Carly Stewart, who she stabbed in the head and killed at an afternoon party in Te Atatū South, that crowded, busy, riverbank suburb in west Auckland.

The paperwork of Operation Puma as laid out in the courtroom might be described as slim. The weapon, a German chopping knife, was found in the kitchen sink; there were a number of witnesses to the attack, including traumatised children; the killing had no forensic controversy about it, and the case was absolutely no whodunit. Browne was handcuffed and put in the back of a police car in the very same minutes that Carly Stewart lay dying from a massive loss of blood. Caught bang to rights, case closed. But an exceptionally young jury – I used to see a couple of them walking around the nearby grounds of Auckland University at lunchtime; they looked like they were on their way to a stage one lecture – deliberated for close to six hours. The possibility of reasonable doubt had surely made an impression as they considered the defence of murderous intent, that Browne was so wasted that she didn't know what she was doing.

Automatism had formed part of that argument in the opening fortnight of the trial. It was introduced by Browne's lawyer, Marie Dyhrberg QC. It required daring and tact, because it's so scarcely used, so odd and unusual; and it presented an opportunity for a learned conversation about free will, the unconscious mind, and other intellectual abstractions. There was this beautiful description of automatism from a court in Ireland: 'a temporary eclipse of consciousness'. It's on speaking terms with temporary insanity and diminished responsibility, although neither are recognised in New Zealand law. Automatism doesn't actually exist as a psychiatric condition, only as a legal term, and the definitions of it are many and varied, all chasing shadows.

But the central problem with automatism in a jury trial is its close association with bullshit. It's the ultimate yeah-right defence.

It sounds made up, a total nonsense. You did it, but you did not know that you did it, and cannot be held accountable for it. Your unconscious mind made you its slave, or not even that, because you couldn't rebel; you were a robot, a puppet, a dim and blameless automaton.

The suspicion that it could only go so far before common sense prevailed was confirmed by Justice Ed Wylie, a kindly, softly spoken soul. He instructed the jury to disregard it. 'I have ruled,' he said, 'that there is no proper basis for the defence of automatism. You will not be required to consider it.' The ruling stripped the trial of its inquiry into the fathomless workings of the mind.

It had been fascinating while it lasted, and it still left open the question of intent. The jury was sent out at midday on a bright Wednesday in spring. There was a tap on the jury door not long after 3pm; Dyhrberg was waiting for the verdict in the courtroom, and said, 'Oh, God.' A verdict after only three hours would surely mean the jury weren't about to waste any more time with the niceties of intent and had already found Browne guilty of murder.

The call went out for Crown prosecutors Nick Webby and Scott McColgan. They finally burst into the courtroom a good 20 minutes later, looking harried and flustered; a lock of hair had fallen over McColgan's scarily suntanned face. Matt Mortimer, a thin, quiet 27-year-old who could pass for 17 and had an insatiable appetite for chocolate, was assisting on his first murder trial. With everyone assembled, the judge took his seat. But it transpired that the jury actually wished to spend more time examining the niceties of intent, and had a question to ask to establish whether intent must be present at the exact time of the killing. 'An intent,' answered the judge, 'can be impulsive.'

It was a simple remark, and it touched precisely on the sudden, awful nature of the killing. The knife concealed behind Browne's back, then the plunge into the side of Stewart's face and penetrating into her neck, cutting the jugular vein – the whole thing was out the gate, no one saw it coming.

Browne, 36, a strongly built, quite beautiful Māori woman with a lovely smile and big hair, arrived at the afternoon party at 47 School Road in Te Atatū South with two bottles of 42 Below vodka, a bottle of Jim Beam and a bottle of Malibu white rum. She duly got trashed. She spilled her drinks, and she seemed well on the way towards being off her face when she was filmed laughing and getting generally jiggy with it on a Facebook livestream. Good times.

There were nine other women. Browne knew only Emmanuelle Sinclair, the host, and Carly Stewart. They'd all met recently at a baby shower for Browne's daughter. A beautician had set up a table to do nails and lashes, for $20 per guest; the killing became known, in every headline, in every story that I wrote in my daily dispatches, as The Pamper Party Murder.

* * *

Three of the women grabbed their phones and rang triple-one after Carly Stewart was stabbed in the head.

The operator said to the first caller, 'What's your address?'

'Forty! No. What?'

'I need you to slow down and tell me the address.'

She shouted, '47 School Road, Te Atatū!'

Another caller was exact: 'Te Atatū South.'

The third caller said, 'Henderson. Yeah. Henderson.'

Everyone was panicking, blood was gushing out of Carly's face and another three of her friends rushed to her side with towels, but each of the callers had it right. Te Atatū is both Te Atatū North and Te Atatū South, the two watery suburbs on either side of State Highway 16, and Henderson stands for pretty much everything across west Auckland, as the centre of the proud, hard-out territories of Kelston, Glen Eden, Glendene, Sunnyvale, Rānui, Massey, and the two Te Atatūs. It's a zone of $2 Shops and laundromats, netball and kapa haka, TENANTS PARKING ONLY and 59 food joints along Lincoln Road. Te Atatū South is on a rise above the Whau River, and the stylish brick house made famous in TV series *Outrageous Fortune* is on Royal View Road. School Road rolls downhill towards the muddy waters of Henderson Creek.

'Beautiful house,' said Corrin Phillip of 47 School Road, picturing the two trees reaching for the sky in the front yard, a garage, picture windows. 'Yeah,' she said, smiling to herself in the witness stand at the High Court of Auckland. 'Nice big house.'

Even nicer inside; the court was shown a video roaming around the lounge and dining room and kitchen and hallway, and it was very tastefully decorated, with timber floors, bookshelves, a red couch against the wall. It was tidy and clean, there were grapes and fresh bananas in the kitchen, paintings.

The first question Crown prosecutor Scott McColgan asked her was, 'Are you known to your friends as Little Corrin?'

'Yeah!' she said, and laughed. 'Little Corrin! That's me!' She was quite loud and also on the verge of tears. Yes, she said to McColgan, she was known as Little Corrin to distinguish her from Carly Stewart's sister Corrine, known as Big Corrine, big only on account of the fact she wasn't tiny like Little Corrin. Big and Little both gave evidence; Big wasn't that big, although Little really was

197

very little, a tiny, passionate woman, who said to the court registrar and the judge through tears, 'Nah. It's okay. I'm good.'

Corrine's sister Patricia also gave evidence, along with party guests shy Helen Wahitapu and athletic Joann Daniela. They were friends, more than that. They were Māori women in their early to late thirties and they loved each other with a fierce loyalty. They called each other 'girls', sometimes 'ladies', also 'sisters': 'The sisterhood. That's us.' They knew each other as children, and now they were mothers of young children, most of them at primary school, mostly girls. They took over the underground courtroom with its snack machine selling cans of Coke for $1 and a choice of biscuits ranging from AFGHAN FRENZY to MEGA CHUNKY CHOC FRENZY. The women stayed close together, were deeply respectful of Carly's parents Reg and Charlene, were open and bright and lovely and shattered.

They were all at 47 School Road on that Saturday afternoon. It looked like a brilliant party. There was a lot of laughter, good music, plenty to eat and drink, the beautician was painting everyone; Little Corrin turned to the camera, and said, 'Yay! I'm getting my nails done!'

She said in court, 'It was a *good* day. It was exciting seeing each other, and we're quite loud girls. I was really, really excited to be going. I'd never gotten my nails done before in my life, and I was happy to be doing it with my sisters. We're family. We love each other. We're there to get our nails done, and to have a little drink on the side was just like the cherry on top sort of thing.'

McColgan said, 'Who was there?'

She named each of her friends, and then paused. 'And,' she said. She turned to her left, and looked past the media bench towards the tall, striking woman with colourful pins in her hair sitting between two security guards. 'And.' Her voice had got louder, and she cried. 'And *her*,' she said, and pointed at the woman. 'Anna. *Anna* was there.'

* * *

'Anna,' Joann Daniela told the court, 'was an outsider coming into our circle.' But there was another woman at the party who hardly anyone knew.

'A white lady turned up,' said Little Corrin.

'I was the only white girl there,' said Justine Evans. 'The odd one out.'

The sisterhood, that tight, protective group of friends for life, acted out the party in court. Justine Evans talked about it too, and the jury was shown police interviews with the four little kids ('Then the cops come and arrested the lady').

The party started at about 1pm. Patricia Stewart, who wore bright blue nail polish in the witness stand, said she left the party to drop off her nephew, and came back again just after 3pm. 'The mood had changed,' she said. 'It felt bad. I knew something had happened, but I didn't know what.'

Justine Evans, 'the white lady', had been introduced to Anna Browne. She said in court, 'I could tell she didn't like me. Looked me up and down. Said something about me being white, and didn't like the way I was dressed … I had on a skirt.' Evans is a small, slender woman. 'She implied I was too fancy. Up myself.'

But Browne also took an instant dislike to another guest who was the last to arrive. Joann Daniela talked about how she was at home and watching the party livestreaming on Facebook: 'I was a little jealous, actually! So I just pretty much self-invited myself.'

She took her two daughters for lunch at McDonald's in Kelston, and bought two bottles of cider for the party. She parked outside 47 School Road on the front lawn. Guests saw her from the front window, and called out, 'Hey, sister! Come in, come in!'

She hugged her friends, and was introduced to Anna Browne. 'She didn't want to know me, so I was like, "Fuck you, too."' Joann wore a Nike Air jacket to court, and moved with the confident, athletic grace of a sportswoman. She said when they were introduced again, a little later, Browne seemed friendlier.

But things got out of control. The beautician packed up her table, and left.

Browne continued to take exception to 'the white lady'. Her insults continued. Guests said to each other: 'What's she on?' Emmanuelle Sinclair, who hosted the party and knew Browne, took her into a kids' bedroom with bunks and an awesome picture of Biggie Smalls on the wall, to try to calm her down.

Emmanuelle got angry with Anna, yelled at her; Anna sat on the floor, and took it. 'There were patches of tension and ill-feeling at the party,' Marie Dyhrberg told the court. 'Not just from Anna Browne. Not all of this ill-feeling is at the feet of Anna Browne.'

Justine popped her head in the door, and Anna got angry again. She scuffled with Emmanuelle. Guests heard a loud thump, and Browne yelling: 'Fucken white teke!'

Crown prosecutor Scott McColgan said to Helen Wahitapu: 'What does "teke" mean?'

And there followed an educational conversation between a Māori woman and a man of colour. McColgan had just returned from visiting his wife's family in Toronto: he lay in the sun until his skin was roasted so deeply, evenly dark that he appeared in court looking like Lawrence of Arabia.

Helen Wahitapu, who has a dry, matter-of-fact manner, said: 'Vagina.'

'And what do you take from that?'

'That someone was being angry with a white teke.'

'Do you know why anyone would be angry with a white teke?'

'No.'

There was another thump inside the bedroom. The door was closed, and it was obvious someone inside was trying to keep it shut, but Joann used her strength to push it open. Anna Browne jumped back into the room. Other guests came in to see what was going on, including Carly Stewart.

'Cuz,' she said, to Browne. 'What the hell are you doing? You've got to calm down, cuz.'

She put her arms around Anna, and said, 'Don't shed a tear.' Anna wiped away her tears. They called each other cuz. They hugged. 'It looked like Carly had it under control,' said Joann.

The others left, some to the kitchen, others to calm their nerves with a cigarette on the deck. Then they heard noises in the hallway outside the bedroom. Carly and Anna Browne had got hold of each other by the scruff of their necks. Carly yelled at her that she was being disrespectful, that her behaviour was totally out of line. Guests broke it up. Joann said she heard Carly say, 'You fucken bitch. This is a fucken family home, how fucken dare you?'

Patricia Stewart took Carly's hand, and said to her cousin, 'Don't worry about her. Just leave her.'

Joann was there, too, and had roughly the same advice: 'Cuz, fuck her. She's fucken nothing.'

Carly said, 'You know what? I'm going to be the bigger person and walk away.'

She went into the lounge, and tried to laugh it off. 'I'm not scared of her,' she said.

Anna had come to the party with two of her sisters. They were her sober drivers, she said. But the sisters left after the scuffle with Justine Evans. Alone, a mess, yelled at, grabbed at, by Carly's definition 'the smaller person' and further shamed as 'nothing', bad news, aggressive, provocative, calling someone a fucken white cunt, a shambles, weepy, an outsider, no longer welcome, no longer remotely jiggy but just totally trashed, she followed Carly down the hallway, then turned into the kitchen. No one saw her pick up the knife. She held it behind her back and walked into the lounge, straight towards her 'cuz', and in a low, quiet voice, described by Joann Daniella as 'a whimper', by Marie Dyhrberg as 'a sob', she called out her name: *Carly.*

* * *

Carly said, 'Yeah, what?'

Guests out on the deck thought Browne punched her. Joann thought that, too. But Little Corrin was right beside Carly, and she saw.

'I saw,' she told the court, and stopped. She clutched at a tissue. 'I saw ... I saw Anna walk in. I saw Anna walk in. She walked straight up to Carly, and lifted her arm. The right arm came up in the air and BOOM, she stabbed her right in the face. We were family and we were standing all next to each other and I saw my sister hold her face and I saw the knife come out.'

Death came shockingly fast. The cops got there quick – seven minutes from the Henderson police station – and leaned Carly forward in an attempt to drain the blood from her mouth. It was called in as status one, life-threatening. A stretcher and a defibrillator were rushed upstairs, but Carly had dropped to the floor and lost consciousness. A heart monitor showed no electrical activity. 'And at that point,' St John's ambulance officer Antony Gabriel said in court, 'we've stopped, and stepped back.'

Anna Browne had kept moving. After she plunged the knife into Carly's head and pulled it out, she walked backwards into the kitchen, then left through the front door and down the steps. She headed right onto School Road, downhill towards slow, brown Henderson Creek. It was a warm afternoon at just after 4pm. She had Carly's blood on her jacket and her jeans and both her shoes.

What thoughts ran through her head, what took hold? She wasn't yet a murderer. Carly was still alive, upstairs at the house where kids were screaming and three of the guests called 111. Browne wasn't familiar with Te Atatū South, wouldn't have known about the 049 Go West bus or the house around the corner on Royal View Road with a letterbox in the shape of an enormous hammer, might barely have registered the gum trees above the creek and the busy weekend traffic on Central Park Drive. Where could she go, where could she hide? She was off her face. Was she totally unaware of what she'd done, or was everything that followed the performance of an outstanding liar?

She turned around on School Road and went back to the house, where she immediately started saying she didn't know what had happened.

The cops at Henderson police station got a call at 4.02pm to attend a reported stabbing. They drove to 47 School Road and arrived at 4.09pm. The first thing they saw were three women at the front of the property yelling at a woman standing closest to the street: Browne, the killer, who the terrified guests thought had come back to kill them, too.

Marie Dyhrberg said in her closing address to the jury: 'When she comes back she's isolated from the group of women who were yelling and screaming "She did it" and pointing to her. She makes no attempt to run and hide from the police or the women abusing her. Just stayed where she was – isolated, hounded almost by a group of frightening women – making accusations she cannot comprehend. Police sirens, people yelling, throwing a stool at her. If she knew what she had done she would have left the scene, fast. But she stayed, bewildered, crying and confused.'

Police notebooks contain some of the best dialogue in New Zealand literature. Someone should publish them. Here's a start; the remarks that follow are taken from the notebooks presented by cops and detectives at the trial.

One of the women pointed at her, and said to the cops: 'She's the one that did it. This bitch, right here.'

Anna Browne was handcuffed and driven to Henderson police station. She said in the car, 'I didn't do nothing.'

She said, 'Where's my cuzzie? What happened to my cuzzie? I don't know what happened. I done nothing wrong. Where's my cuzzie? Where's my cuzzie? Where's my cuzzie?'

She meant Carly Stewart, who she'd killed.

The car turned the roundabout on Alderman Drive to the Henderson station, and Brown began thrashing around in the back seat, screaming and yelling. She continued to scream and yell for the next hour in custody: 'I didn't do nothing. Where's my cuzzie?'

She said at Henderson police station, 'Are you saying I did it?'

A detective said, 'The finger points at you.'

She said, 'All we were doing was drinking, then something happened and I woke up here.'

She had been placed in a suicide gown – a white smock that couldn't be torn. There are photos of her wearing it in the prosecution's photo book. Her hair is long and straight, and her arms and legs are bare. She said, 'Why am I in this shit garment?'

She said, 'Are people saying I did it, that I stabbed her up?'

Again, the detective said, 'The finger points at you.'

She said, 'It's bullshit. Why did I attack her? Why did I do that to her? What do they say? I didn't do shit.'

She said, 'Damn that PCP shit.'

She said, 'I didn't do nothing.'

She said, 'Where's Ems?' She meant Emmanuelle Sinclair, her friend, the party host. 'I want her to tell me what happened.'

She said, 'They're all friends. I'm the only outsider. What did I do? Tell me. Tell me. Tell me.'

The cops wrote in their notebooks that she smelled of alcohol. They noted that it took seven officers to hold her down in custody. They noted that she grabbed at her hair and tried to climb the walls, that her mood went from happy to sad to angry, that she wouldn't sit still, that she talked about another person being with her in the cell, that her pupils rolled back and forth so all they could see was the whites of her eyes.

And then she said, 'Fuck I'm hungry.'

A detective said, 'I'll get you a pie.'

'All good,' she said.

He said, 'What kind of pie would you like?'

'Mince,' she said.

He said, 'Okay, we'll get you one.'

'Sweet,' she said.

* * *

205

The kitchen knife that killed Carly Stewart was displayed in court inside a Perspex case. It was suspended in the middle of it. It looked like a kind of objet d'art, like Damien Hirst's famous installation of a tiger shark preserved inside a large cabinet; exhibit 10 was similarly a thing of menace and horror. It had a hard black plastic handle, and the blade was long and sharp. It didn't look expensive and it didn't look cheap. It looked like it was part of a set.

The knife was presented to defence witness Dr Krishna Pillai during cross-examination. He took the stand after the prosecution had called the last of its 36 witnesses – their own forensic psychiatrist, Dr David Street, a whispery-voiced fellow from Pennsylvania. He was the second American to give evidence. Prosecution had also called Dr Chip Gresham, an ESR scientist who studied at the University of Massachusetts. He was thin and wiry, but with big, tough hands; Gresham is an active rock climber, and was due to climb in Spain when the trial finished.

Dr Gresham was called to give evidence relating to the alcohol and drugs found in a urine sample taken from Browne after her arrest. She proved positive for traces of methamphetamine, or P, which she said she'd smoked three or four days before the killing. There were also traces of amphetamine, contained in Ritalin, which she took for her ADHD. Dr Gresham said he didn't expect that P would trigger 'bizarre behaviour' three or four days after it was smoked.

'May it please your Honour,' said prosecutor Nick Webby after Dr Street had spoken on the subject of Anna Browne's state of mind, 'that is the evidence for the Crown.' There was a 15-minute adjournment, and then Dyhrberg opened for the defence. She spoke for 20 minutes. She said Brown had elected not to give evidence, and that she would call two expert witnesses, one in forensic psychiatry, and the other in toxicology.

She stood facing the jury, and said: 'The defence says you will not, on the evidence you have heard, be able to find that Anna Browne, beyond reasonable doubt, intended to kill ... Anna Browne has no recollection of stabbing Carly Stewart. But she does not say, "I didn't do it." She does not say she did not deliver the fatal blow, but she does challenge murderous intent.'

Dyhrberg has a beautiful speaking voice. It is posh, but not overbearingly so; and along with her short hair and her thin smile, she looks full-on Judi Dench.

She said, 'The defence says that due to Anna Browne's intoxicated state, she did not mean to kill and she did not know the risk of death.' She paused, and then said very simple words: 'She didn't stop to think.'

The foreman of the jury was maybe 24, 25. Dyhrberg looked at him, and said: 'If you find there is no murderous intent ... you will find Anna Browne not guilty of murder, but guilty of manslaughter.'

Browne wore a loose red top tucked into her knee-length black skirt. Her hair was in a bun. She looked like she was on her way to church.

* * *

There was a phantom in the courtroom at her trial, the old, shabby ghost of one of New Zealand's greatest wretches – Tony Dixon. Dixon, who smoked epic amounts of P and took a Samurai sword to two women, then shot and killed a bystander in a service station; Dixon, who pleaded insanity, and rolled his eyes in his head to make himself look like a crazy person, and cut his hair into a shape to make himself look like a complete moron. There were so many parallels with Browne, right down to the use of a blade.

207

'She was thrashing about and moaning incoherently,' said constable Grant Moreland, of her behaviour at Henderson police station. 'She was trying to climb the walls and what-not.' What-not! Seriously deranged what-not. Like Dixon, she made a great show of rolling her eyes back in her head; like Dixon, who engaged in imaginary conversations with someone called Sid, Browne spoke to someone who wasn't there: 'Oh, stop doing that!' she scolded the hair-puller who didn't exist.

Like Dixon, she was diagnosed with antisocial personality disorder; like Dixon, she was accused of 'malingering', that strange, rather Victorian term that means to feign symptoms. Dixon had the relatively straightforward task of presenting himself as a lunatic. Browne, though, had to meet the subtle requirements of sane automaton. It was always going to be difficult. The judge in a sane automatism case in Britain described the defence as 'a quagmire of law seldom entered nowadays, save by those in desperate need of some kind of defence'.

There are two species of automatism. Insane automatism is classified as having internal causes, which essentially means a disease of the mind – mad, crazy, a lunatic of some stripe. Non-insane or sane automatism is due to external influences, or events which befall a person, such as a blow to the head, emotional shock, or excessive alcohol and drug use. Sleepwalking also comes under that classification. Shakespeare gave the world a celebrated automaton: Lady Macbeth. The great scene where she washes her hands ('Out, damned spot!') while sleepwalking fulfils the definition of an unconscious or involuntary act. She can walk with a lighted taper and perform actions but has no idea what she's doing. 'Her eyes are open,' observes the doctor. 'Aye,' replies another witness, 'but their sense is shut.'

One of the very few New Zealand cases where sleepwalking inspired the automatism defence was in 2013, when a man was charged with indecent assault. He'd woken up in the night at a friend's house, and climbed into bed with the man's daughter. When he was dragged off the girl, he said groggily: 'What? This is my wife!' He had a long history of sleepwalking, when he would often have sex with his wife without being consciously aware of it. Curiously, the jury returned a verdict of not guilty 'by reason of insanity'. Sleepwalking is not a disease of the mind.

At Browne's trial, Dr Street made mention of a sleepwalking automaton who entered a lounge, picked up a cushion from the sofa, and proceeded to urinate on it. Street did not add whether the man left the cushion up or down.

The first instance of automatism as a defence in murder trials was in 1955, in England, when a man violently attacked his young son with a mallet, and threw him out of the window into a river. The judge instructed the jury, 'If his actions were purely automatic, and his mind had no control over the movement of his limbs, then the proper verdict is not guilty.' There it was, the debut appearance of that now-you-see-it, now-you-don't word in a court of law: *automatic*. It was described another way at the trial as a rhetorical question: 'Did he know what he was doing when he struck his son with a mallet? If he did not, then he could not be held responsible.'

Another test case, still cited in literature on the subject, was a 1963 strangling in Northern Ireland. George Bratty had given a ride to a woman called Josephine Fitzsimons. His recollection of what happened is like a man peering through fog and trying to make out a few vague outlines: 'I had some terrible feeling, and then a sort of blackness ... Just with that, I took one look at her, and caught her and threw her over the back seat. I caught her with my two hands.' The court accepted automatism as a defence with this lovely Jack-and-Jill description: 'It is a defence because the mind does not go with what is being done'.

Browne maintained she had zero recollection of the killing of Carly Stewart. Nothing, just thick fog. Dr Street accepted she had likely experienced an alcoholic blackout at some stage that afternoon. Automatism, though, was out of the question. 'The more complex the behaviour, the more remote the possibility … It doesn't stick.'

Someone in the twilight zone of automatism exists as a dream-like creature, capable of anything, unchecked, a free spirit; they're too exotic, too fabulous, to perform the ordinary chores of the conscious and wide-awake drudge. Street removed Browne from her very interesting role as a visitor from another planet of altered consciousness and placed her at 47 School Road as a nasty and calculating drunk. The characteristics of automatism weren't met, he said. 'Most of the time when there's violence involved with automatism, it's kicking, it's scratching. People aren't planning things. Any planning just precludes it.'

He pointed to Brown's progress down the hallway to the kitchen to choose a knife, to her ability to identify Carly and call her name, to the fatal blow itself: 'It sounds like the blow she delivered was fairly co-ordinated.'

And yet Robert Schopp writes in his study *Automatism: A philosophical inquiry*: 'The defence applies to those who perform complex actions in a co-ordinated, directed fashion, but with substantially reduced awareness.'

There was support for the automatism argument from Dr Pillai, a forensic psychiatrist called by the defence. These shrinks get around: he met with Tony Dixon on the day he took his life.

Like Dr Street, he thought Browne's behaviour at Henderson police station was evidence of a blackout, or delirium. But Pillai went further, and said it was consistent with automatism.

In his assessment of Browne, Dr Pillai wrote: 'It is worthwhile considering whether she may have been acting under the influence of an external cause, that being alcohol intoxication, and was without conscious intent at the time of the offending, and that it may constitute evidence of sane automatism.'

There it was, plainly stated, in open court – automatism, the power of the unconscious to make things happen independent of the empty vessel who performs the terrible deed. A trial judge in the US made this breathtaking proposition: 'An act committed while one is unconscious is in reality no act at all. It is merely a physical event or occurrence.' The ethical and legal prospect, then, was that the horrible slaying of Carly Stewart was no more than that: 'merely a physical event or occurrence'.

This bleakest of possibilities was cut short by Crown prosecutor Scott McColgan in cross-examination. That was when he called on the registrar to produce exhibit 10. The murder weapon – that hard black plastic handle, that long, sharp blade – was placed in front of Dr Pillai. 'That was the knife,' McColgan said, 'she used on Ms Stewart.'

He swept through the remainder of his cross-examination with the knife in plain sight. Yes, Dr Pillai conceded, there was an element of choice in Browne selecting the knife. Yes, he admitted, the fact that she held it behind her back was evidence of deceit. There was more, and then, devastatingly, right at the close, McColgan asked: 'Given the evidence about pre-stabbing, and during the stabbing, and immediately after the stabbing, how likely is it that Ms Browne was acting as an automaton?'

Dr Pillai said, 'I think the evidence suggests there was some conscious activity.'

McColgan asked, 'And it's consistent, isn't it, with somebody who has the capacity to form an intent?'

Dr Pillai said, 'Yes.'

It was over. Automatism had flown, had returned to its strange, vague twilight. Intent, too, was a lost cause. Browne's defence had gone as far as it could. Her team were superb in the courtroom. Barbara Hunt, a small, vivacious woman who wore the collars of her white shirt up, clawed back valuable ground in cross-exam. She was absent on the day of the verdict, to be in Wellington where her husband, Gerard van Bohemen, was appointed a judge of the High Court. Kirsten Martelli, assisting, had to start work on another trial. Marie Dyhrberg waited alone. Her closing address was a masterclass, right from the start: 'What happened that afternoon was so inexplicable, so unforeseen, that something extraordinary must have occurred for the day to turn deadly. And that extraordinary intervention was something which was in Anna Browne's mind ...'

But it wasn't extraordinary. It was the banality of killing, a stupid act of violence. Anna Browne ended Carly Stewart's life and the verdict declared that she meant to do it. She was reckless, impulsive, homicidal. The idea formed as she deviated from the hallway to the kitchen. 'She wasn't there for the chips and dip,' Nick Webby told the jury. She knew what she was doing. She was wide awake.

Chapter 11

Missing: Murray Mason

Accrington 0 Gillingham 2
Barnsley 4 Oxford United 0
Burton Albion 1 Rochdale 2

I asked everyone who knew Murray Mason, found dead at the age of 76 in the Auckland Domain in the winter of 2019, 'What did he look like?' They described a tall, thin man, who walked everywhere and always at speed ('Striding with purpose', one friend put it), carried an umbrella and a shopping bag full of fruit and books, had blue-grey eyes, thin hair, a bushy moustache ('That's how you used to see him. That's exactly how he looked, the little beer drops on his moustache,' said another friend, standing in front of a photograph of Mason hung next to portraits of his parents on a wall in his house), and a drinker's red and haggard face. 'Cadaverous,' said a guy who used to work with him. 'A reasonably long face,' said an old schoolfriend, who would meet him at a Queen Street pub on pension day every second Tuesday morning. And then he said: 'It was a sad face, actually.'

Word went around after Mason's shocking death that there'd be a kind of wake, held at one of his watering holes, The Albion, a dark and quiet nineteenth-century pile opposite St Matthew's church in downtown Auckland. It was thought that maybe four or five old codgers might turn up. But the place was absolutely packed; reports vary, but there was at least 60 people, maybe over 100. They included a son whom he hadn't seen for over 30 years, and a brother whom he hadn't seen since he was four. There were warm and emotional speeches. His life had meant something; his death was felt as a genuine loss. They came to celebrate a kind of urban legend.

No one knew the whole story of his life. He left his past behind, travelled light, moved in secrecy. His life was none of anyone's damned business. One thing about him: he hated being followed. If he said goodbye, went on his way, and saw that you were keeping an eye on him as he walked down the street, he would not be happy about it. He operated in darkness. One friend recalled: 'I met him once at the Countdown near the waterfront and took him back to our place for dinner, at the bottom of St Georges Bay Road in Parnell. We had a few wines and at about 11 he said, "Which way is Newmarket?" I pointed him the way, and he walked up the hill and off he went.' A perfect getaway, slipping into the dark night.

The more people I spoke to about him, the guiltier I felt, because he would hate this story, hate the fact it was asking questions of him and tracing his whereabouts. The point of his existence as an old man who wandered the streets of Auckland at any time of day or night was to keep his head down, avoid scrutiny, live in peace. But I was also conscious that we shared a kind of bond. Mason, too, had worked as a journalist. He spent most of his professional career with the *Herald*. His face – as seen in the portrait on the wall at his friend Ivan Davis's house in Glendene – looked familiar. It's likely I saw him now and then at the newspaper's former, glorious

214

premises in Albert Street, where he worked as a sub-editor on the business desk.

Gavin Ellis was his editor. All journalists talk in stories; they may not be true, but they're based on real events. He said, 'Have you heard the story of the Masonette? There was a room at the *Herald* that had been set aside for women members of the staff where they could go and lie down if they weren't feeling well. There was a rumour that Murray used to kip down there at night when he wasn't feeling up to going home after a hard night. It's all hearsay, but the room became known as the Masonette.'

A 'hard night': Mason smoke and drank. Everybody in journalism did, it was as compulsory as shorthand. But he chainsmoked, and drank as fast as he smoked. The smoking yellowed his teeth until they fell out; according to his ex-wife, it's why he grew the moustache, as deep cover. He stopped smoking. He never stopped drinking. Not one person though described him as an alcoholic, including an alcoholic.

'See that guy over there, asleep? He might have known him,' said a helpful librarian at Auckland Central Library. We approached the old drunk dozing in a chair in a quiet corner. The librarian gently woke him up. He gave his name as Jack; he was a large man who wore numerous layers of black wool, and he smelled bad. He said, 'Yes, I know who you mean. He used to sit there.'

He pointed to a chair in front of a small desk. It seemed like just about the loneliest spot in the entire library.

Mason waited at the front door of the Central Library for it to open every morning. He was a familiar sight. It was where Gavin Ellis last saw him. 'He was sitting there engaged in a book. He had notes on him, and he gave me the impression he was studying.' Other friends thought he was completing a university

215

degree – mathematics, someone said, and someone else thought mathematics, too. Another wondered if it was a study of Egyptian hieroglyphics, which Mason could read. There were various other speculations made at his wake about his library project, where he sat surrounded by books and paper, and was intent on writing page after page.

Jack the library drunk said, 'I thought he must be writing a book. He used to write a lot, he had all these papers and was writing onto them.' He never saw him drunk, never saw him aggro; he figured Mason was some kind of scholar, on serious business. 'He was here every day. This was his preferred spot.' Jack looked again at the deserted table. 'I used to see him every day, and next thing ... yeah.'

Coventry 1 Scunthorpe 2
Fleetwood 0 Wimbledon 1
Peterborough 2 Bristol Rovers 1

* * *

We think of downtown Auckland as a happy, tragic mass of students and professionals, drunks and beggars, tourists and shopkeepers, as a zone of commerce and conspicuous excitement. Mason was among a loose group of old-school Kiwi blokes who passed through the valley of Queen Street almost unnoticed.

Certain names kept coming up, of guys who drank with Mason, were part of his crowd – Shorty, Trevor, Frank, Mike, Big Pete. Solitary men, for the most part, they came in by bus, and drank deep at their favourite watering holes. Mason had a kind of itinerary. It included The Right Track, a sports bar on Fort Street. I called in one lunchtime and figured I'd come across someone who knew Mason. John Mitchell, 80, stood at the bar; he said, 'Oh yes. A really good guy. He was always really polite and so nice. I'd see him here a couple of times a week, and I tell you what, I never saw him drunk.'

We got to talking about the fact Mitchell only had one leg. He explained that the other leg got infected when he slipped on wet leaves and got it stuck in a gutter.

I walked around the corner to the QT Tavern, a sports bar at the wharf end of Queen Street. Mason was a regular there, always sat at the end of the bar with a $7.80 pint of Speight's Old Dark. Bar manager Paul Budd said he'd worked at QT for eight years. 'When I first started here, there'd be a group of about 15 old guys. Over the years you'd hear about another funeral, and another one … Jeez. If they all got together now, you'd be lucky to get seven or eight. It's quite sad.'

QT is where Mason would meet his friend from school, Peter Warlow, on pension day. It was Warlow who described Mason's sad face. Big Pete, they call him; an ex-butcher, he took up a lot of room when I called into the tavern on another lunchtime. He sat at the bar next to Mason's favoured position. He turned and looked at the empty stool quite a lot while we were talking. 'I miss Murray,' he said. 'I still can't bloody believe he's gone. I expect him to come in any minute. He was a fantastic joker.'

'He was that,' agreed Michael Fenwick, who I met at QT on yet another lunchtime. I enjoyed these visits. There was something reassuring about standing at the bar with men who liked a tall, cold glass of beer at midday, and were in no hurry to go anywhere; it was as though they were maintaining a proud New Zealand tradition of masculinity in the heart of downtown Auckland. 'He was quite

217

particular with his friends and pubs,' said Fenwick. 'He could move around pubs quite a bit, but if something ticked him off, he'd say. "That's it, I'm out." He banned himself.'

He said that Mason liked to talk about a kind of holy grail of pubs, celebrated as an ideal establishment for the drinking man: The Coach & Horses, in Soho, made famous by the journalist Jeffrey Bernard. 'He could describe it in detail,' Fenwick said. Mason had gone there on a pilgrimage on a trip to London. You could have worse role models than Bernard, but not by much. Bernard was a wreck, a mess; famously, his weekly column in *The Spectator* was described as 'a suicide note in instalments'. Bernard, like Mason, worked in journalism; like Mason, he had an enormous capacity for alcohol, but carried himself with some dignity; like Mason, he claimed a stool at the end of the bar as his spot, his place in the world.

One of Mason's regular ports of call was Spitting Feathers, on Wyndham Street, where he'd sit at the end of the bar and drink two $5 bottles of Heineken at lunchtime. If the seat was taken, he'd hover nearby. He occupied the same spot at The Albion on Hobson Street, except that he had privileges and certainty. 'That corner was pretty much reserved for him,' said bar manager Julie Hanson. She pointed to a stool at the end of the bar. He drank $10 bottles of Lion Red, always from the same glass: 'Every time he came in, we'd get the glass from the fridge. It's still in there. Everybody knew it was his. It was one of the first things that I learned when I started here.'

Hanson, an attractive young woman with dyed red hair, and the only person in this story under the age of 50, is from Germany, and began work at The Albion in 2018. 'It's a safe place,' she said. 'As a regular you get to know the staff and the staff know you.

You feel like you're at home. That's why people keep coming back. Murray was always very nice and polite, and had interesting stories to tell. I remember him talking about travelling in London; he said he always regretted not travelling earlier, that he didn't start travelling till he was in his fifties.'

She looked over at the empty stool. 'He always came here before he went home,' she said. 'Every single night, he said, "Thank you Julie, I'm going home." For sure he said that on his last night.'

I said, 'His last night?'

She said, 'The last time I actually saw Murray was the night he died. He said goodbye, and he walked out the door. It was about midnight.'

* * *

Portsmouth 1 Luton 0
Shrewsbury 0 Bradford 1

There was a lot of conjecture after he died that he was homeless. Police made their first inquiries at the City Mission. None of his friends believed it; the Mason they knew looked after himself, dressed reasonably well, bought supplies from the supermarket, was never drunk or at least never so drunk that he was legless. But how well did anyone know him?

He talked a lot about sport, also the importance of education, was sometimes argumentative (Paul Budd at the QT Tavern asked him to leave maybe three or four times in eight years; 'He could be a cantankerous old man but there was no malice'), but generally he was a quiet presence at the end of the bar, held his drink, never swore, was marvellously polite and respectful. He had a code of conduct. 'Murray was straight as a die,' said Peter Warlow. 'If he wanted to say something, he would come out and say it.'

He seldom spoke about himself. Now and then he might mention a marriage that ended, a family he left behind.

'Murray would open up to me,' said Warlow.

I said, 'Like about his marriage?'

'He didn't tell me very much about that.'

I really went to great lengths to talk to those who knew him, which is to say I bowled up to some people in the office. 'He was always very secretive,' said *Herald* sub-editor Mark Freyer, who worked alongside Mason for years. Well, not exactly alongside: he recalled Mason taking stories to the Shakespeare, and subbing them over a drink. 'Guarded,' he continued. 'You couldn't get anything from him.'

'Well, he was very, very kind to me,' said sub-editor Faith Lee. 'I came here from the *Rotorua Post* and he looked after me. He was a lovely man.'

'But you couldn't get anything out of him, could you?' said Freyer.

'He was a lovely man,' she said.

Richard Dale, an illustrator at the paper, was walking past, but stopped to listen. 'Ah, yes, Murray,' he said. 'He was always affable. Plus he had a Nietzschean moustache which I always admired. He was like those old-style New Zealand guys, the kind who lived in boarding houses, and smoke and drink too much. He was a man who seemed to have fallen from somewhere. His death was particularly tragic.'

Adrian Blackburn, 80, worked with Mason, too. He said, 'The last time I saw Murray, his face was reddish and he looked down on his luck. But he didn't look like he was at the bottom of the heap and sleeping on Queen Street.' Certainly he thought of Mason as a heavy drinker. 'There are plenty of people around journalism as you would know who abuse demon drink. I've done it; you've probably done it, too. This is low-dose.' We met at The Albion; Blackburn ordered something disgracefully low-alcohol.

I was given Blackburn's number by another ex-journo, Gavin Ellis, who had last seen Mason at the library. Ellis said, 'He obviously looked down on his luck. But there was a certain dignity about the guy, Steve. He held himself well. And when I'd see him walking along the street, he wasn't a shuffling shambles or anything like that.'

Blackburn put me in touch with Bruce Morris – Auckland has more ex-journos than current journos – who worked with Mason in the early 1970s. When I phoned, he'd just come back from hospital: his mother-in-law, Joy, had been knocked over in a hit-and-run in Henderson. She was recovering from her injuries, but tests discovered cancer. She died on Christmas Day 2019.

Morris was in shock when I called. Even so, his instincts for a newspaper story were sharp, and right on the money. Only a few minutes after I started asking him about Mason, he said, 'You're obviously coming at it from an angle of a bloke who nobody knew much about.'

Morris didn't know much about him. 'He never really spoke much about his family. I knew he had kids … He was just one of the blokes. I'd occasionally drop him off home. He was always a very quiet guy. Very popular in that no one ever had a bad word to say about Murray. He was always at the pub never saying very much … It was an odd thing, really. He was always like a loner within a circle. It's strange, isn't it?'

That was when Mason lived with his wife and their four children in Glendene, in west Auckland. He went to look at the house two years before he died with his good friend Ivan Davis, a barman at The Albion. It was Davis who hung the portrait of Mason next to photos of his parents on the wall of his lounge. He was cut up about Mason's death; the sadness was deep, and enduring. I met him at his Glendene home above the Whau River. He said, 'Murray came here one day in 2017, and we had a few beers, and he said, "Do you mind if we go for a walk around the area?"

'I said, "Yeah, sounds good to me." So he took me on the walk he used to run. Cos he loved running, long-distance running.

'We went all over. He loved it. Hepburn Road, Barrys Road … We went through the Glendene Reserve and he goes, "I need to go see the old home."

'So we got there, and you could just see in his face that the memories must have come back about that house. I thought, "I'll just leave him here for a sec." I just wanted him to have a moment to himself cos I could tell he was sort of standing there and thinking. After a while, he said, "Right. Let's go." '

Mason didn't say anything about it, and Davis didn't ask. 'He was very, very private. I never delved into his personal life.'

'He was always a very quiet guy,' said John McCaulay, 74, yet another ex-journo who worked with Mason. We met at a tearoom in my neighbourhood in Te Atatū. He is a very urbane fellow from the other, richer side of town, Parnell. I asked him what he thought of Mason's work. I liked McCaulay at once; he was a journo's journo, someone who respected the trade, was aware of its limitations. He gave Mason the highest compliment you can ever give to a reporter. 'He never made a mistake,' he said. 'He typed with two fingers and his copy was always clean. When he wrote, he only had to do it once.'

Sunderland 2 Charlton Athletic 1

Wycombe 0 Blackpool 0

* * *

Mason's daughter Rachel Wise followed him into journalism, and she acknowledged it was driven by some deep need to impress him, even to win his love, although she knew that was probably futile. She is associate editor at *Hawke's Bay Today*. I interviewed her on a Friday afternoon in Napier. We sat on the foreshore. The surf clawed at the gravel beach. It got dark. There were lights like fires at the town of Haumoana across the water. We spoke for over two hours, and just about every second of it was an unrelenting story of trauma and unhappiness and grief.

She said he sexually abused her. He was violent, full of loud and hectic rage, but equally as capable of tense and seething rage – he'd give her the silent treatment, the longest was for six months. He came home plastered, and was either a nasty drunk or, preferably, comatose. It was a long and disturbed reign of terror which ended when he upped sticks and took off, leaving his wife and kids penniless in a shack in the King Country. He stayed in touch for a little while, but only as a kind of threatening stalker, and then he disappeared from their lives, completely, for over 30 years, until the police got in touch to say he was found face-down in a ditch in the Domain. 'Mum looked at me,' she said, 'and it was like, "Yes!"' She mimed a high-five, and laughed.

One after another of her stories crashed like the surf in front of us. This one: 'One of his first stories in his scrapbooks was about mice they were growing cancer in, and he had these very gruesome photographs of mice with cancer. Knowing how much I liked animals, he took great delight in showing me those photos. And when we move to Ōwairaka, there were wild cats living in the hedges and we tried to adopt a kitten. He told me in great detail

223

how he'd killed it by putting a needle through its fontanelle. I would have been five then, maybe six. He was quite proud he knew how to do that.'

And this one: 'He'd come home after work drunk and dishevelled, very late quite often, shouting, hitting us kids. We never quite knew what we'd done to deserve it or how not to get into trouble. He was an imposing person, physically and psychologically, because he had very firm ideas on everything and prescribed ways of how things should be done. We were pretty good at sticking to the rules, otherwise he'd lash out, usually with the back of his hand, and he was quite deft at kicking you.'

Also this one: 'I remember us running out of petrol once; this was years down the track, when we were in Raetihi. He pushed the car all way the way from Horopito to Raetihi [14 kilometres]. He wouldn't stick his thumb out or walk to get a gas can. When we got to a downhill, we'd jump in and coast down the hill. And this was all done in absolute silence. Murray hadn't spoken to me since I was fourteen or fifteen; this was when I was sixteen. I'd offended him somehow and he decided that he was no longer going to speak to me. He wouldn't even acknowledge me. If I was walking down the passage, and he was walking the other way, he'd just knock me over and walk over the top of me. I didn't exist.'

There were other stories ('He didn't hold with fun', 'He liked to call us imbeciles – he never used a short word when a longer word would do'), including one too heinous to report. They all came pouring out. 'You're very easy to talk to,' she said, but the compliment was misplaced. As a journalist, she would have known that a good interview is entirely at the discretion of the person being interviewed; if they talk, it's because they need to talk. Mason was a black stain on her life. She felt compelled to describe it.

A black poodle dragged a piece of driftwood across the beach. A very tall man walked past with a very short man. I said to her, 'As journalists we meet so many people and routinely feel for them, have empathy or affection, find something about them attractive. But I'm not feeling anything for the man you're talking about. He seems entirely loathsome. What were his good qualities?'

Journalists always try do their best when they're the ones who get questioned. Wise couldn't or wouldn't come up with an answer, but she made up for it with the gold all journalists hope to be given: a devastating quote. She said, 'I have gone through my life disliking him immensely.'

* * *

How does a life begin to unravel? Where do things start to go so wrong that you end up being despised by your own family until you disappear, and you move through the rest of your days as a kind of ghost? I spoke with his ex-wife, Claudia. She was in good spirits when I called her at her Waipawa home; she wandered around watering the plants and calling out to various pets, and said in a sing-song voice, 'It was a huge relief when I heard he died.' Yes, she said, her and Rachel greeted the news with high-fives.

Of course she's thought a lot about Mason over the years and tried to fathom why it was that he made her life hell. Her stories about his abuse were just as dismal as her daughter's, but they had another quality: she made the narrative of Murray Mason's life sound gothic, doomed.

I asked, 'What was his central problem, do you think?'

She said, 'Apart from the drink? I think he had psychological problems and the drink made everything worse. He was adopted when he was four. His father died of pneumonia and his mother was an alcoholic, and couldn't cope. He was the youngest of her children and so he was the easiest to foster out … He probably was an angry, bewildered little boy.'

'I don't think he ever loved anyone,' said Rachel, once again devastatingly. 'I don't think he was capable of it.'

But he had gone through a trauma as a child. Torn from his family, he was taken in by a couple who Claudia described as cold, remote. His adopted mother was often 'unwell'. When she was particularly unwell, Mason would stay with a family who were wealthy Hawke's Bay landowners.

His daughter Rachel said, 'They had a beautiful mansion built from kauri. Murray used to talk about it all the time. He'd say: "It had a hallway that was big enough for a cricket pitch." I think that was where he got this idea that he wanted to be landed gentry, in particular Hawke's Bay landed gentry, which is a breed unto itself … He was green with envy that that wasn't him, that that was supposed to be his life.'

Her mother laughed. 'Yes, I've heard Rachel's theory. There may be something in it. He did seem to have a chip on his shoulder about life in general and his lack of success in it. He was hellbent to get money. He always had grand ideas about making a fortune and being someone important. But everything he tried turned to custard.'

They met when they were working one summer at the Peter Pan ice-cream factory in Waipukurau. He was a catch: tall, handsome, athletic, he'd been Dux at his school, outstanding at cricket and athletics, and was studying for a Bachelor of Science. Claudia was a solo mum; Rachel, who was four when they got married, only ever called him 'Murray', never 'Dad'. The couple moved to Auckland and had three children of their own. Mason got a job with the government research institute, the DSIR, and moved over to journalism in 1969 when he was approached by the *Herald* to take on the science round.

One of the great attractions of newspaper journalism in the twentieth century was as a refuge for scoundrels, wastrels, layabouts, loners, deviants and drunks. It didn't require talent, but it demanded stamina. It was like going to sea. The voyage took men away from their family and plied them with alcohol and kept them in tobacco. The trouble was that it also returned them to their family. Claudia said, 'He started spending more and more time at the pub. I used to hope if he came home on time, that was fine; if he came home slightly late, he'd be belligerent and argumentative and nasty; if he came home really late, you'd hear him spewing up in the toilet and then he'd crash into bed. I hoped he would either come home early or come home late. I didn't like the in-between bits.'

Colleagues from those days looked back on the trade without attaching a lot of glamour to it. Their tone was flat, resigned, vaguely ashamed. 'Alcohol was an ever-present part of journalism,' said Gavin Ellis. 'I mean I had issues with alcohol till I stopped drinking … The pub was a second office for many journalists.' Ex-journo John McCaulay remembered the hours: 'We'd start work at 8, go till 11 when the pubs opened, and knock off again at half-past 2. The Occidental was the place.' Ex-journo Bruce Morris dragged me into the bar, so to speak, in his memoir. He said: 'Journalism is full of alcoholics, and all of us drink too much – you probably knew better than I. No one sits in judgment on that, and perhaps we should. I wrote a note to Rachel and said, "I look back now and regret we didn't do anything about it." We didn't see it as an illness, we just saw him as another pisshead journo.'

Claudia saw him as just another violent and disturbed pisshead husband coming home after dark with a head full of beer and rage and the need to create the one thing he was best at: damage. 'It wasn't great,' she said. 'He became more and more violent and aggressive as the alcoholism got worse ... He was obnoxious to Rachel. Physical abuse. Psychological abuse. And the other abuse. That was the absolute last straw once she told me what had happened. I couldn't stand to be in the same room as him. I'd have pushed him face-down in that ditch,' she said, meaning the Auckland Domain on the Friday night of his lonely death.

She told stories too heinous to repeat. I asked her, 'What were his good qualities?' She said, 'I don't think I could come up with anything.' But there was a pause, and the sound of her footsteps as she walked around watering her plants, and she said, 'He was a highly intelligent person. I think that's what attracted me in the first place. But it didn't stop him being a nasty person. He used to say the family was dragging along on his coat-tails.'

He'd had it all going for him. At school he was Dux, good-looking, fast ('Built like a sprinter,' said his schoolmate Peter Warlow); as a young man, he had a university education, a steady job, was raising a family, and he had ideas on how to get ahead. It was the ideas that did for him. He was the kind of man who feels cheated by life – and he had been cheated, his mother throwing him out of the house like an unwanted chattel – and busily, angrily sets his mind to getting even. Some people fight their way to the top; with no less energy and wild ambition, Mason crashed and burned his way to the bottom.

* * *

228

His first failed venture was a macadamia farm in Ōkaihau, in the Bay of Islands. The family moved from Auckland and Mason got to work. 'Murray had done a lot of research beforehand,' said his daughter. 'This was going to be his big money-making scheme.' John McCaulay was impressed when Mason told him about it. He said, 'He was ahead of his time, really. He did soil analysis and developed a concept to use unproductive land, in gulleys and creeks.' Thousands of macadamia plants were put in. Money was growing on trees. It couldn't fail. Rachel: 'But then something went wrong, and we were pretty much frogmarched off the property.' Claudia: 'I never did find out what he had done that bust the whole thing open. We had to move out.'

Sue McCauley, the author who wrote one of the most famous novels in twentieth-century New Zealand literature, *Other Halves*, was housesitting for the Masons at the exact moment it went bust. Her partner Pat – a younger Māori man; their scandalous romance was the subject of *Other Halves* – worked on the farm. They liked the Masons; Murray was quiet, Claudia was a character, 'wacky and hilarious', who gave animals the run of the house, including chickens and a rat called Ratty. 'Claudia asked me to take Ratty to the vet because he was ailing, and the vet said, "Oh, yes, Ratty's come in a few times."'

She took up the story of the day the macadamia experiment came to a sudden halt. 'It was horrifying, actually. They'd gone on holiday and we stayed in their house – Claudia had copious animals that needed feeding. Murray's business partners arrived. They pulled Pat aside, and said, "Murray's no longer your boss. We're kicking him out."

'And Pat said, "Does Murray know this?"

'And they said, "No, you can tell him."

'And he said, "No, I'm not going to tell him." So we actually moved out a day or so before they were coming back. We didn't want to be there and confront them with this information. We never did know why it happened. It was awful. They had to get out of the house and find a place to rent. It was very strange. The partners simply said, "We've voted him out. He's no longer running this place." And that was that.'

Claudia and Rachel were never told why. Mason had no choice but to pack up and leave – and then jump into his next big adventure, when he bought the *Waimarino Weekly* newspaper in Raetihi, that small, appropriately gothic town on the cold and exposed volcanic plateau. Again, the family were uprooted; again, it ended in disaster.

I spoke with Nancy Anderson, who sold the paper to Mason. She claimed: 'On the day he was supposed to pay us, he took off to Nelson in the car – we supplied him with a car. We didn't know where he was. Couldn't find out anything. He came back a couple of days later and said he didn't have enough money to pay us. We ended up taking him to court … It was a really good profitable business when we sold it. But he drove it downhill in six months.'

I think it would be fair to describe Anderson as somewhat bitter. She said she'd read a story about Mason's death. 'I sent it to the kids, and they all just laughed.'

Raetihi was the beginning of the end for Mason's life with his family. It stopped there, and so did the newspaper. 'It got into bad financial strife, and he couldn't drag it back again,' said Rachel. 'He even had a donations bucket on the desk to try and keep it alive. The owners went from friendly to snaky and Murray started to disappear for long periods of time.

'He'd come back, and wreak havoc, argue, throw things – one night he held a knife at my throat. He'd done that when I was a kid; I woke up and there he was with a carving knife. But this night [in Raetihi], we were on either side of the ironing board, and I had the iron. He backed off.'

They lived in a 'hovel', Rachel said, next to the caryard made famous in the film *Smash Palace*. They froze, got by on a pittance; the walls started moving in. Claudia said, 'It was bleak, and his moods got worse and worse. He left, and we moved into the vicarage. I went to get drawings from the bank, and they came out and said, "I'm sorry, you can't have anything." We were in massive arrears. I can remember how my knees felt like buckling. It was the most horrible sensation. You've basically got nothing. We'd been living on a pittance for quite a while, and there were four children and no food. And then after he shot through, the bailiffs and the police and the traffic cops all came down to the property and confiscated our two vehicles. That was humiliating, this procession of our two cars going up the main street of Raetihi. I got offered a job doing housework and paid off the arrears and got the car back.'

I said, 'You hero!'

She said, 'I had to get on with it. But I do recall applying for family assistance. You had to line up in front of everyone at the Post Office to have an appointment with the social welfare office. I had to take bills to show how much electricity we used, that sort of thing, and that I spent ten dollars on petrol. Well, this young man, he'd come in from Taihape, he looked at me, and said, "Do you have a receipt?" And, honestly, I'd never felt so miserable and put-down and demoralised. I just went home and cried. I cried all the way home. It was a miserable time, but life was better without him in the family.'

There had been another business flop – more of a farce, really. Rachel: 'He was going to make his millions by growing potatoes.' Mason planted 3 acres and designed the perfect potato-harvester. But the equipment didn't work, and the family had to pull out 3 acres of potatoes by hand. 'He also hadn't worked out how he would market these potatoes. In the end we had a mound of rotting potatoes in the back yard.'

The macadamia king, the newspaper tycoon, the potato king – years later, when he made his last stand, fighting for life in the Auckland Domain, he was found the next day with no proof of address.

* * *

Accrington 1 Charlton Athletic 1

If he hadn't died in such a tragic and mysterious manner, if he'd just lived out the rest of his days in the same quiet, undetected way he'd come to perfect; there'd be no story, no investigation, no digging. I was always aware there was something unseemly about my efforts to uncover his curious life. He didn't deserve it. He was just a nice old man going about his business, and he was so well-liked, too, so admired and respected; even his closest friends were surprised at the turn-out for his wake at The Albion. But he wouldn't have drawn such a big crowd if he'd gone quietly. The mourners were shaken by the nature of his death. They, too, were attracted by its tragic and mysterious manner.

It was a dark and stormy night. No, really; it was pouring with rain, cold as Hell, and Mason set out from The Albion at about midnight. He'd settled in for the evening in his usual spot when it was cold: in front of the gas fire.

'A funny story about that fireplace,' said Ivan Davis, The Albion's former barman. 'Murray came in one night and it was a bloody cold night. It was freezing. Murray was like, "Do you know how to light that thing?"

'I said, "I've got no idea, man, but I'll give it a go." So I went over there and I found the ignition alright. I was fiddling with it for bloody ages. I couldn't smell gas, and then I thought, "What if I just push it in and turn?"

'And then BOOM!, I went flying backwards. Singed my eyebrows, lucky I didn't get third-degree burns. Murray just stood there with a cheeky little grin on his face, and said, "Well, you got it going, Ivan."'

He'd sit back on the couch by the fire and watch sport on the TV screen above the fireplace. He loved his sports, especially cricket. Ivan said, 'He knew past, present, you name it. Past players, past coaches, he knew them all.'

Talking about the friend who he'd lost made Davis cling to good times, good memories. He said, 'I think the best time I ever had with Murray was his last birthday: twenty-seventh of December. We had such a good day. We met at The Albion; Peter Warlow was there, and another mate from Blockhouse Bay. We had a catch-up, and the cricket was on. There was one Ashes test on in Australia, and the Black Caps were playing some other game. Murray was just in his element, between two TVs, watching the cricket. Oh, it was a fantastic day.'

He always carried an umbrella. He needed it that night, with the rain lashing down as he said his farewells and set off into the night. His son Davin later followed his father's likely route. Down

Wellesley Street West and on to Queen Street, then up the rise into Wellesley Street East, past AUT to Symonds Street, then a clever turn onto a walking track from St Paul's Church and beneath Wellesley Street, emerging onto Grafton Road and then across Stanley Street – and, finally, into the darkness of the trees and bush of the Domain.

I followed that route, too. It's a long walk just to get that far. Naturally I did it in the daytime. It's very pretty to slip inside the Domain and follow the track that Mason walked – a loner, an ex, who went his own way; his last steps were taken on Lovers' Walk. Steps lead onto the track. A nice, very shallow creek flows beside it. Sunlight winked on the water.

But Mason was there at night when it was pitch-black, and freezing cold, and the ground was wet, and the likeliest explanation is that he slipped and fell down the bank and into the creek. He tried to crawl back up the bank, but couldn't get a hold. He crawled along the creek and beneath a small bridge. He got to the other side of the bridge. The water would have been up, because of the rain, but probably not very deep. It would certainly have been extremely cold, and dark, and loud with wind – no one would have heard him if he cried for help. His torch was shining when they found him lying face-down in the creek. It was held tight in his hands.

'I've been there,' said Ivan Davis. 'It was hard. But I needed closure. You know, when I was told he was found in a creek, I thought of the Whau River. But it was just a little bit of water. Was he face-down in mud? I wanted to find out.'

He went there with a mate for support. I'd walked it the morning before I interviewed him; together we traced our movements, and Mason's last moments.

'Yeah. So, Lovers' Walk. He's walked down there. He's stepped a little bit to the left and gone down to where the creek is. You can see where he's taken out a sapling on the way down. He's tried to stop himself with his umbrella. You could see the marks where he's dug it in.

'He's tried to pull himself up. But, shit, he's seventy-six years old and he just can't get up. He's got his torch and he's gone under the bridge, crawled along under there, and tried to get himself to where the track was lower. But he couldn't make it. And they found him with his fists clenched around the torch. When they prised his hands open, his torch was still shining.

'I said to my mate, "Come whatever, Murray's time was up."

'He said, "What do you mean by that?"

'And I said, "He's a fragile man, you know, and it's a shitty night, he's got wet, he's lost a lot of heat." It just needed one person to be walking that way. But it was after midnight. His time was up.'

Doncaster 0 Peterborough 0

* * *

Why was he in the Domain, on an unlit dirt track on a wet, filthy night, and where the hell was he going? 'Well, he was going ... somewhere,' said his drinking friend Michael Fenwick. 'And that is the mystery.' No one to this day knows where he was headed. Someone said he had a room in Kingsland. Someone thought Eden Terrace. His school friend Peter Warlow was convinced it was Parnell: 'He used to always go through the Domain. He took a bit of a detour the night it happened. He was definitely headed for home. I'm sure it was in Parnell ...'

235

Mason was found without any proof of address, or a set of keys. It's possible he was sleeping rough, but it doesn't add up: Mason didn't smell, his clothes were clean, he looked after himself. Also, he was hardly penniless. 'He always had money on him,' said Albion bar manager Julie Hanson. 'He would easy spend at least seventy dollars a day here.'

His entire manner and way of being was independent, self-contained. Ever since he left his family, his MO was bedsits and rooms in boarding houses. 'Dad quite liked his bedsits,' said his son Davin. 'I can remember after Mum and Dad split up, we'd visit him in Wellington, my brother and I, but we couldn't stay with him because he'd just have a room. I was told he had a place like that in Parnell.' In recent years, John McCaulay remembered dropping him off at a concrete block of flats in Newmarket, and another time Mason told him he was boarding in Mt Roskill. He also lived on Waiheke Island.

The only mention anyone made of a partner was when Sue McCauley told a strange story about him. She and her husband Pat were living in the Wairarapa, in the late 1980s, when they ran into Mason. She said, 'He came to stay with an apparent woman who drank quite a lot. I remember she took beer off to bed so she'd have a bottle there to drink first thing in the morning. She wore high heels all around the place; we were sort of semi-rural and she was there in stilettos. Later we visited them in Wellington, and this person showed me her linen cupboard, which she said was her pride and joy, and what a pleasure it was to run around after Murray.

'I said to Pat on the way home, "No woman talks like that. That is not a woman."

'And he said, "Well I knew that from the moment I first saw her. She's a man."'

He moved back to Auckland sometime in the 1990s, friends thought, and resumed subbing at the *Herald*. When Ivan Davis met him in 2002, Mason was working as a cleaner at The Albion. His real occupation – his mission, his purpose – was the strict itinerary he kept of drinks and watching sport at The Albion, The Right Track, Spitting Feathers, QT and a few select other pubs, in between his regular hours of study at Auckland Central Library, where he put pen to paper and made copious notes. These last 20 years of his life were his halcyon years. He always had money for a drink. He sat at the end of the bar and was never short of company. 'He was a good man. A very intellectual, very nice man. It was nice to have known him,' said Karl Watkins, who drank with him at The Albion. 'He could talk to people from all different walks of life. He didn't care if you were a doctor or a lawyer or you were homeless; he always treated people with respect. He was one of those old-school people with manners. He didn't like swearing in front of women. He thought that was bad form.'

There was that Mason, the one who was wonderful with children. Ivan Davis said, 'He loved reading, and my daughter, who is nine and coming up to ten, she loves reading as well, and Murray would say, "Please don't let that stop. Keep her reading. It's very, very good for her." For her birthday last year he gave her a card and twenty-five dollars, and said to me, "Make sure she buys a good book." She used to call him Old Man Murray.' He was Uncle Murray to John McCaulay's kids: 'He'd read my daughter a story and the room would go all silent, and I'd go in and Murray would be sound asleep on her bed. He used to really love kids.'

And there was that other Mason, from an earlier time, who was violent with his wife, and his daughter said had sexually abused her.

Rachel Wise and her mother, Claudia, hated Mason. They had good reason to hate Mason. But the way he died – that was something else again, something that demanded a reckoning. 'It was awful,' Rachel said. 'Awful. When they rolled him over, because he was face-down, he had a torch clutched in his hands, and it was still going – that turned my monster into a sad little old man, who died cold and alone and unloved in a creek in Auckland Domain. Even my mother, once she got over thinking it was wonderful, ended up in buckets of tears and said, "He was cold. I can't bear to think of him cold and alone."'

The last time they had anything to do with him was at Christmas 1987. The marriage had split up, but Mason begged to come home and see his family at Christmas. He spent most of the day standing by himself out by the back fence, gazing down the paddock: 'He was like the spectre at the feast,' said Claudia. She'd moved home to Hawke's Bay by then. Once or twice Mason drove up from Wellington and left long, raving letters thrown over the front gate – 'I'd find all these cigarette butts outside the gate, like he'd been standing there for some time; that was scary' – but she never saw him. The first she heard of him after that was when the police phoned to tell her that he was dead.

According to quite a few of his friends, Mason had planned to visit Claudia, Rachel and his son Davin in the Hawke's Bay in 2019. He also made casual mention that he'd already built bridges with his estranged family, and as such planned to travel there by bicycle. John McCaulay: 'The last time I saw him, he'd been in touch with his family, and the plan was to bike down to Wellington and then bike to Waipawa and spend Christmas with his family. He was delighted.' Ivan Davis heard much the same story. 'There was talk of doing a bike ride to see them.'

There were two problems with his plan. One, the likelihood of Mason, at his age, attempting the ride was somewhat … ambitious. I asked Davis, 'Do you think he could have done it?'

He said, 'To be honest, no.'

The other problem was the veracity of his claim. 'Not long before he passed away, he got in contact with his boy,' said Peter Warlow. 'They got very, very close.'

I said, 'Did Murray tell you that?'

'Yes,' he said.

But he hadn't been in contact with Davin. He hadn't spoken to Claudia or Rachel. There was no reunion that anyone knew about, no emotional return of the prodigal ex-husband and ex-father. He might not have been telling stories he knew to be false. He might have been telling stories he wanted to be true. His friends believed him; Mason seemed to, as well. Police gave Davin Mason his father's possessions when his body was found. They included a 3B1 Warwick notebook. Mason had written a to-do list, which included: *Buy new phone and set up … Pack books in storage. Get prescription from doctor … Plan possible HB [Hawkes Bay] trip.*

Davin said, 'He was looking at building those bridges. He wanted to come back here. Well, he's right here, actually. He's sitting on my mantelpiece in front of me. So in a roundabout way he's come home.'

I asked about what other papers or notebooks Mason had on him when he died. He said there were pages and pages of lined A4 paper. He'd had to dry them out. They'd got wet in the rain that night and in the little creek in the Domain.

His father made a record of every book he'd read from 2009 to 2019. He numbered each book as he went along and got to 570. They included classics such as *The Adventures of Tom Sawyer* by

Mark Twain and *Our Man in Havana* by Graham Greene, modern New Zealand novels such as *A Briefcase, Two Pies and a Penthouse* by Brannavan Gnanalingam, and a lot of sports books.

There were yet more pages of A4. In small, neat handwriting, Mason had recorded English football results. Page after page, the teams in blue biro, the dates in red: this is what he'd been working on at the Auckland Central Library. This was his supposed thesis, his epic and enduring project.

Plymouth 1 Wycombe 1
Rochdale 0 Barnsley 4
Scunthorpe 0 Fleetwood 5

In all the pages that Davin photographed and emailed to me, there's not a single spelling mistake. Mason, the reporter who only had to write things once; Mason, the journalist who went to work to record the words and actions of others; Mason, the sub who took pride in accuracy, with his love of statistics and facts, the beautiful tidiness of them, the way they were impervious to the mess and loose ends of the life people lead behind closed doors. Left alone, a ghost from a past he abandoned, he could bend his back to an important and consuming task for countless hours in a quiet nook in the library.

Peterborough 1 Doncaster 1
Portsmouth 3 Plymouth 0
Shrewsbury 1 Bristol Rovers 1

He'd come to a peace in his final years. He had friends who loved him. He had his itinerary, his routines. He knew where he was at all times, but no one else knew – to others, he was always passing through, always on the move. He's managed to keep his destination that night in the Domain a secret.

Davin thought he might have come close to solving the mystery. Among Mason's possessions was a key to a storage locker on Waiheke Island. The combination was in a notebook.

He said, 'I'd been planning to get up there and clear it out and was hoping to find a bit of information there. That was the only thing that could connect him to where he lived or whether he was living anywhere.'

He left a pause. I was on the edge of my seat. And then he said, 'But three weeks ago, it burnt down. The storage locker on Waiheke Island burnt down. It burnt down.' He kept repeating it in disbelief. 'I got a phone call from the manager and he said, "It burnt down and nothing's been saved. Everything is lost." So we don't know what was in it.'

It was his final mystery. His friend Michael Fenwick had said of him, 'If he didn't want you to find him, then good luck.' Even in death, he simply disappeared. But it was the same when he was a small child: he was made to disappear, ripped away from his family, placed elsewhere.

His brother Richard showed up at the wake at The Albion. Davin had found out about his father's past. 'Murray Edward Wyatt was Dad's name,' he said. 'Murray Edward Wyatt, born December 27, 1942, at Takapau.' Mason wasn't even his real name. He'd gone through his entire life as someone else.

Chapter 12

The redemption of Grace Millane: Sentencing Kempson

A few days before Kempson was due to be sentenced at the High Court of Auckland for the murder of Grace Millane, I ran into Crown prosecutor Robin McCoubrey. It was nice to see him. He spoke half-English, half-Kiwi – he emigrated to New Zealand from London in 2008 – and you never knew which vowels he was going to come out with next. We asked each other if we'd had a nice summer, and we both confirmed that we had. McCoubrey is a stout fellow with a smooth face. He had a very big sandwich in his hand and was keen to sit down and fill his face with it. I said, 'Well, see you Friday.' He nodded. Of course he knew what I meant. And then I said, 'I'm looking forward to hearing Simon Moore's judgment. He's going to *sing*.'

McCoubrey laughed, and said, 'I think that's exactly the right word.'

Friday came, and Justice Moore sang an aria, a dark, sombre 6,154-word composition in major and minor keys that completed his outstanding work on the Millane trial and brought a desperately sad and wretched story to an end. 'Please stand,' he told Kempson. 'You appear before me to be sentenced for the murder of Grace Emmie Rose Millane.' He sentenced him to 17 years without parole. 'Stand down,' he said. Kempson was taken away; he wore the same dark suit and white open-necked shirt he wore at the trial, had the same dumb, blameless face, with dark rings under his eyes and no hope for any redemption or mercy in his eyes. The public gallery was full. The press benches were full – I sat in the jury box with a few photographers. Everyone stared at Kempson. But there was nothing to see. A man of 27, tall, dark-haired, no one you'd notice in a crowd, although he was quite handsome, and was widely considered at school, at Aotea College in Wellington, as 'skux', the compliment that meant hot. He got the girls. He got Grace.

Summer had relaxed the courtroom. People chatted and laughed before proceedings began at 9am. Video screens were set up in preparation for Millane's family to read their victim impact reports from their home in Essex; when I walked in, Millane's mother was on the screen, dandling her grandson in front of the camera. But in obedience to some invisible sign, the courtroom abruptly fell silent about five minutes before Justice Moore was due to appear. It was just like old times. The Millane trial was the quietest I've ever witnessed, and here was that same tense and awed holding of breath.

It remained suspended in silence as the clock ticked towards 9am. And then Justice Moore arrived, bowed deep from the waist, and took his seat. He'd had a haircut. His splendid white bouffant was settled closer to his head. Kempson stood with his hands clasped in front of him. His father sat in the public gallery. No one could comprehend or begin to imagine the grief and loss felt by Millane's family; no one could even guess the broad outline, or have the faintest idea, of the particular deep shame felt by Kempson's father.

Millane's brother, sister-in-law and mother each read their reports, and each broke down. I made a recording of the sentencing and afterwards, listening back to it, I could barely make out any language. It was all incoherent wailings and great sobs of grief. But I could make out one word, repeated over and over. The reports were all addressed to Kempson. They were like letters. It was very personal. 'You,' they said. 'You.' The word came out like spit, like a little parcel of hatred. 'I torment myself over what *you* did to my Grace,' said Gillian Millane. 'The terror and pain she must have experienced at *your* hands.' She wished that she had been able to protect her daughter. She wished that as a mother she had saved her life. 'I should have been there, but she died terrified and alone in a room with *you*.'

Who were they talking about? Who even was Kempson? So little was known about him; a few details emerged at sentencing. Moore referred to his pre-sentence report, which mentioned his 'complex needs', and that a psychologist would have to 'assess a suitable treatment plan while you are in prison'. There was a glimpse into his past: 'The report writer has concluded that your childhood and upbringing has been affected by various traumatic influences which have impacted on your transition to adulthood and your ability to make good decisions and the right decisions. There may be, as the pre-sentence report writer also touched on, some mental health issues. But none has been diagnosed.

'I accept that you had a volatile upbringing and that may well have influenced the person you are today. It may well have led you to lie to those you wanted to impress by pretending you were a man of affluence and social standing. In fact that appears to have been your modus operandi when attempting to impress the women you met. But I struggle to see the connection between that presentation,' he said, 'and what led you to strangle Ms Millane to death.'

And then Moore sang the first of his two long and sustained tragedies. Much of it reads like hard-boiled crime fiction. Sentences slam shut like doors. He began with the rendezvous at Sky City – the Christmas tree, the humid evening – and ended with Kempson ambling through Albert Park beneath the crimson pohutakawa. The following is in his own words.

* * *

I turn to the facts.

Ms Millane was 21 when she arrived in Auckland on 20 November 2018. She grew up in Essex. She was the youngest of three children. She graduated from the University of Lincoln in September 2018 with a degree in advertising and marketing. As with so many young people in her position she decided to spend a year travelling the world before returning home in about June 2019 for a family wedding.

On 26 October 2018 she flew out of Heathrow bound for Lima, Peru. After a month or so travelling in South America she arrived, as planned, in Auckland. Almost daily she was in touch with her family and friends. It was obvious to them that she was thoroughly enjoying herself.

Ms Millane used the dating application, Tinder. She was travelling alone and, unsurprisingly, wanted to meet others.

On Friday, 31 November 2018 she matched you on Tinder. The following day, which was Saturday, 1 December 2018, you messaged her and agreed to meet up in Auckland's CBD for a

245

drink. You met outside Sky City. Your meeting was captured on CCTV. It was there that Ms Millane sent her parents a photograph of the Christmas decorations set out on the forecourt. That would be the last communication the Millanes would have from their daughter who was to celebrate her 22nd birthday the next day.

The time was about 5.45 pm. From that moment until approximately 9.40 pm, when the CCTV picked up Ms Millane following you out of the lift onto the third floor of the City Life Apartments where you were then living, most of your movements were captured on CCTV.

You and Ms Millane visited a number of bars over the next four hours or so. Neither of you had any food during that time and judging by the till receipts and invoices a good deal of alcohol was consumed. It is fair to say you both must have been drunk. How drunk is difficult to gauge. But certainly not so drunk either of you seemed unsteady on your feet.

Your last stop was the Blue Stone Room behind the City Life Apartments. The CCTV footage shows you both were plainly enjoying each other's company. At one point Ms Millane messaged her close friend, Ameena Ashcroft. She told Ms Ashcroft that she was on a date with the manager of an oil company who lived in a hotel. This was followed by the message, 'cocktails all round' and then a reference to her birthday the next day and getting 'smashed'. She also told her friend she clicked so well with you. That was the last message she ever sent.

Exactly what happened from the moment Ms Millane first stepped into Apartment 308 we will never know. Only two people were witness to those events and one is not alive to tell us. The jury had only the account you gave the Police in your second interview on 8 December 2018. By their verdict they plainly rejected your claim of consensual sexual activity gone wrong. That is unsurprising given not only the elaborate and detailed lies you told in your first interview, but also the patent untruths which peppered the second.

So what happened? In your second interview, conducted in the presence of counsel two days after the first, you gave a reasonably detailed version of what you said happened. This was the version which was promoted at trial as the true account despite containing demonstrable lies. In several respects you tailored your story so that it would match not only what you already knew of the Police investigation, such as your movements captured by CCTV, but also what you knew the Police would likely uncover. For example you would have known that the post mortem would probably reveal that Ms Millane had a blood nose which bled into the carpet. You knew the Police would find out where you went the next day, what you bought to do the clean-up and how you disposed of Ms Millane's body. You insisted that Ms Millane's death was some terrible accident arising out of a casual, consensual, sexual encounter involving manual strangulation. You told the Police that she was the initiator and that you were 'new to all that sort of stuff'. I accept that at some point you and Ms Millane must have discussed BDSM practices but any claim that this was somehow novel to you runs contrary to the evidence the jury heard from other women you had met on Tinder; women you told about your sexual preferences, including your liking for rough sex and possibly strangulation.

You also told the Police that you and Ms Millane took intimate photographs of each other … I am satisfied that the photographs found on your phone were taken after you killed her. I am satisfied you disclosed that detail because you knew the Police would have your phone and discover those photographs. You also knew Ms Millane's phone could never be checked because you had thrown it away three days earlier. You did not tell the Police about the pornographic searches you made before and after you took the photographs.

In your interview you said that because you were sweating you went to have a shower. Improbably you said you fell asleep in the shower. When you awoke you went back to your bed. The room was dark. You said you assumed Ms Millane had left. It was only in the morning that you discovered her lying lifeless on the floor. You said you panicked. You said you didn't know what to do.

But you didn't ring an ambulance. You didn't call the Police which, had this been the tragic accident you insisted it was, would be expected. Instead, you embarked on a well-planned, sustained and co-ordinated course of conduct in an attempt to conceal any evidence of what had happened in your room. For example, just after 6.00 am you used your phone to search for 'car hire Auckland'. Then you searched for 'large bags near me'. Shortly afterwards you tellingly searched for 'rigor mortis'.

Then, just before 8.00 am, you messaged 'M' [name permanently suppressed]. You had matched her on Tinder a couple of weeks before. You sent her a message which read, 'Morning, how are you today?'. Then you sent an identical message to another young woman you had met a month before.

You and 'M' agreed to meet later that day in a Ponsonby bar. Then you made more searches on your phone. You searched for carpet cleaner, rug doctors and rigor mortis (again). You searched for large bags.

You also searched for 'time in London' no doubt because you knew it was Ms Millane's birthday and that it wouldn't be long before her family became concerned at her uncharacteristic silence and would sound the alarm (which is just what they did).

The jury saw the CCTV footage of you at The Warehouse in Elliott Street checking out the suitcases before buying one and taking it back to your apartment. The jury also saw your movements at Countdown buying cleaning equipment. Then you took a taxi to pick up the rental car which you would later use to transport Ms Millane's body to the Waitakeres.

At no point in this sequence is the faintest impression given that you were a man in a hurry or that you were a man panicking. Indeed, the very opposite is the case because as I mentioned, later that day you were socialising with 'M' at the Ponsonby bar. It was at that bar you told her the story about your friend who had been charged with manslaughter after a consensual strangling had gone wrong and how full the Waitakeres are with bodies … We will never know why you said those things.

Mr Brookie points out that the date with 'M' had been arranged the previous week and that maintaining the meeting in an attempt to continue a semblance of normality is not unusual. Whatever the reason, what cannot be overlooked is that while you and 'M' were together, Ms Millane's body was back in your room.

After you and 'M' parted company you returned to your apartment before heading over to Countdown again, this time to hire a Rug Doctor to clean the carpet.

Later that evening you squeezed Ms Millane's body inside the suitcase, wheeled it out to the car and placed it in the boot.

Early the next morning, which was Monday, 3 December 2018, you drove out to Kumeu where you bought a shovel before heading into the Waitakere Ranges and burying Ms Millane in a shallow grave which you attempted to conceal under foliage and fern fronds.

Then you went to The Warehouse at St Lukes and bought an identical suitcase, an action plainly designed to put the Police off your trail. You knew they would find out you had bought a suitcase from The Warehouse early on Sunday morning. You needed a duplicate, but not from the same shop. It needed to be bought from somewhere you thought the Police wouldn't look. In fact, in your first interview with the Police, you made reference to the suitcase claiming you had bought it to move personal items.

Then you went to a car cleaning booth. You washed the car and left the shovel there.

Your final act in this sequence was dumping Ms Millane's personal effects including her phone in a rubbish bin in Albert Park. They have not been recovered.

So those are the facts.

* * *

So all that remained was to determine the exact length of time Kempson ought to rot in jail. Crown prosecutor Brian Dickey was invited to address the court. There are people who affect a casual demeanour, and then there are people like Dickey who will likely have a casual demeanour on his deathbed. It comes naturally to him. He plunged his hands in his pockets and said he didn't really have much to add to his extensive written submissions to Justice Moore, but that it wouldn't hurt for him to say in open court that he was seeking a minimum of 17 years' imprisonment.

And then Dickey quoted a section of the Sentencing Act which is seldom used in New Zealand criminal law because of its extreme nature: section 104(1)(e). It was the (e) that did all the heavy lifting; it was the (e) that peered out from the shadows. It stated that a minimum of 17 years' imprisonment was required 'if the murder was committed with a high level of brutality, cruelty, depravity, or callousness'.

Brutality, cruelty, depravity, callousness: strange to see the terms for violent barbarism quietly enshrined in law. Dickey briefly reminded the court of the special brutality and cruelty required to strangle Grace Millane to death. And then Dickey briefly reminded the court of the special depravity and callousness of the way in which her body had been disposed. Brutality, cruelty, depravity, callousness: section 104(1)(e) was reserved for behaviour on a cold and distant shore. Kempson had stood on that shore. It was as though section 104(1)(e) was made for him, that it had been waiting for him to slouch towards it.

Dickey's address ('depravity', etc) made good copy. He was duly quoted in every story that appeared after the sentencing, and every story made mention of his remark that Kempson had 'eroticised' the death of Grace Millane by taking intimate photographs of her body after he had murdered her. Ian Brookie, Kempson's lawyer, said that claim was wrong. Kempson insisted that he photographs were taken when she was alive. But I didn't see that reported. I saw hardly anything Brookie said in his address – mitigating factors, comparable cases, general remarks ('This is a court of law, not a popularity contest') – that was quoted.

And nor did I see any report which carried an extraordinary speech that Justice Moore gave after he had sentenced Kempson to jail. In journalese, it qualified as an outburst; in English, it went against prevailing thought, it held to a standard, it constituted an attack.

251

'Mr Brookie,' Justice Moore said. Brookie looked a bit startled. He got to his feet.

Moore said, 'While the defence of consent did not persuade the jury to acquit, it needs to be said that it was entirely proper of you to have raised that defence. You have been publicly criticised, along with your colleagues, in social media and other media forums for doing so. And that is wrong.

'And it reveals a concerning misunderstanding of the duties of defence counsel in criminal cases. We are blessed to live in this free and democratic society. When people are charged with criminal offences they are not only entitled to a fair trial, but in this country, they will receive a fair trial. That is guaranteed under our Bill of Rights Act. Anything less, no matter how repugnant the offending, will dangerously erode our precious system of justice. Everyone must be presumed innocent until they are proven guilty beyond reasonable doubt.

'It is your duty and the duty of those who also represented Mr Kempson to do what you did in the defence of your client. You ran the defence in a strong and competent fashion that the courts in this country would expect of you.'

He straightened some papers, and said, 'I shall retire.' And they were the last words heard in the High Court of Auckland in the matter of Kempson.

But had anyone been listening to his speech or taking note? It could easily have blown up in his face. It was a provocation, and it rejected feminist critique of the consent defence: 'And that is wrong.' His speech was a rallying cry on behalf of the status quo, and maintained the principle of the presumption of innocence. But was Justice Moore wrong? Was he out of line, was he misreading or patronising the very serious, very passionate opposition to the consent defence?

Not long after sentencing, the UK government announced it would consider how it could curb the same 'rough sex' defence used in Kempson's trial. A campaign group called We Can't Consent To This revealed that 30 women and girls had been killed in what was claimed to have been consensual violent sexual activity.

But Justice Moore's passionate little speech went no further. No one paid it any mind. It didn't fit the narrative.

* * *

The narrative of Kempson was narrow, predictable, and it didn't go anywhere near telling the full story of who he was and how he had ended up adrift, living at CityLife, with no job and seemingly no prospects, with only fabrications and delusions of grandeur to go on, and his looks. Kempson's narrative was set out and ready to go as soon as he was found guilty at his trial: the only acceptable version of Kempson was of a man who was and always had been manifestly evil.

Journalists had found a few people who knew Kempson. No one had a good word to say about him. He was a loser who didn't have a job. He had been asked to leave a share flat because he was so creepy and weird. He lied, compulsively.

'He maintains his innocence,' said Brookie at sentencing, but who cared? The jury had declared his guilt. It rejected Brookie's defence that 'her death resulted from an impulsive act borne of poor judgement and risk-taking, exacerbated by alcohol', as Justice Moore summarised it. The verdict was absolute. There could no longer be any question of innocence. The issue was punishment.

Dickey had spoken for five minutes; Brookie spoke for twenty. He came up with a very nice euphemism for the things Kempson did to Grace after he killed her: 'the post-death conduct'. He noted the absence of premeditation. He pointed out the absence of a weapon. He argued that there was no evidence of a sustained violent assault: 'Beyond the pressure to the neck,' he said, 'there is no attack.' But there was no getting beyond the pressure to the neck, because the pressure to the neck was what killed her.

He proposed that a starting point for Kempson's sentence should be 12 years. Twelve, he said, was 'appropriate'. Seventeen years, he said, was 'over-pitching'. He referred to comparable cases – a father who killed his son after it was discovered he'd spent the father's life savings, a man who killed his ex-partner with a baseball bat and dismembered her body, a man who lured a woman to his address and killed her after a sustained depraved attack – which he described as somehow 'far worse'. The killers had all received less than a 17-year sentence. 'This is not a case involving a high degree of brutality, cruelty, depravity, or callousness,' he said; 'no more than any other murder case.' Justice Moore later paraphrased Brookie, thus: 'He says that compared with other cases this is not one out of the ordinary.'

But the killing of Grace Millane wasn't just another murder. It *was* one out of the ordinary. There was the killing itself, the intimacy of it, the suffering it caused, the duration of an agony – the blood nose, the loss of consciousness – and the decision to continue strangling her while she lay beneath him, inert, naked, literally defenceless. And then there was, as Brookie tried to euphemise it, 'the post-death conduct'. The watching of porn while she lay dead on the floor. The little pathetic errands to buy a suitcase and stain-remover and a rental car. Her body half-in, half-out of a suitcase bought from The Warehouse while he went out on a date in a Ponsonby bar. The shovel. The drive to the Waitākere Ranges. Christmas 2018, beautiful summer weather, and her body dumped by the roadside in a shallow grave.

Everything about it was a section 104(1)(e). Everything about it was 17 years without parole. Nothing about it inspired clemency. The fact that he appeared as a first offender was a vast and fatuous irrelevance. Justice Moore: 'As for your previous relative youth and good character, quite frankly given the enormity of your offending I can give those factors little or no weight … I can find no factors shifting my view of your culpability or justifying any leniency.' His sentencing notes referred to just about the only other person in New Zealand criminal history who stood on that same barren shore as Kempson, and occupied the same foul mess of brutality, cruelty, depravity or callousness: Clayton Weatherston.

Justice Moore reached back into history for a definition of callousness. He was quoting the nineteenth-century theologian Richard Bentley when he said, 'Callousness does not require prolonged activity. It involves a lack of feeling, empathy and sensibility, once colourfully described as a "numbness of the soul".' Bentley prefaced that colourful description by calling such men 'destitute of common sense'. Kempson, through the centuries; Kempson, excoriated.

And then Justice Moore sang the second of his two long and sustained tragedies. The language changed. The sentences were longer, more expansive. There was concern for balance, for accuracy. But it was no less emphatic than his opening aria and it grew darker and darker until there was no light left. It began with death and ended with burial. The following is in his own words.

It is common ground that Ms Millane was murdered by manual strangulation. In your second interview to the Police you gave a description of how you held her arms and then her throat. You gave no detail of how long you held her throat or what pressure you applied. The evidence on that point came from the pathology. At the trial there was some discussion about the four mechanisms which could cause death through manual strangulation. For a variety of reasons given by the experts, venous obstruction was regarded as the most likely. The experts said that it requires some effort to kill by manual strangulation. It cannot be achieved by the kind of gentle or low level consensual touching you suggested in your interview.

Mr Brookie points out that you may not have appreciated Ms Millane was in difficulty until it was too late, a scenario which he says is supported by the absence of defence injuries. But the jury, by its verdict, was necessarily satisfied that at the time you had your hands around Ms Millane's throat, you intended, at the very least, to cause her the sort of bodily injury which you knew was likely to cause her death and were reckless whether she died or not.

On the question of timing, both Dr Garavan and Dr Stables agreed that the 90 seconds, apparently suggested by Dr Healy as being at the lower limit of her range, was too short to cause death if the mechanism was venous congestion. Both agreed that it would take some period of sustained pressure, measured in minutes, to cause death. Dr Stables did not give a precise answer on the question of timing but Dr Garavan favoured a period of between five to ten minutes, possibly longer due to Ms Millane's youth and apparent health. In giving that range he was aware of the probability Ms Millane was intoxicated and how alcohol may have affected that timing.

It was also common ground that at some point during her strangulation Ms Millane would have lost consciousness and gone limp. When in the sequence that occurred cannot be fixed. But for her to have died it required you to have knowingly maintained sufficient pressure past that point and continued to apply that pressure until she died. Again, that is necessarily implicit in the jury's verdict. We do not know whether Ms Millane struggled but it is likely she did. Most certainly she would have been aware of what was happening to her. Your admission that she had a nose bleed and the finding of her blood at the scene supports the conclusion that her nose bled as a result of the pressure you applied to her neck. But there is also the pathological evidence. First, there was the significant and deep bruising to Ms Millane's neck. Dr Stables described it. Bruises only form while someone is alive; while their blood is circulating. The extensive and deep bruising on the left side of her neck described by Dr Stables means that Ms Millane must have been alive long enough for that bruise to form after the assault to her neck. This further supports the conclusion she died from venous congestion and that the process of strangulation occurred over time and required sustained and prolonged pressure.

Although by the time Ms Millane's body was recovered there was some decomposition, all experts were agreed that the bruising to her upper left chest, arms and elbows (by my calculation six separate bruises) was consistent with physical restraint. The bruises to the inside of her upper arms, described by Dr Stables as 'concerning', were regarded by him to be consistent with restraint injuries caused by the assailant's fingers. Dr Garavan was more equivocal on this bruising but, of course, it was Dr Stables who conducted the post-mortem and actually examined these marks. The lack of defence injuries and an absence of your DNA under Ms Millane's fingernails is also consistent with her being forcibly restrained.

I also have regard to the evidence of 'A' [name permanently suppressed] who described a sexual encounter she had with you a month before you met Ms Millane. She described being restrained against her will and violently struggling against your weight. She believed that she would die and although the mechanism of suffocation in that case was different, the parallels of restraint in a sexual context are obvious.

I agree with the Crown that manual strangulation is a particularly intimate and intimidating form of physical violence. By definition Ms Millane was at but an arm's length from you. On your account she would have been facing you although I accept the room may have been darkened at the time. However, no matter what way the mechanism of death by strangulation is viewed, it requires close physical and intimate proximity.

This is not a case where the strangulation was driven by rage or a loss of self-control. On the other hand neither is it a case where the killing was for a motive such as covering up another crime. I also accept it was not premeditated in the way of other comparable cases. Viewed in isolation, the actual mechanics leading to Ms Millane's death may not meet the threshold of a high level of brutality, cruelty, depravity or callousness when compared to other cases. But to stop there would be to view your offending in a vacuum and that I must not do.

There are other factors which need to be considered and the first of these is Ms Millane's vulnerability. There can be no doubt

258

that she was vulnerable. Certainly she was vulnerable in the sense that she was a young woman on her own travelling in a foreign land. You were a complete stranger. She trusted you. Her messages to her friend reveal that she believed the lies you told her about yourself. She trusted you enough to go into your room with you alone. That certainly placed her in a position of some vulnerability. But, in my view, what then happened after she entered your room made her particularly vulnerable.

On your admission you were both naked. You were engaged in the most personal and intimate of human activity. You are a large and powerful man. She was diminutive. On your account she asked you to hold her arms and then her throat. On your account this was happening while you were having sexual intercourse. In that position and in those circumstances, Ms Millane was particularly vulnerable. You were in a position of total physical dominance. In my view that meets the definition of particular vulnerability.

The next aggravating factor which particularly goes to callousness and depravity is your behaviour after you had killed Ms Millane.

I start with what you did immediately after Ms Millane was murdered. I find as a fact that Ms Millane must have died at some time before 1.29 am on Sunday, 2 December 2018. That is because at that time you undertook a Google search of the Waitakeres. Self-evidently, you would not have done that unless you knew that Ms Millane was dead and you were researching possible places to dump her body. That the Waitakeres were, in fact, where you concealed her supports that conclusion. It is also reinforced by the second search conducted five minutes later when you looked for 'hottest fire'.

259

But what then followed over the next three minutes provides an insight into your state of mind at that time. Ms Millane's lifeless body was with you in that room when you searched for and accessed four pornographic sites. The title to the first was extremely explicit. The next three related to teenagers and slaves.

Then, over the following three minutes, you took seven photographs of Ms Millane's dead body. These photographs were highly sexualised and grossly intrusive. In one your hand is visible. Such a violation of a victim's body is relevant to the section 104(e) assessment, even when it occurs after death.

Then, over the next quarter of an hour or so, you went back to the same porn site and searched and viewed eight further images. To borrow a phrase from the Court of Appeal, this was 'hardly the spontaneous outpouring of remorse that might point away from callousness'.

This conduct also strongly supports the statutory requirement of callousness and depravity to a high degree. It is plainly a serious aggravating factor. It was conduct closely connected in time to Ms Millane's death. It is rightly described as depraved. These were not the actions of a man in panic. Far from it. Your actions reveal a complete disregard for your victim. This conduct is inextricably connected to the manner in which the murder itself was committed. It is conduct which underscores not only the total lack of empathy you had for Ms Millane but the sense of self-entitlement, objectification and sexualisation that is reflected in other parts of the evidence.

And then you set about covering your tracks by searching for car hire businesses, buying suitcases and cleaning products. Again, this conduct on its own would not attract the application of section 104. But it must be relevant to a broader, contextual assessment of callousness. That you also contacted other women and went to a bar with one of them must also be relevant to this assessment.

When you got back to your room after meeting with 'M' you set about squeezing Ms Millane's naked body into the suitcase. You then carried it downstairs and put it in the back of the car. That conduct compounds the other indignities you had already subjected her body to.

The next morning you buried her before embarking on further, elaborate activities designed to shift the eye of suspicion from you.

In my view you can claim little credit for showing the Police where Ms Millane's body was buried. At the trial we heard that the Police, through cellphone polling off your phone, were already close on your heels and would certainly have discovered Ms Millane in short order even without your help.

But your attempts to divert suspicion did not end there. I have already discussed the two Police interviews undertaken on 6 and 8 December 2018. Giving false accounts to the Police may also support a finding of a high degree of callousness, particularly where the behaviour involves attempts to avoid detection and the return of a loved one's body to their family.

* * *

Kempson was taken away, removed from sight. Justice Moore retired. That old familiar silence – its hush, its awe, its respect – stayed in place. The video screens where the Millane family had made their statements continued to show a room in the family home. Earlier, in sentencing, Justice Moore had talked about their victim reports. 'I have listened carefully to the statements read to the court by Gillian Millane, Declan Millane and Victoria Millane,' he said. 'I have closely read David Millane's statement. I have received and read statements from Ms Millane's uncles and aunts from both sides, her grandparents, her cousins, her godparents and her many friends. They make harrowing and desperately sad reading and it is impossible not to be moved by both the sincerity and love implicit in the tributes and the fathomless sense of loss her death has brought to so many. I need to say no more.' Here, then, was the beautiful epicentre of Justice Moore's aria, its heart, its dying fall. The public gallery filed out of the courtroom. The lawyers stood and arranged their papers. The court crier walked around and turned off the video screens. The camera had been pointed at a wall in a room in the family home. There was one object on the wall: a framed photograph of Grace, happy, beaming, alive. It was the last thing I looked at before I left the courtroom. Kempson had gone, been obliterated. It wasn't about him anymore. It was about the memory and life of Grace Millane.

Acknowledgements

To the family and friends of Socksay Chansy, Nigel Peterson and Murray Mason for their time and their forbearance. I have never performed 'the death knock' – the routine practice many journalists experience, of knocking on the door of the family of someone who is not long dead, and asking, 'How do you feel?' – but these three stories essentially function in the same way. Socksay's father and cousin were very generous, as were Nigel's parents and Murray's daughter and ex-wife. I thank them for putting up with a stranger who visited their grief.

The stories on the trial of Grace Millane and sentencing of Jesse Kempson appear for the first time. The remaining chapters have been revised and reshaped from their original publication in the *New Zealand Herald*, where I am proud to work and count myself fortunate to be surrounded by many of the best journalists and editors in New Zealand. My thanks to the *Herald* and its parent company NZME for permission to republish these stories, and to managing editor Shayne Currie in particular.

Court reporting is one of the more collegial rounds in journalism. My thanks to Sam Hurley from the *New Zealand*

Herald, Edward Gay from Stuff, and Anneke Smith from Radio New Zealand, who were present at most of the trials featured in *Missing Persons*. I looked up to their high professional standards and am grateful for all their help.

My thanks also to HarperCollins. Journalists write, and move on; publishers expect rather a bit more time, patience, and care. *Missing Persons* exists in the first place because of Alex Hedley, and the final product owes a great deal to Lachlan McLaine and Kate Stone.